Dr. Stoll has helped me understal most important decision we make learned how to make effective everyday nutritional decision as an athlete, a coach, and now a father that have brought health and success to my family and athletes.

—Brian Shimer,
USA Bobsled Men's Head Coach
5 Time Olympian and Olympic Medalist, 2002

I have benefited enormously from Dr. Stoll's personal health counseling and guidance. Mainly due to his help, I was able to rebound from a very serious health crisis to the point that I am now enjoying renewed vigor and physical activity. The book you hold in your hand contains excellent advice, and I say this not merely because of Dr. Stoll's excellent credentials and thorough research, but beacuse I have personally applied his advice to my life and have seen the results.

—Rev. Cliff Boone, PhD

Dr. Stoll has managed to combine three conceptual truths that are oftentimes separated in unrelated sources in order to provide a dynamic tool that speaks to the complete person. *Alive* brings health to the body, wholeness to the soul (mind, will, and emotions), and growth to the Spirit in an unprecedented format.

I personally recommend it as a pastor and as an individual who experienced guidance, encouragement, and results within its inspired pages.

—Doug Anderson,
Senior Pastor Rose Heights Church
Tyler, Texas
www.roseheights.org

Dr. Stoll's Bible-based health transformation instructions come to us in perfect time. All of humankind is now dealing with one of our largest and deadliest ever health deteriorations. Increased mutations in our DNA from inheritance and environmental insults make it more important than ever to take immediate action to protect and enjoy our health at all ages. In his new book, *Alive!*, Dr. Stoll leads us down an easy, understandable path. Take action! Change your health and improve your purpose with his guidance.

—Aaron Tabor, MD, Anti-aging Gene Therapist
and founder of "Jesus Daily" on Facebook

In his book, *Alive!*, Dr. Scott Stoll provides a clear, effective path to physical health teamed with spiritual well-being. If we are to be truly effective in our lives, we need to heed Dr. Stoll's call to treat ourselves as God intended. This is a must read!

—Curtis Wallace,
Chief Operating Officer/General Counsel
T.D. Jakes Enterprises, LLP

Families today especially need the wisdom contained in this book! If you are sick and tired of being sick and tired, it might be time to reassess the biblical principles relating to healthy eating. Dr. Scott Stoll provides a balanced, thoughtful approach to the important area of health and diet.

—Kevin Swanson,
Radio Host, Generations Radio

Alive!

40 Days to Lifetime Health

Alive!

*A Physician's Biblical and
Scientific Guide to Nutrition*

SCOTT STOLL, M.D.
Foreword by Walt Larimore, M.D.

CREATIVE ENTERPRISES STUDIO

FORT WORTH, TEXAS

Alive!

Published in association with Creative Enterprises Studio, 1507 Shirley Way, Bedford, TX 76022. CreativeEnterprisesLtd.com.

Unless otherwise noted, all Scripture quotations are from the New King James Version (NKJV®), copyright © 1979, 1980, 1982, Thomas Nelson, Inc., Publishers.

Cover Design: The Dugan Design Group

Interior Design: Inside Out Design & Typesetting

ISBN 978-0-9826143-3-4

Printed in the United States of America
11 12 13 14 15 TS 7 6 5 4 3 2 1

$\mathcal{T}$o my beautiful bride, Kristen: Thank you for your endless encouragement, tireless support, ever-listening ear, and unconditional love. This book would not be possible without you, my love.

My children—Dawson, Gabriel, Samuel, Joy, Elijah, and Faith—thank you for your love, regular prayers that "Daddy would finish his book," and questions at the dinner table, such as, "How many pages do you have left, Daddy?" This book is for you, for your future, and for your children's children. I love you.

And finally, all praise and thanks be unto our great God and King for His wisdom, patience, and eternal grace.

Contents

Contents

Foreword

$\mathcal{B}$ookstores are full of all sorts of health care books, diet books, and books on nutrition. But this book isn't like *any* of them.

You can find countless Internet websites that claim to answer every conceivable question about your health while offering you myriad supplements and health aids. But the information you'll find in this book is different from what you'll find on any of those sites. These resources provide lots of information, yet few attempt to give the insight you need—from both a medical *and* a biblical perspective—to become and stay highly healthy.

While we are a more health-conscious society today, we seem to be less healthy in many ways than our parents and grandparents were. Yes, we have more and more new drugs almost every year for a growing number of diseases. Antibiotics can cure most of the infectious diseases that killed earlier generations. Our hospitals are full of the latest high-tech gizmos to diagnose and treat any number of disorders or ailments. Yet, the complexity of health care sometimes is more harmful than helpful.

We may be living longer than previous generations, but I don't sense that most people are necessarily healthier or cared for better. Health is not just an absence of illness or an increased life span. As you will learn, it is much more than that—it's thriving; becoming truly alive.

This book is written by a devout follower of Jesus primarily for followers of Jesus and the churches they attend. But, irrespective of your personal spiritual journey, the principles in this book are universal—they are designed for all men *and* women.

Alive! is based upon the principle that your Creator gives *you* the obligation and responsibility to, in large measure, determine your own destiny with regard to becoming and remaining highly healthy. Family history and genetics play a role in health, to be sure, but it is increasingly obvious that our lifestyle decisions play a much larger role—particularly our decisions about what to eat, how to fuel our bodies and minds.

Dr. Stoll wants you, the patient, to take charge of your health. In the critical game of your life, he believes, as do I, that you must learn to be your own health-care quarterback.

This book will help you understand yourself and teaches you to discover the disciplines that will make you a more healthy you. If you're afraid this will be heavy stuff, just begin reading. You won't encounter highbrow medical terminology here; what you will find is a conversation with a trusted physician who realizes that most of his readers don't have medical training. Between his stories, you'll gain insights that reveal the great breadth and depth of Dr. Stoll's experience and of his own study of medicine and the Bible.

As a physician, who has worked with thousands of doctors across the country, I am convinced that too few health care professionals know or apply the information found in this book. As a medical journalist and speaker, who has spoken with tens of thousands of people across our wonderful land, I've found that many, if not most, are not aware of the principles in this book, which could improve not only the quality of their lives, but also increase the quantity of their years. But, from Dr. Stoll's teaching, you will learn practical and easy-to-apply tips and tools to begin improving your health over the next forty days. If you are wise enough and diligent enough to apply what is taught here, it will transform your life and your family's life.

Ready to start? Ready to begin your journey toward a more healthy you? Find a comfortable chair, for once you start reading, you won't want to stop. Grab a highlighter to mark the information you won't want to forget. And don't forget to write your name in the front. You're sure to loan it to a friend. Better yet, give it to him or her. It's one of the most important gifts you could give to someone you love.

—Walt Larimore, M.D.
Family Physician and Best-Selling Author

Preface

If you read no further than this preface, I want to highlight the most important truth in this book—Jesus Christ. You can eat well, take vitamins, and exercise, but ultimately each of us is destined to live out our years on this earth and then die because we live in a fallen world subjected to sin, disease, and death. We will then stand before our Creator and give an account for our lives and how we responded to God's gift, Jesus Christ. If you have not considered the life of Jesus Christ, His claims, His sacrificial death, and His historical resurrection, I want to encourage you to stop everything and study His life.

Your physical health is temporal, but your spiritual health is eternal. You may gain superior health and a few extra years by eating well, but if you miss Christ, you will lose out on the blessing of eternity in heaven. The good news is that you can be saved and have a relationship with God through Jesus Christ. The New Testament book of Romans tells us that "If you confess with your mouth the Lord Jesus and believe in your heart that God has raised Him from the dead, you will be saved" (10:9). Your eternal destiny will be sealed, and the remainder of your life on earth will be filled with purposeful joy, renewed hope, forgiveness, and grace.

The most important decision you will make during your life is, how will you respond to Jesus Christ, the free and generous gift of God? This will determine where you are going when your time on earth has been completed—your eternal destiny. The second most important question that naturally follows is, how then should you live each day?

Many people answer the first question with very little research or careful investigation and often accept only the vague reasoning of a friend, a book, a sage, or their own fallible logic to arrive at a conclusion, failing to consider the full weight and risk of the decision. Many have never taken the time to research the potential answers to the question or to weigh the consequences of that decision. If you have never considered the life of Christ, who He said He was and what He asks of you, I pray that this book will serve as an introduction to Jesus Christ.

Your answer to the second question should be the driving motivation of your life every day. If you have decided to follow Jesus, then it is my prayer that this book will serve to inspire you to live in a way that brings honor, glory, and worship to His name. Colossians 3:17 says that whatever you do or say, you should do it all as a representative of Jesus Christ. *All* encompasses every aspect of your life: every thought that you think, every minute of every day, and every word that you say.

This book is about one area of your life that is often forgotten—your body and its health. Your body is the Lord's, and as a wise steward of the body given to you, you should manage it lovingly and utilize it completely for His glory.

Every morning when your feet hit the floor and your eyes see the rising sun crest the horizon, you should make a decision about how you will live and for whom you will live. Will it be Christ or for self? Ask yourself, how will I live today?

Glorify Him in All Things

We live in a fallen world where sin and decay are ever present, and sometimes we encounter situations that lead to illness or injury despite our best efforts to eat well and take care of our bodies. It is in these times that we need to remember that God uses challenges and suffering to draw us closer to Him and to serve as a witness to the world. But Romans 8:28 tells us that "all things work together for good to those who love God, to those who are the called according to His purpose." The bottom line is that we should live in a relationship with God that reflects His glory and enjoy glorifying Him in all things.

We do not need to be in optimal health to serve and worship Him, and we should be of service and bring glory to Him at all times and in all circumstances. I believe that we should pursue optimal health because we are stewards of our bodies; they are His temples, and it is our spiritual service of worship.

You Are Hidden in Christ

Our hope is not in this world and its systems but rather in God's perfect plan. The world's systems are at war with our bodies, minds, and spirits, and I believe it is an attempt by the enemy to steal and destroy every aspect of our lives. The enemy has come to kill, rob, and destroy through every possible tool, including the industrialized, modern diet that leads to disease, disability, pain, and premature death. God's gift is food, and this gift has been corrupted for the purpose of destroying us.

There is a solution. If we return to God's original provision of food for life on planet Earth, we can find renewed health, disease reversal, and energized life. We will also find a renewed relationship with God as we begin to understand His gift of food and the relationship that is fostered when we intentionally partake from His "garden." God also provided the proper fuel for our bodies in the foods of Eden when He created every green plant, seed-bearing plant, and fruit on Day 3 of creation. These foods sufficiently feed and fuel the body and lead to optimized function, renewed strength and energy, disease resistance and even reversal.

Day 3 Foods

Every diet today is given a name, but names tend to create groups and followers with dissenting groups arguing for the benefits of their "better" plan. The diet described in this book is not a vegetarian or vegan diet plan, high-protein, low-carbohydrate, low-fat, or any other named diet. Each of these dietary plans can be unhealthy, and the life application can be misconstrued because of philosophical bias. I want you to begin to conceptualize that you are eating the food God created as His original provision in the first garden—foods that promote a healthy, strong body; prevent disease; and even help the body begin to heal itself and reverse disease. So if someone asks you what dietary plan you are following, you can say simply that you are eating the foods God provided for health and life.

This book is not about legalism, dietary laws, asceticism, or religious food restrictions. We have freedom and liberty in Christ, and we are not confined to strict dietary laws. Yet, diet is one of those closely held belief systems that can lead to arguments—sometimes heated—and then categorization followed by separation. Within Christian circles, it can be equally divisive as groups and individuals take a stand and attempt to defend their positions, often with unspoken assumptions and misunderstandings. Therefore, I have not named a diet, nor do I promote a named diet. I encourage you to return to foods that God created, supported by the Bible and science.

Transformational Days

During the next forty days, I want to share with you the time-tested conclusions of my journey that included thousands of hours of research, a review of thousands of articles and hundreds of books, and time spent mentoring with the world's leading nutritional authorities. The simple answer to the majority of our health problems can be found in returning to God's original provision of food for life found in Genesis 1:29. Today, science is discovering and uncovering the eternal wisdom of God's provision of food for this planet. The growing body of scientific evidence confirms that making a simple shift in diet to foods that God created not only prevents disease but also has the power to reverse disease. I will also share with you the humbling revelation of God's perfect plan for food that was designed to draw you back to a daily, or bite-by-bite, relationship with Him.

Forty Days

The forty chapters in this book represent a forty-day transformational journey toward a biblically balanced understanding of health. The first set of days begins with a study of who you are in Christ and why your body and health are important to God. The next series of days walks you through a basic explanation of how your body works, reveals why food can cause or reverse disease, and offers a biblically based solution that is in harmony with current scientific research. The final few days of your journey will guide you through the steps that will help you make lifelong, lasting change and inspire you to finish strong. It is my prayer that the next forty days of your life will be transformational, both spiritually and physically, through the revelation of His Word and a concise presentation of science. Many people have already experienced tremendous change by following God's plan, and you can, too, during your forty-day journey to lifetime health.

Acknowledgments

$\mathscr{M}$y special thanks to my wife for her insights and additions to this book that make it real, tangible, and grounded. Ron and Cheryl Stoll, my wonderful parents, for their investment of time in my life and this project.

Cliff Boone for his spiritual contribution and oversight and providing sound biblical footing on whhich to build.

Don Stillman for his invaluable contributions and assistance in marketing the book.

Eric Muller for the artistic rendering of concepts and creative contributions.

Greg Stoll for his prayers and encouragement.

Brian Shimer for his endorsement, friendship, and encouragement.

Richard Wood and Ian Serff for their creation of the "Healthy Plate" images and cookbook.

Friends and family who have helped to develop this information and patiently listened to presentations and read through numerous pages.

The physicians and researchers mentioned in this book for their investment in research that strengthens and solidifies the recommendations for a plant-based diet.

Mary Hollingsworth for her skillful editing and incredible organization, Creative Enterprises Studio, that helped bring the words and book to life.

My patients who have shown me that change is possible for everyone and the amazing healing potential of God's original provision of food plants.

Quick Reference Guide to Nutrition

$\mathcal{O}$ne of the questions people ask most frequently as they begin to shift toward a healthy plant-strong diet is, "What am I going to eat?" Dietary change can seem overwhelming, but with slow, diligent effort, a lifelong change can be made in just a few weeks. Within three to six months, it becomes an effortless part of daily life. Keep the vision before you and diligently work each day toward that goal. The list below is a brief overview of daily suggestions for breakfast, lunch, dinner, and snacks. More comprehensive recipes can be found at Day3Health.com.

General Daily Recommendations
Breakfast
Green Smoothie
Steel-cut oats with berries and black walnuts or pumpkin or sunflower
    seeds
Lettuce/berries/seeds or nuts with homemade dressing
Organic herbal teas
Fresh vegetable juices

Lunch
Raw vegetables of choice
Salad or greens used in lunch
Vegetable pita pockets, collard wraps, organic low-sodium vegetable or
    wheat wraps filled with a variety of vegetables, hummus, and greens

Hummus and vegetables, such as broccoli, cucumbers, carrots, celery, and cauliflower

Nut butters

Small cooked dish, such as lentils, beans, vegetable-based soups and stews, maybe leftovers from previous meals

Dinner

Large green salad or use a variety of leafy greens

Cooked dish, such as vegetable-based soups, stews, beans/lentils, and whole grains, such as quinoa, millet, buckwheat, and bulgur

Steamed vegetable

Fruit

Water

See the perfect plate in the resources section

Beverages

Spring water—may be flavored with lemon, lime, cucumber, mint, orange

Organic herbal teas with no sugar added

Freshly made vegetable and fruit juices

Almond or hemp milk—small amounts

Green powder drinks, including wheat grass, barley, spirulina—a blue green algae—chlorella

Seasonings

All fresh herbs, ground herbs (organic is preferable), onions, garlic, sodium-free vegetable seasonings, nutritional yeast (cheese flavored)

Snacks

Raw fruits and vegetables/hummus

Smoothies

Banana ice cream

Dehydrated vegetables and fruits

Fruit pies—no sugar added

Kale chips—dehydrated

Green bars

Avoid these foods that work against your health

All added sugars, including white/brown, high-fructose corn syrup, cane sugar, rice syrup, turbinado, agave nectar, maple syrup

Processed foods in boxes, bags, and cans

All added oils, including canola and olive oil

All sweetened beverages, including teas, processed juices, carbonated beverages

Added salt, table salt, and sea salt

Alcohol

Nicotine

Dairy, including milk, cheese, butter, yogurt, and ice cream

Occasional Food List—one to three times weekly (may need to be temporarily removed if you are fighting disease)

Organic free-range animal products (chicken, wild caught fish, beef, bison, or wild game)

3 to 4 ounces per serving (the size of a deck of cards)

7-Week Solution

Note: You can add juicing (three vegetable to one fruit) any time during the 7-week process to increase the nutritional content of your day

Week 1

Simply add a smoothie for breakfast:

- 1 frozen banana or 1 cup of frozen mango
- 1/2 cup unsweetend pomegranate juice
- 1/2 cup water
- 1 cup of frozen berries of your choice
- 1 to 2 leaves of dark, leafy greens, such as kale, bok choy, or collard greens

Week 2

Continue morning smoothie and add one healthy dinner, using the "healthy plate."

Please visit Day3Health.com for recipes.

Week 3

Smoothie for breakfast and add two healthy plate dinners.

Remove processed foods from the cabinets, cupboards, and refrigerator, using the suggested list of foods to avoid.

Week 4

Smoothie for breakfast and add three healthy plate dinners.

Begin to transition lunches to include raw vegetables, such as peppers, carrots, or cucumbers.

Cut down on total caffeine consumption by one-half or use one-half regular and one-half decaffeinated coffee.

Week 5

Smoothie for breakfast and four healthy plate dinners

Eliminate meat/animal products from lunches, and add suggested items from the list above or from Day3health.com.

Week 6

Smoothie for breakfast and add five healthy plate dinners.

Create a healthy lunch everyday. Pack it during dinner clean-up the night before to simplify the preparation

Week 7

Smoothie for breakfast, healthy lunch daily from the suggested list, and add six healthy plate dinners.

Balance Your Plate for Optimum Health!

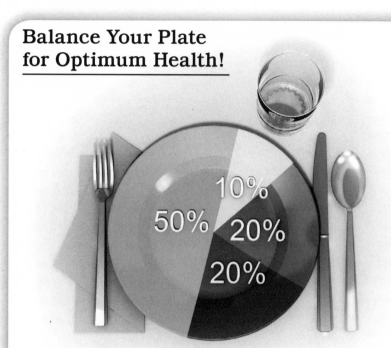

Each healthy meal should be proportioned like the plate above.
SECTION 1 will dominate your plate (about 50%) this would include a leafy green salad and raw vegetables. (This can be placed in a large bowl.) **SECTION 2** will be about 20% of your plate. This would include all of your lightly steamed or cooked vegetables. Remember not to overcook your vegetables. **SECTION 3** will be about 20% of your plate. This is the cooked portion of your meal and will include bean, lentils, whole grains, stews, soups and possibly a small serving (deck of cards) of animal products. **SECTION 4** will be about 10% of your plate. This is the fruit and the occasional bread portion of your meal.

Healthy nutrient dense recipes designed to help you create a healthy plate everyday!

And do not present your members as instruments of unrighteousness to sin, but present yourselves to God as being alive from the dead, and your members as instruments of righteousness to God.

Romans 6:13

Alive!

40 Days to Lifetime Health

Day 1

My Story

*L*et's go! Join me on a unique forty-day adventure that will draw you closer to Christ and renew your health and strength so that you can serve the Lord with all your heart, mind, soul, and strength. I am excited that you have chosen to spend the next forty days passionately pursuing a healthier body to bring glory and honor to the Lord. Your body and health are important to the Lord and should not be neglected, but instead should be offered up in love to Him as a living sacrifice of praise each day.

This is a book about health, but more importantly, it is an opportunity for you to draw nearer to the Lord as you begin to understand who you are, who He is, and how then you should live. You see, He is worthy of our very best in every aspect of who we are, because God gave us His very best, Jesus Christ (1 Corinthians 10:31).

Epiphany

On a typical afternoon in my medical practice nearly a decade ago, I heard a patient say something that made me stop and reconsider the way I practiced medicine. It was a comment I had heard nearly every day in my work and a comment that often made me smile. I had never stopped to really consider the significance of what my patients were telling me, but it was a quiet cry for help hidden between a smile and a laugh. The closer I listened, the more frequently I heard patients, friends, neighbors, and family all making the same statement: "Dr. Stoll, help me; I am falling apart."

I'm sure you have heard your friends or family say it as well. Sometimes we have to hear something several times before we truly listen and understand, listening with our hearts and not just our ears. One afternoon I truly listened, and then I saw the tears and frustration come pouring out as my patient described how her life had been painfully impacted by disease.

In response, I asked myself a very difficult question: *What am I really doing in my practice every day to improve the quality of my patients' lives?* Initially, my honest answer was that I was simply managing the symptoms of diseased bodies.

That answer begged another question, *Am I a health-care practitioner or disease-care practitioner?* I was doing very little to help improve the health of my patients; very little to promote healing, regeneration, or restoration; and I was offering very little of eternal value. In medical school I had been taught to manage the symptoms of disease and, thus, attempt to improve the quality of people's lives. But I felt as though I was fighting only half the battle, and a losing one at that! Every disease was a symptom of a diseased body that would eventually yield to failure in other areas. I felt like Lucille Ball and her friend Ethel during the episode when they were working at a chocolate conveyor belt. The belt speed increased, and chocolates kept coming faster and faster with nowhere to put them. In the end, they had stuffed chocolates everywhere possible but failed to keep up with the task.

During my practice of medicine, I have become aware of an almost palpable momentum of disease as it begins to insidiously take hold in one body system after another. This progressive spread of disease creates the perception of falling apart and with it lost quality of life, purpose, and opportunity to serve the Lord and others. When I finally understood the true implications of "falling apart," I found a new motivation: to help people regain their lost quality of life, stop the runaway train of degenerative disease, and find the eternal meaning of their lives.

I spent thousands of hours reading more than two hundred books and more than ten thousand peer-reviewed articles, met with experts from around the country, and studied under great physicians like Dr. Joel Fuhrman. My research led to some shocking yet exciting conclusions:

1. The majority of the degenerative diseases that we face today are preventable and, in fact, reversible.

2. Pain can often be eliminated without medications, and we can live healthy, high-quality lives well into our eighties, nineties, and beyond.

3. After comparing the scientific information with the Bible, I learned that we have strayed from God's original provision of food.

The Lord then began to bring Christian brothers and sisters, pastors, and missionaries through the doors of my practice, and sadly I heard the same stories. Some were unable to continue in their current positions due to disease, others had to leave the mission field, and many had to dramatically alter their service to the Lord because of disease. Through observation and study, I began to realize that the Western diet and lifestyle had infiltrated and infected the lives of Christians and the church and their opportunity to serve as hands and feet of Christ was amputated by degenerative disease, pain, and disability. It caused me to ask myself, *How would the church today be affected if this trend could be reversed?*

As I began to work with brothers and sisters in Christ, I was blessed to see the spiritual benefits of a renewed healthy body. For example, Janice was a missionary from Jamaica, who returned to the United States and abandoned her mission field because of high blood pressure, reflux disease, back pain, and borderline diabetes. Rather than try to treat each disease individually, I spent time teaching her the primary underlying cause—an unhealthy diet and lifestyle. She joyfully embraced the basic lifestyle changes that I shared with her, and within three months, the majority of her diseases had completely resolved. Soon thereafter, she returned to Jamaica to continue her work serving the Lord with a healthy, strong, and resilient body. For Janice, her body, mind, spirit, and service were all intertwined, and the physical change rippled into every area of her life.

Today, I believe many Christians are like Janice and have unknowingly and subtly embraced a culture of food and lifestyle that is now causing millions to suffer from a host of degenerative diseases. These diseases slowly and insidiously steal away their quality of life, their joy, and opportunities to serve the Lord. It is my prayer that this book will serve as an educational tool to help you better understand your body and what it requires for health, introduce you to a healthy diet and lifestyle, and inspire you to serve the Lord with all that you have, including your body.

Some have asked why I have become so passionate about health and prevention. My answer is that I wish each of you could spend a day with in me in my office listening to my patients. It is a rare window into the future and a unique opportunity to view the spectrum of every disease from its seemingly benign infancy to devastating maturity. Every day I see the ravages of disease and the broken lives strewn in its path. People whose dreams and hopes have been crushed under the weight of disease. Parents who are unable to hold or play with their children, grandparents unable to travel to see family, lost jobs, homes sold due to pain and disease, income checks consumed by health-care expenses, daily planners filled with health-care visits, and lost vitality due to medication side-effects. Eventually, their lives are reduced to the full-time management of the diseases that hold them hostage—they become slaves to disease.

Take a Minute

Spend some time right now prayerfully committing to walk this forty-day journey to its completion, finishing strong. Ask the Lord for His wisdom, understanding, and strength to guide you as you seek honest introspection and a renewed commitment to serve Him with all of your heart, mind, strength, and soul. And dedicate the next forty days and the rest of your life to the Lord, willingly surrendering your personal desires, pleasures, and plans for His greater glory. Ask Him prayerfully to lead your thoughts and decisions and bring about changes in your life that will bring Him greater glory.

Day **2**

Crisis in America, Crisis in the Church

*E*mily is a forty-nine-year-old woman who was obese most of her adult life and addicted to food. She was suffering from high blood pressure, fatigue, elevated cholesterol, and borderline diabetes. Her quality of life was poor, and she was struggling every day just to keep up.

Emily is a gifted artist who admittedly spent her energy and life trying to create significant works of art to inspire others and point them to God. Gradually over time, she began to sense a conviction that she was desecrating the greatest work of art, God's handiwork, her body. Prayerfully she repented and decided to make a lasting change to bring glory to God in the way she cared for her body. Over the course of a year, her body and her life were transformed. Her high blood pressure resolved, she lost nearly one hundred pounds, normalized her blood sugars and cholesterol without medication, and found new vitality and energy. Today, she is alive and actively serving the Lord with renewed vigor and passion both at home and in the community.

Martin was a fifty-five-year-old elder of his church who strived to serve the Lord with a sincere and passionate love both at church and at home. He suffered from many of the same diseases that afflicted Emily: high blood pressure, borderline diabetes, elevated cholesterol, and obesity. But he did not recognize the severity of his condition and the critical risk of his lifestyle and diet. He was a loving and faithful husband, the father of two sons, and a respected and valued long-term employee at his workplace.

On a typical Monday, Martin arose full of life, ate his breakfast, and drove to work to begin his workday. He arrived at work on time and greeted his staff and then turned to walk to his office. Midway down the hall, without warning, he suffered a massive heart attack and tragically died. That fateful day, the family lost its patriarch, leader, provider, husband, best friend, and father. The church lost an elder, and the community lost a true representative of Christ. It was an incalculable loss . . . that could likely have been prevented.

Here are two lives lived out on a similar path to about the same age but with dramatically different outcomes. Emily consciously chose to take a new pathway by changing her diet and lifestyle that led her to a new destination and hopeful future. Martin, unaware of the full risk of his diet and lifestyle, continued down a common and comfortable pathway that ultimately led to a catastrophic end. The divergence of their lives came when Emily recognized the signs pointing in a different direction, toward a healthy body for God's glory, and she chose to take the path less traveled.

Some people scoff at the importance of health, diet, and lifestyle, but as you can clearly see, this is a life-and-death issue. In our current culture, diet and health are commonly relegated to a less-important category of life, and decisions are either neglected or postponed until it is often too late. Diet is minimized and considered something that is used to merely control weight when the scale or doctor tells you that you are too heavy. This confusion leads many people to live for comfort and pleasure, unaware that the diet and lifestyle they choose each day will directly impact opportunities to serve the Lord, lead their families, and serve others.

At least three times per day you make important decisions that accumulate over time and eventually lead to a future of health or disease, to life or premature death. Today our nation has become so dietarily confused and ambivalent that our citizens don't understand which foods support health and which ones breed disease. As a result, Americans merely eat for pleasure, convenience, weight management, cost, or tradition and suffer the dire consequences of those decisions.

A World at Risk

Headlines in America and around the world decry the declining health of its citizens and the exponential expansion of their waistlines. Obesity rates have skyrocketed in America and are rising at epidemic levels. The latest statistics reveal that 68 percent of all Americans are either overweight or obese and in thirty states 30 percent of our children are obese. If this trend does not stop, it has been estimated that by 2020 about 81 percent of men and 68 percent of women will be overweight or obese according to the *Government Foresight* study update.[1]

Once thought to be only an American problem, now every industrialized country in the world is facing a crisis of poor health and obesity. In fact, China is now the latest country to succumb to the disease-promoting modern Western diet and has the fastest-growing obese population in the world. Leading newspapers and major magazines have detailed the obesity epidemic and speculated on potential causes and recommended solutions to halt the world's ever-expanding waistline. Due to the publicity and obvious association, obesity has become the "smoking gun" and is cited as the cause for the rising disease rates and burgeoning health-care expenditures. This has led to a plethora of interventions, including diets, surgeries, pills, and plans to treat obesity.

I would propose that obesity is not the cause of our health crisis, nor is it the primary cause of the increased rates of heart disease, diabetes, and cancer. Overweight and obese bodies are merely visible symptoms of an entrenched and deeper-rooted problem—dangerous dietary and lifestyle habits (just as a runny nose is not the cause of a cold but merely a visible symptom of a more insidious viral or bacterial infection). To paraphrase the famous Pogo quotation, "I have met the enemy and he is me"[2]— the food I eat, my activity levels, stress levels, toxic exposures, and sleep patterns.

If we as a nation continue to focus only on weight, we will miss the opportunity to identify the true underlying cause and create a long-term inexpensive solution to the obesity epidemic and health-care crisis; and it is not another fad diet! In fact, when the primary cause is identified, we will find that some normal-weight people—a group that is completely missed if we focus only on weight—are just as unhealthy and at equal risk for many of the same diseases as those with overweight bodies. It is imperative to understand that weight is merely an easily measurable marker of a much larger problem and that some people are more suscep- tible to weight gain than others, but all are at risk of disease when eating the modern Western diet.

What is the fundamental origin of our current crisis? It's an inactive lifestyle and a nutrient-poor diet full of processed food and chemicals, excessive animal products, sugar, and salt.

Weight gain, like so many of the degenerative diseases, is the result of genetic susceptibility combined with accumulated environmental influ- ence. In this case, the environmental factors are food, activity levels, toxins, and stress. If someone is not susceptible to weight gain but instead to heart disease, a poor diet may not lead to weight gain but will still lead to heart disease. It is essential that we begin to understand that our lifestyle—the food we eat, exercise (or lack of it), stress, and toxic exposures—will either support and protect our genetic weaknesses or expose the weakness and allow the manifestation of disease.

Every day you hold the future of your health in your hands and habits. What will you choose today?

Is the Christian Church in Better Shape than America?

As I contemplated this question several years ago, I assumed that as followers of Christ we would be generally healthier, more fit, leaner, and exhibit more self-discipline in the care of our bodies. However, as I researched this important question, I was stunned and saddened to learn the results: Christians today as a whole are in worse shape than the average American!

America is facing a crisis of health and obesity, but an even greater crisis, one that is not discussed in the news or in our pulpits, is occurring in the chairs and pews of evangelical churches across the nation and around the world. The church, followers of Jesus Christ, is more unhealthy, overweight, and obese than the general American population. I hope that this news stirs up righteous indignation deep within your gut. It is just not right that we, as His followers, His ambassadors to the world, and the redeemed bride of Christ should be more overweight and unhealthy than the secular culture. Step back now and look at the statistics and consider how we are representing Christ to the world in our appearance, how we are being stewards of our bodies.

A *Pulpit and Pew Study* from the Duke School of Divinity interviewed twenty-five hundred pastors and found these results:

- 70 percent of Americans are overweight or obese.

- 76 percent of evangelical Christians are overweight or obese.

- 76 percent of evangelical pastors are overweight or obese.[3]

Purdue University sociology researcher Ken Ferraro was quoted as saying, "America is becoming known as a nation of gluttony and obesity, and churches are a feeding ground for this problem."[5]

What happened to our churches? These stunning statistics highlight a growing and tragic situation in the church today, and I believe they should be a clarion call for us as followers of Christ to step up and make some lasting lifestyle changes. We should be the example of health, not obesity and disease. The excessive body weight is merely a visible marker of an insidious process that is leading to diseased bodies, disabled lives, and compromised Christian service around the world.

Obesity in the Religions of the World:

- Baptist: 30 percent

- Pentecostal: 22 percent

- Methodist: 19 percent

- Catholic: 17 percent

- Mormons: 3 percent

- Jewish: 1 percent

- Muslim, Hindu, Buddhist: 0.7 percent[4]

As Christians begin to lose their health, they become focused on their own lives, pain, diseases, and sufferings, which leaves them less able to focus on the needs around them. The ability to rise up and go forth, to see and meet the needs around us is greatly diminished, and the living, active church slowly dies from within.

A simple glance at the prayer list each Sunday highlights the growing magnitude of the problem—pages and pages of brothers and sisters fighting largely preventable diseases, such as cancer, heart disease, diabetes, autoimmune disease, and arthritic pain. Some pastors are overwhelmed by the number of church members with physical/health needs and spend much of their week visiting members in the hospital. Prayer is important, and it is important to pray for the needs of our brothers and sisters in Christ, but consider for a moment how the prayer list might look if the majority of church members were healthy.

- For what would we pray?

- Where would our hearts be focused?

- How would a healthy church serve differently?

- How would the tone of our prayer time change?

This is exactly where the physical and spiritual dimensions collide; they are inseparably interwoven, and one will directly impact the other.

During the past thirty years, we, as His followers, have been slowly desensitized to a host of deceptive and destructive cultural forces. We have dropped our guard through the gradual but effective program to make something that should be shocking become normal and acceptable. It is a systematic process that little by little preys upon our natural ability to adapt to anything new, including food and lifestyle. Adaptation is an elegant mechanism woven into our DNA that helps us to survive in every environment or condition. But it can also be a tool of the enemy that slowly wears down our defenses through a methodical and progressive presentation that builds upon a gradual acceptance of new standards of excess. I believe that our lifestyles and our diets today would prove shocking to the members of a church in 1900. They may have even said we were living in excess, gluttonous, and indulging our every desire to the destruction of our bodies, minds, and spirits.

Renewed Church

"Is there good news?" you might ask. Yes! There is a growing number of Christians who recognize the importance of being good stewards of their bodies, and they have decided to pursue a healthy lifestyle, not for their own profit but for the Lord. I sincerely believe that God is moving in the hearts of Christians to reform food and to reclaim our health from a culture of disease and death.

During the next forty days, I will introduce you to some of these brothers and sisters in Christ who have dramatically changed their lives, their health, and their walk with God by simply changing their health habits. The Bible and science agree on an inexpensive solution that has the power to prevent and even reverse many of the most common degenerative diseases that afflict millions. And you can do it. God promises that you can do all things through Christ who strengthens you (Philippians 4:13).

Take a Minute

Spend some time this week studying the pervasive impact of the modern Western diet in the lives of people around you, at the grocery store, convenience store, and at church. Now consider the numerous ways that the burden of disease has affected the church. Pray for the church, your brothers and sisters who are in need around the world. Pray for a renewed love for Christ, vision for their lives, stewardship of their bodies, and a church that decides to fully return to their First Love.

Day **3**

Eternal Perspective of Health

Can you remember a time in your life when you stood beneath a majestic ink-black night sky, far away from the light pollution of cities, and gazed deep into the starry heavens? Countless twinkling stars stretch from horizon to horizon, filling every corner of the vast black canvas. Perhaps you stood frozen in reverent silence, awestruck by the vast enormity and magnitude of the universe and the seemingly innumerable stars. Maybe you can remember feeling very small and humbled at your place in time and space on this small blue planet that is hidden away in a tiny cul-de-sac of the universe. Isn't it amazing to consider that you and I will live all our days on this small blue planet 93 million miles from a medium-sized star, our Sun, in a small corner of the Milky Way galaxy, one of an estimated 170 billion galaxies in the observable universe? It makes you feel extremely small and insignificant, yet you are very significant to God.

Every day the Sun sends its life-giving rays 93 million miles to warm the land and oceans of our small planet. Our Sun is not just a quiet golden ball that we see crest the horizon each morning or slip behind the mountains at night. The Sun is really a 10,000-degree giant ball of plasma that dwarfs our little planet. In fact, over 1 million earths would fit into our Sun. This life-giving Sun is just an averaged-sized star in the 100 billion stars in the Milky Way galaxy.

The largest star that has been identified in our galaxy is Canis Majoris, interpreted as the "big dog" star. It is a massive star about 4,900 light years from Earth (that's about 6 trillion miles multiplied by 4,900)—a really long trip! To give you an idea of its immense size, just imagine for a moment that the earth is a 1-centimeter blue marble, Canis Majoris would then be an enormous ball rising one-and-a-half miles in diameter above that small marble. That is the equivalent of approximately twenty-six football fields stacked end to end in both height and width. Let's place that little marble at the bottom of that first football field, way down in the end zone and gaze up at the twenty-six football fields rising above the marble. Now imagine yourself somewhere on that little marble. Do you feel small and insignificant? I surely do. And Canis Majoris is just one of 100 billion stars in our Milky Way galaxy.[1]

As we move out of our galaxy, we find that the Milky Way is only one of hundreds of billions of galaxies in the known universe, each with millions to billons of stars. And this is only what astronomers have been able to measure to date in the observable universe. The size and scope of the universe is beyond comprehension, both in the magnitude and number of stars.

Creator King

Have you ever stopped to really consider the origin of the matter contained in the 170 billion galaxies and trillions of stars, the orderly arrangement, and the immutable universal laws that govern the universe? In Colossians 1:15–17 we read this:

He is the image of the invisible God, the firstborn over all creation. For by Him all things were created that are in heaven and that are on earth, visible and invisible, whether thrones or dominions or principalities or powers. All things were created through Him and for Him. And He is before all things, and in Him all things consist.

Jesus Christ created every galaxy, star, and planet. Genesis 1 and John 1 reveal that Jesus spoke the stars into existence by the power of His word. Jesus called into existence the mighty Canis Majoris and the 100 billion stars in the Milky Way galaxy. That is truly the power of the spoken word!

In this passage, we see that all things were created by Him and for Him and that He holds all things together. Jesus Christ holds the fabric of the entire universe together. Every atom, planet, star, and galaxy is held together by His power and is under His control. Knowing this should bring great comfort to all of us—He who created the universe knows each of us on the deepest level right down to our subatomic particles, is intricately involved in every aspect of our lives, and upholds us by the power of His word.

Some have asked, "How can He know all of the people and events in the world?" But in the context of the size and scope of the known universe, the earth, the pale-blue dot in the vast universal ocean, all of its daily earthly activities are just a fraction of the daily activity in the universe. All things are possible with God (Matthew 19:26).

Creator-Redeemer

This infinitely powerful King and Creator could have sat upon His throne in the perfect heavenly realm for all eternity admiring His handiwork. Instead, He chose to leave. He humbled himself by putting on human flesh and chose to walk the hot, dry, dusty roads of a world that He created long ago but had fallen. His own creation, created in His image, did not recognize or welcome Him with praise and celebration but arrested Him, brutally beat Him, spat upon their Creator, and eventually nailed Him to a tree—a tree that He created and knew would one day be His own cross. And even while He hung on that humiliating cross, bleeding and dying, His creation mocked Him, wagging their heads and calling out, "You who destroy the temple and build it in three days, save Yourself! If You are the Son of God, come down from the cross" (Matthew 27:40). They didn't believe.

Jesus could have called ten thousand angels and freed Himself from that cross, but He chose to remain there, to bear the burden of sin debt once for all time and suffer and die because He first loved us. Even while we were still His enemies, living selfishly, He loved us and had compassion on us. Why? Because He knew the future; He knew the hope and abundant relationship that would follow His brutal death, and He willingly accepted the penalty for sin and gave Himself for your salvation, saving you from certain eternal destruction and amazingly inviting you to become an adopted son or daughter and partake of the richness of His inheritance. The Creator-King, who called into existence the great Canis Majoris and trillions of other magnificent stars, took on the frailty of human flesh to conquer sin and death that you might one day be crowned in glory and become an adopted child of the living God. The offer is free to all, but love is always a choice. God desires a relationship with you, but the choice is yours: will you choose to follow Him?

Jesus' death and resurrection have reconciled all things, including you, to God, and He will present you without blemish or stain before God. As a Christian, this should be the overarching context of your life, saturating all your decisions and plans. The unifying principle in life should be Jesus Christ first in all things.

Steward-Servant

Jesus Christ is the Creator and owner of all things, and as a result, you are a steward of everything within your reach during your time on this earth. You are a steward of your body, time, family, talents, money, and resources, and the goal of your life is to manage everything in the best interest of the owner, Jesus Christ. In the context of this book, this includes your body and health, and I believe it is our responsibility to do all that we can to build a strong and healthy body for His glory.

Remember that the One who called stars into existence and created the earth in all of its fullness, designed your DNA and knows your name. As Psalm 139 so beautifully reminds us, He is intimately acquainted with all of your ways. If you do not know about Jesus Christ and would like to have a relationship with Him, please contact us at Day3Health.com. You will find that you can have a personal relationship with Jesus Christ, a blessing beyond description, and a promise of peace, hope, purpose, and eternal destiny. You will also learn the great joy of the promise that, even though our outward man is perishing, yet the "inward man is being renewed day by day" (2 Corinthians 4:16).

Take a Minute

If you know Jesus Christ, please take a few minutes right now to spend time in prayer, thanking Him for His great sacrifice and surrendering every aspect of your life, all that you are and have while on this blue dot in the universe, to Him. Consider every aspect of your life, including your body and areas where you have not surrendered fully. Lay them down before Him. Contemplate the fact that the One who created the magnificent stars, such as Canis Majoris, died for your salvation, and He asks that you glorify Him with every aspect of your life. May your prayer today be the classic words of the great hymn "I Surrender All":

> All to Jesus I surrender,
> All to Him I freely give;
> I will ever love and trust Him,
> In His presence daily live.
>
> I surrender all,
> I surrender all;
> All to Thee, my blessed Savior,
> I surrender all.[2]

Day 4

The Gift of Life

$\mathscr{A}$s each of my six children grew in their mother's womb, we studied pictures of the miraculous growth and development at each stage as each child transformed from a single cell to a fully formed and functional baby in just nine months. It is still one of the greatest miracles that defies explanation and points to our Creator's magnificence. As I held each of those precious babies in my arms and looked in wonder at their small fingers and perfectly formed features, I could not help but consider the lives that are laid out before them—the joy and sorrow, victory and defeat, dreams and all of the realities of life on this earth. Each of my little ones was given the gift of life and a future full of days yet to be lived and opportunities to live them with eternal purpose. And as followers of Christ, they will have endless days with their Creator and loved ones lived out in the perfection of the new heaven and new earth.

Currently, the average person lives approximately eighty years. Multiply that by 365 days per year, and we find that on average each of us has approximately 29,200 days to spend on this earth. If you are like me, you have already started to do the math for your own life, and yes, those days do go quickly once you pass forty. "As for man, his days are like grass; As a flower of the field, so he flourishes. For the wind passes over it, and it is gone, and its place remembers it no more" (Psalm 103:15–16). Excluding any unforeseen events, you can count on those remaining days to comprise your life history on earth, documenting how you spent your days and hours. How will you live your days, and who will you spend your time serving? What will stand on the scales of eternity opposite the days of your life when you stand before God?

Tested by Fire

First Corinthians 3:13–15 tells us that all of our works of this life will be tested with fire and only those things that are of eternal value will withstand its purifying heat. How often in my own life have my heart motives been selfishly lived for those things that are temporal, as I spend my days, hours, energy, and money on temporal wood, hay, and straw that will be consumed by holy fire. It is important during your life to pause and take stock of your days, your plans, and your goals, and then prioritize them based on the impending trial of your 29,200 days. Everything will be judged by your heart motives applied to each situation and every day.

Our 24/7 culture is saturated with distractions that make it easy to lose sight of the bigger picture. We quickly become entangled in the affairs of the world. We have become like busy rats, running the maze of life, looking for the way out and the next delicious morsel yet forgetting our greater calling and final destination—servants of the living God, ambassadors to a world in need, and citizens of heaven.

Living for the Lord

Everything in your life is spiritual; it should be lived fully for Christ and not for yourself. Your days are numbered, and one day you will give an account for your life, every moment and every aspect of your 29,200 days. Knowing this, the most important question to ask yourself every day is, "How then should I live today?" From the moment your eyes open with the rising sun to when you finally lay your head to rest, consider how you should live, plan, decide, and take action to bring glory to the Lord.

First Corinthians 10:31 says, "Therefore, whether you eat or drink, or whatever you do, do all to the glory of God." Each day and in every way we are to live fully for the Lord. That little three-letter word *all* encompasses in totality every area of your life. "Whatever you do" includes everything from the time we wake up until the time we go to sleep, and I believe that includes the care of your body. I don't know about you, but that verse is a great challenge for me because I can't honestly say that I consciously seek to serve the Lord in *everything* that I do *every* day for His glory. It is a great calling to represent our Creator, our Savior, and our King in every aspect of our 29,200 days on earth, and it should be our goal to pour out our lives and bodies in all of our 29,200 days as living and holy sacrifices that are pleasing to the Lord. And by His grace, wisdom, and with His strength, it is possible.

Representing Jesus to the World

You have probably represented something in your lives such as a business, a music or performing arts school, a team, a family, or a church. There is an extra sense of responsibility attached to the task at hand because your actions and conduct reflect the character of the one who trained or sent you. Your appearance, demeanor, manners, and attitude are all brushstrokes that begin to paint a picture of the one you represent.

This is true of our lives as followers of Christ. We represent Jesus

Christ to the world, including His character, ideals, life, love, forgiveness, hope, promise, and joy. Your attitudes, actions, words, and physical appearance serve as the living expression of the King of kings. Have you ever stopped to consider how you represent Christ to the world? What do others think about Jesus after spending time with you? The temptation is to consider how we are representing ourselves and to worry about how we were perceived. But as His ambassadors to the world, we need to think beyond ourselves and live to bring glory to Him. Each of your 29,200 days is a marvelous opportunity to represent Him authentically to people in desperate need, who live without hope during this fragile and often painful life.

Denying Self

Every day when you awaken and set your feet on the floor, you are called to put on Christ, deny yourself, take up your cross, and follow Him (Mark 8:34). This self-denial and all-embracing pursuit of Christ is never easy, and it is a daily battle against our fleshly desires and the strong cultural influence. Our modern culture is fueled by the service of self and the individual pursuit of pleasure, so it stands in direct opposition to the calling of Christ to turn from your selfish ways, take up your cross, and follow Him.

Taking up your cross is a great challenge, and the audience that read Mark's letter deeply understood the significance of that calling of Christ. The prisoners of Rome were forced to take up their cross and carry it to the place of execution, signifying absolute and final submission to Roman authority and power. Jesus used this phrase to illustrate the call to fully submit our entire lives to Him every day. Every moment of every day we should be denying the draw of our selfish desires and committing to follow wherever He leads.

Today one area where the pursuit of personal pleasure is evident is in our modern culture of food. Eating has become a sport, exciting entertainment, and opportunity to satisfy appetites, relieve stress, and ease pain, rather than an opportunity to nourish and strengthen the body by enjoying the foods God created. As a result, our nation and our churches have become overweight, diseased, and ineffective. I would even argue that as representatives of Christ we are not displaying to the world an accurate picture of our magnificent Creator and Savior. Every aspect of our lives, including our bodies, should be honed and shaped to reflect the glory of our Lord, not for our own glory or self-satisfaction but to demonstrate our love and respect for the One we represent and serve.

Cultural Current

All of us live out our 29,200 days and operate within a culture that influences our ideas, philosophies, work, diet, habits, families, and beliefs. The influence is often very subtle, and change occurs at a slow, almost imperceptible rate, but it is always advancing. These incremental, imperceptible changes added together over time result in dramatic and striking outcomes. Stop and think for a moment about the cultural changes that have occurred in the last fifty years here in America, including social mores, acceptable language, religious beliefs, entertainment, advent of easy credit, and for the purposes of this book, dietary consumption.

During the past forty years, our culture of diet, food, activity, and lifestyle has dramatically shifted toward habits that promote disease. All of the advertising, processed foods, food trends, convenience, flavor enhancements, pleasure eating, and modern manufacturing are like the strong Mississippi River current. On the surface it appears quiet, peaceful, and lazy, but the strong undercurrent powerfully directs its course toward a known destination—disease. American health is now adrift on a strong cultural current that leads to a host of degenerative diseases, including heart disease, diabetes, and many cancers.

The strong Mississippi River current pulls ships downriver with very little effort expended, but if the ship is turned around, the engines must labor and strain against the mighty current. Similarly, riding our modern cultural current of food and lifestyle and lounging on the lazy river is effortless and fun. But remember, the current always leads to a destination, and as you will see in later chapters, this cultural current leads to sick, unhealthy, diseased bodies. Do you know where your "ship" is going?

Popular foods, restaurants, preservatives, salt, sugar, processed foods, low consumption of vegetables and fruits are part of the cultural current, and it is quite easy and pleasurable to ride the current for a while. But we know that if you do what everyone else is doing, you can expect to get what everyone else is getting. Simply looking downriver, you can begin to see what may await you in the future: degenerative disease, pain, lost quality of life, doctor visits filling up your calendar, expensive co-pays, deductibles, missed opportunities, and a potentially shortened life span. Is that where you want to go?

To change direction requires energy and effort, and the going is slow at first, but once you pick up steam, the journey becomes easier, and the sense of purpose and direction will make the work meaningful and often enjoyable. How can you change direction? Just as the boats on the river do. First, take an honest assessment of where you are and where you are headed. Second, grab hold of the wheel and begin turning your boat around. Third, start paddling!

Start today by evaluating your life and direction and then dedicate your body to the Lord. Commit to make lasting dietary changes, remove the processed foods from your pantry and cupboards, take a walk, find time to rest, and make a commitment to learn more about the care of your body. Stroke by stroke, applying consistent effort, your ship will begin to move in the right direction. Don't give up!

Take a Minute

Because you're reading this book, it is likely that you have somewhere around 15,000 days or fewer on this earth to live for the Lord. I don't want this to be a downer day, but it is important to consider your days and then ask how you will live out each day. Remember that the end of your days on this earth is just the beginning of endless days with God, but these days hold great value eternally. I encourage you to be aware and on alert because the cultural current will insidiously steal away your days, your health, your strength, and your ability to live effectively, serving the Lord and others.

Take time now to prayerfully consider how the cultural current has influenced your life and your decisions, and commit to make to make a life-altering change of direction so that each of your days can be lived out fully for the Lord.

Glorify God in Your Body

$\mathcal{E}$very day you see your body in the mirror—sometimes it's quite a surprise! You use it to accomplish the day's work, give and receive love, achieve goals, and sometimes abuse it. But have you ever considered who owns your body and its primary purpose?

Today, many secular philosophical views about the body have become secretly woven into our Christian concepts of health. For example, Plato taught that the spirit is the only thing of worth, and the body is temporal; therefore, little time and effort should be focused on the body. It is corrupted and will one day pass away; the spirit is the only thing of eternal value. This philosophy leads Christians to believe that they should not be concerned about the body and that any effort or time spent on the body is wasted.

Existentialism (man determines himself and his world) and humanism (every individual has the right to give meaning to his/her life) have taught us that your body is *your* temple. Every decision is yours alone, and the body is to be used for personal pursuits and pleasures. Modern song lyrics such as "It's My Life," and "I Did It My Way," highlight this philosophy that has become the refrain of our modern culture, igniting the fires of self and pleasure.

Fatalism has deceived us into believing that we have little control over the outcome of our future and our health and that we shouldn't place too much emphasis on long-term planning because our bodies will be replaced in the future. Some may believe that it is a sinful world, and their bodies are subjected to sin; therefore, they can't do anything to fight the fallen world. Or they may believe that all disease is genetic and they can't change their genes.

In Christian circles a form of fatalism creeps in when discussing health and care of the body. Many Christians mistakenly believe that because the body is not yet recreated and is temporal, that we should not place any emphasis on healthy maintenance of the decaying body, saying, "It will just pass away one day and be replaced with an eternal body." But, again, this is a worldly philosophy that misses the mark and ignores the biblical mandates to do our best with everything we have to glorify God. It also ignores the very real and potentially tragic consequences of ignoring destructive lifestyle patterns, such as food addiction.

Think about the Biblical Body

These secular views stand in stark contrast to the biblical view of the body. Your body is important to God, and He is interested in how you manage, use, and maintain your body. Psalm 139 eloquently reveals that God is intimately acquainted with all of your ways from the time you were knit together in your mother's womb until your last day on this earth. Sadly, because of sin, your body, your earthly tent, has been corrupted, and it will feel the sting of death and decay. Second Corinthians 5:1–10 promises that we have a new body fashioned by God awaiting us and that one day mortality will be swallowed up by life.

Take heart, because just as your spirit has been renewed, your body will also one day be transformed into the likeness of Christ, and you will be given a new, perfect body for all eternity, free from the bondage of sin and death.

You Are a Vessel

During your time on this earth, your body is a vessel of the Holy Spirit and is supremely precious and holy to God. We are encouraged in 2 Corinthians 5:15 with these words: "And He died for all, that those who live should live no longer for themselves, but for Him who died for them and rose again." And just a few verses earlier, we are given the challenge to make it our ambition to please Him knowing that one-day we must all appear before the judgment seat of God to give an account for what we have done in our bodies, whether good or evil.

With these verses as a foundation for your life, it should be your loving and joyful response to surrender your body, with its earthly desires and appetites, to the Lord and dress yourself in holiness every day for His glory. Paul tells us the body is for the Lord, and the Lord is for the body, and that our bodies should be dedicated to bring glory to God. Later, in 2 Corinthians 6:16 we read these incredible words about our bodies: "And what agreement has the temple of God with idols? For you are the temple of the living God. As God has said: 'I will dwell in them/and walk among them. / I will be their God,/and they shall be My people.'" Your body is now His temple. These are life-changing perspectives from the Bible and the antithesis of worldly philosophies. We are not called to serve self and live for our own pleasure, but we are called to sacrifice self and make it our aim to bring glory to God in every aspect of our life, including our bodies.

Your Body Is His Temple

Have you ever asked yourself whom you are glorifying with your body? It is a strange question to consider, but it quickly clarifies your motives, especially when the answers are placed in the context of the supremacy of Jesus Christ: "For you were bought at a price; therefore glorify God in your body and in your spirit, which are God's" (1 Corinthians 6:20). This simple, short verse establishes a lifetime context for the management of your body. As a Christian, you have been given a high calling to live a holy life, glorifying God with your body. You were purchased with the incomparable and invaluable blood of Christ, and you have been redeemed from certain eternal death. In response to God's free and immeasurable gift, you are asked to glorify Him. The word *glorify* means "to bring worship, praise, and honor, in your body, to the Lord continually every day."[1] Please reread that last sentence and consider the application of that truth to your life.

I hope this will challenge you, because it certainly has caused me to reconsider my own life by asking, "Is Christ prominent or preeminent in every facet of my life, including my body?" A second follow-up question is, "Do the choices that I make each day about how I use, maintain, and manage my body bring glory—worship, honor, and praise—to the Lord?" These are difficult and uncomfortable questions to ask yourself, but they are critical questions to contemplate as you begin to make changes in any aspect of your life, including your diet and health habits. If you truly grasp the high calling on your life, it will serve as unending motivation that will transcend the ups and downs of life.

Compare Temple Perspectives

The warm afternoon sun gently reaches its soft golden rays through an open stone window in the upper walls of the palace, and a gentle breeze cools two men seated at a large circular cedar table. David, sitting with his son Solomon in his private quarters, carefully takes one scroll from a large bundle and unrolls it. The yellowed parchment is filled with a detailed plan for the complete rebuilding of the temple of God, and each succeeding scroll reveals even greater detail. You can almost feel the intensity in David's voice and see the sweat on his brow as he sits next to Solomon, fervently reviewing the meticulous plans that were given to him by "the hand of the Lord."

David's passion was to build a temple to honor the holy name of the Lord, and every detail of the temple was to be of the highest quality material and best workmanship. The first part of David's prayer in 1 Chronicles 29:10–14 reveals his passion for God and his vision to bring God honor by sacrificially building the best temple possible:

Therefore David blessed the Lord before all the congregation; and David said:

Blessed are You, Lord God of Israel, our Father, forever and ever. Yours, O Lord is the greatness, the power and the glory, the victory and the majesty; For all that is in heaven and in earth is Yours; Yours is the kingdom, O Lord, and You are exalted as head over all. Both riches and honor come from You, and You reign over all. In Your hand is power and might; in Your hand it is to make great and to give strength to all. Now therefore, our God, we thank You and praise Your glorious name. But who am I, and who are my people, that we should be able to offer so willingly as this? For all things come from You, and of Your own we have given You.

David truly understood the majesty and supremacy of God and his personal responsibility to offer his very best to the Lord.

Once the temple was completed and dedicated, God said to Solomon, "And the LORD said to him: 'I have heard your prayer and your supplication that you have made before Me; I have sanctified this house which you have built to put My name there forever, and My eyes and My heart will be there perpetually'" (1 Kings 9:3). From that day forward it was maintained meticulously and treated with the greatest reverence because it was the place where the Lord dwelt and interacted with mankind.

Fast-forward with me now to another table, this one small and austere, where another man sits, sweat on his dusty brow, laboring over a parchment that is a letter to the church in Corinth. Paul, calling upon the knowledge of Solomon's temple and contrasting it to the new covenant in Christ, writes to the Corinthians, "Do you not know that you are the temple of God and that the Spirit of God dwells in you? If anyone defiles the temple of God, God will destroy him. For the temple of God is holy, *which temple you are*" (1 Corinthians 3:16–17, emphasis mine).

Later in the letter, Paul again asks the question, "Or do you not know that your body is the temple of the Holy Spirit who is in you, whom you have from God, and you are not your own?" (1 Corinthians 6:19). He was emphasizing to the Corinthians and to us that we have a special calling—that our bodies are important to God, and that together as a body of believers today we *are* the living temple of God.

During Old Testament times, the Jewish people recognized the temple as the dwelling place of God where God interacted and dwelled among His people. Today, there is not a great temple where God dwells, but instead He tells us that our bodies are now His temple. It is an amazing and miraculous shift in location, and it is a critical distinction to understand because of the far-reaching ramifications. God's word to Solomon, during the temple commemoration, is His word to us today, "I have heard your prayer and your supplication that you have made before Me; I have sanctified this house which you have built to put My name there forever, and My eyes and My heart will be there perpetually" (1 Kings 9:3). The ancient Hebrews lived to bring honor to God and provide a place for Him to dwell among humans, and I believe we are called to have the same sense of reverence and responsibility toward God's New Testament temple— our bodies. "Foods for the stomach and the stomach for foods, but God will destroy both it and them. Now the body is not for sexual immorality but for the Lord, and the Lord for the body" (1 Corinthians 6:13).

There is a silent war being waged today for your body. The secular culture, created and infused by Satan, entices us with alluring ideas of personal pleasure, the pursuit of happiness, and comfort at the expense of our relationship with the Lord, our health, and our service. Satan has organized the culture to once again draw our attention away from Christ and to refocus our thoughts and desires back to ourselves through a carefully cultivated propaganda blitz of personal pleasure. Paul teaches us that our bodies are actually parts of Christ and are, therefore, of great importance to Him. Your body is not to be neglected or abused; it is very precious to God because it is His temple and an instrument to be used for His righteous plans. It is important to remember that once you accepted Christ, you were forgiven, purchased from slavery to sin, are now a new creation in Christ, are owned by Him, and you are now an adopted son or daughter of the Most High God. Our goal in life should be to live through our bodies to bring glory and honor to His name and receive the high calling of Christ. When the day comes that we each stand before Him, may He turn to you with a warm smile and arms open wide and say, "Well done, my good and faithful servant."

Take a Minute

Today, spend some time prayerfully considering how you have used your body for both your own honor and glory and for the Lord's honor and glory. If necessary, repent for the decisions that you have made that selfishly feed fleshly appetites, activities that have defiled your body, and perhaps for a general lack of care or concern for the Lord's temple. Ask the Lord to reveal to you where humanistic philosophies have crept into your life and are directing your behavior. Prayerfully recommit to do your best to bring glory to His name in every aspect of your life, including maintaining your body, no matter what it takes or how great the challenge may be. He gave everything for us, and we should be willing to do the same out of a heart of gratitude for our salvation. Remember, it is all about Jesus, and even our pursuit of health should be for His glory and not our own.

$\mathscr{Day}$ **6**

Stewardship and Lawnmowers

$\mathscr{H}$ave you ever borrowed something from a friend or neighbor? When I was a boy, my father always taught me to return everything we borrowed in better condition than when it was loaned to us. It was something he learned from his father and his uncle while working on the farm in Nebraska. They taught him that the way he treated the borrowed items directly reflected his respect for the owners, and it was an opportunity to honor the owners by carefully managing their possessions.

One Saturday morning, we tried to start our old mower, but it sputtered, coughed smoke, and refused to spring to life one more time. My brother and I thought we had escaped a Saturday mowing job, but my dad, undaunted by the challenge, quickly called a neighbor, and within a few minutes a running lawnmower was in my hands and my feet were in the field. After hours of mowing in a hot, dirty field, we finished the job, and our neighbor's mower looked as if it, too, was finished. Dirt and oil created a thick black layer on the engine, the decking was covered in weeds and dirt, and the blade was dented and dulled. I rolled the mower onto the driveway and was about to go inside for a little well-deserved rest and a glass of ice water.

My dad, even though hot and tired, knelt down with a soapy rag and started to meticulously clean off the old grease and grime. Watching my father's dedication inspired my brother and me to join the cleaning party. The three of us spent a solid hour scrubbing, polishing, and even waxing that old lawnmower, striving to make it look as new as possible. We even used Q-tips to clean out the small spaces! Amazingly, the labor became almost fun as we began to imagine the response of the owner when we returned his old mower polished with a new coat of wax!

Sweaty and dirty, we stepped back to admire our work, and we began to laugh because that old dirty mower now sparkled in the sunlight, and not a speck of dust could be found on the engine. We could hardly wait to put it in the truck and return it to our unsuspecting neighbor. Almost giddy with anticipation, my brother and I rolled the mower out of the truck and placed it on our neighbor's driveway. When he walked out of the house, he stood in stunned silence, and then a big smile filled his face followed by a great laugh. An even bigger smile lit up our faces. He called his wife to come out and look at the mower, and you can imagine that she was initially not too thrilled to stop what she was doing to come outside and look at an old mower. But as soon as she rounded the corner, a bright smile filled her face, and she began to laugh too. I suddenly understood what my dad was teaching me: it wasn't the clean mower that created joy for the owner, but the respect, honor, and love demonstrated in our stewardship. The hard work in the hot sun that day quickly melted away, and a warm sense of satisfaction filled our hearts as the owner praised our care and concern for his old mower, saying, "It has never looked so good."

Your Body, God's Lawnmower!

I often think my body is like that old lawnmower. It is a machine created for a purpose and owned by someone else. Have you ever stopped to consider who owns your body? The culture today would scream out, "You are the master of your ship; you control your own destiny, and your body is yours to do with whatever you want!" Growing up in this culture, it is easy to begin to unknowingly accept its unwritten belief and assumptions. So who really owns your body, and if someone else owns it, what is your responsibility to the owner?

Turning again to 1 Corinthians 6:19–20, we learn that our bodies are not our own but are really on loan from the Lord, and their purpose is to bring glory and honor to Him. Verse 19 begins with a rhetorical question, "Or do you not know that your body is the temple of the Holy Spirit who is in you, whom you have from God, and you are not your own?" God is the rightful title-holder of your body and the owner of all creation; you and I are merely stewards of everything He has given us, including our bodies. We are owners of nothing, stewards of everything.

If you and I are stewards of everything, including our bodies, then it is important to understand the role and responsibilities of a steward. So what is a steward? A steward is one who manages the owner's assets in the best interest of the owner. The last part of that sentence says "in the best interest of the owner." That statement is the key to stewardship. We must get to know the owner well enough that we know His plans and desires and then use everything that we have been given to achieve His goals, not ours. Responsible Christian stewardship is the careful management of God's possessions for His plans and purposes, with the goal of returning everything to Him in the best condition possible, just as my family returned the old lawnmower that we borrowed to our neighbor. This biblical perspective of stewardship should be a driving force behind your life, in the pursuit of health, and in the management of your body. Your body is not your own but has been bought with a price, and the Lord calls you to glorify Him with your body.

Wise Stewards

In Matthew 25:14–30 we find the story of a man who left on a trip and entrusted his possessions to the care of his three servants. After a long time, the man returned and asked his servants to give an account for the way they had managed his possessions.

The first two servants had wisely invested the money he had given them, trying to make the most of it, knowing they would have to give an account to their master and return the money to him. Their master praised their diligence, saying, "Well done, good and faithful servant; you were faithful over a few things, I will make you ruler over many things. Enter into the joy of your lord" (vv. 21, 23). These are the words we all hope to hear from our Master one day.

The third servant only had excuses and insults for his master when asked how he had managed his possessions. As a result, he was rebuked for his laziness and wickedness and cast out from his master's home.

Everything you have, including your body, is on loan from the Lord and should be maintained and used to serve His purposes and plans and to further His kingdom. That includes careful attention to eating foods that promote health and not disease, regular exercise, consistent rest, and balance so that your body is as strong and healthy as possible for the work at hand.

Atrophy is the reward for apathy in every area of our lives, including our spirits and our bodies. Diligence and discipline are rewarded both temporally and eternally and should be a mark of our lives as followers of Christ and stewards of His possessions.

Overcoming Challenges

Today, many Christians avoid making dietary changes or adding exercise to their daily routine because it causes them to be uncomfortable or challenges busy schedules. Why is it such a struggle? A primary reason, I believe, is because the focal point has become self and personal comfort in our temporal lives and a lost perspective of who we are in Christ and God's greater plan. However, what if these challenging lifestyle changes were instead built upon the concept of stewardship and in the light of the Owner's plans and purposes? Suddenly the task becomes exciting and purposeful as we shift our focus from ourselves to the rightful owner and His response, rather than our own desires for immediate personal pleasure. Instead of returning an old, dirty, run-down "mower" to its owner, we can return a mower that is in the best condition possible—polished, clean, and ready for service.

Take a Minute

I encourage you to begin prayerfully surrendering your body, your health, and your entire life to the Lord. Imagine for a moment that you are standing in front of the King of kings, presenting your body and your life to its rightful owner, the Lord of all creation. What will He say about your life and your care of all that was entrusted to you? Ask yourself right now, as a steward, how well you have maintained and used your body for His glory. If the answer makes you uncomfortable, then spend some time prayerfully repenting and committing to create a new plan to improve the condition of the Master's possession—your body.

Day 7

God's Original Diet Plan

And God said, "See, I have given you every herb that yields seed which is on the face of all the earth, and every tree whose fruit yields seed; to you it shall be for food. Also, to every beast of the earth, to every bird of the air, and to everything that creeps on the earth, in which there is life, I have given every green herb for food;" and it was so (Genesis 1:29–30).

*E*very year a host of new diets appears on the shelves of bookstores, magazine covers, and late-night infomercials. Each claims new insight, touts scientific discoveries, and promises breakthroughs that will make weight loss easier, faster, and painless while enjoying all of the foods that we have *grown* to love . . . in more ways than one! Have you ever stopped to ask what was God's original plan and provision for food? Did He have a plan or establish a diet for optimal health?

Many Christians today look to the world for guidance on the best dietary plan and have neglected to return to God's Word for His wisdom and guidance. Just a quick glance at the general condition of Christians in the pews across America, and we can see the result of this decision to follow the culture: the church is overweight, sick, run-down, and falling apart. Sadly, we rarely hear sermons on the subject of health and God's perfect plan for our bodies. The stewardship of the body is a forgotten topic, and Christians are suffering unnecessary disease because of the "worldly wisdom" of this age.

As a direct result, I believe that our ability to go forth, share the gospel, and serve those in need has been desperately compromised. One fellow believer, who recognized this in his own life, said, "I have become soft inside and out, selfish, and in my diet and disease I end up thinking only about myself, my disease, and my lost quality of life." It is an unbroken selfish circle.

God's Original Provision

Imagine for a moment the garden of Eden. What images spring to your mind? What colors do you see? How do the land and soil appear? The lush, green plants; bubbling, blue springs of water; and warm, yellow rays of sun fill the garden in my mind. But I don't see a pizza parlor, convenience store, or fast-food joint on the corner by the big palm tree, do you? Seriously, have you ever stopped to consider what Adam and Eve ate? They ate directly from God's original provision of food—the plants and trees that He planted in that first garden. All of the wonderful fresh produce picked ripe from the plants or trees was fully satisfying, health sustaining, and with a taste that is beyond our comprehension.

In the beginning, our Creator fashioned an elegant system of food to nourish the body, provide energy, and cultivate an ongoing relationship with His creation. Importantly, I believe He added taste so that the process was intensely pleasurable and deeply satisfying. This is His gift. The complex experience of eating and feeling fully satisfied physically and emotionally was truly spiritual. Adam and Eve were sustained and made complete every day through God's bountiful and beautiful provision of food. Every day when they reached up to take and eat from the plants in the garden, they were in communion and relationship with their Creator, Provider, and Sustainer. Their hunger drew them back to the garden and into relationship with God. Every pleasurable bite nourished their bodies and gave them an opportunity to worship.

Returning to Genesis, we can begin to uncover God's original dietary provision. Genesis 1:29–30 tells us that God created the green plant for food and every seed-bearing plant and tree to provide nourishment for the body—a plant-based diet, rich in nutrients that provided optimal health and complete nourishment for the body. It was the perfect diet comprised of perfect foods. It was not until after the Flood that we see God's first direction on the consumption of animals.

After the Flood, the world changed dramatically, including the climate, soil composition, and plant variety and availability. Common foods that were once abundant and a part of the daily diet became scarce, and animal foods perhaps filled in the deficits. God spoke to Noah after the Flood, saying, "Every moving thing that lives shall be food for you. I have given you all things, even as the green herbs" (9:3). God did not intend harm and, therefore, we can conclude that eating animal products is not evil or forbidden. It is important to recognize that it was not God's original plan for life, but it appears to be an adaptation to the changed world. First came the green plant and then the animal products, which is the opposite order of our diets today, which consist largely of processed foods and animal products. In later chapters, we will explore some other changes in our world that have further altered the food chain and increased the need to consume more plant-based foods.

Imperfect World, Imperfect Food

It is not earth-shattering news to tell you that today we live in a world vastly different from that original garden. Catastrophes dating back to the Flood have continued to change the face of our planet, including the health of our soils and crops. The extensive use of pesticides and aggressive farming have depleted our soils and polluted the food chain. And the industrialization of food produced new man-made processed food in boxes, bags, and cans that fill our diets with calorie-dense, nutrient-poor foods that result in overfed, overweight bodies that are starving for nutrients. America and a growing number of countries are overweight on the outside and emaciated on the inside.

Depleted Fields

Agricultural studies confirm the progressive decline in nutrient value of foods by demonstrating statistically significant declines in the nutrient content (vitamins, minerals, antioxidants, and phytochemicals) of food, due in part to both farming practices and the selection of plant varieties that produce high yields.[1, 2] Organic farmers will tell you that the health of the plant depends on the health of the soil, and our soils today are deficient. Combine this with the fact that 90 percent of Americans don't eat the minimum government-recommended four to six servings of fruits and vegetables per day, and you can begin to see that the average American's intake of vital nutrients from plant-based foods is grossly deficient.[3]

For millennia, scarcity was the driving force behind food choices and ultimately the diet-related diseases. People suffered from both a lack of food and variety that led to diseases of vitamin and mineral deficiencies. Today we live in a unique period of human history. America and many of the developed countries have created feasting opportunities that never existed before through refrigeration, fast food, a restaurant on every corner, 24/7 grocery shopping, prepackaged food, snack foods, and convenience stores. The new abundance of processed foods led to an overfed but still nutritionally deficient population that is susceptible to a host of other diet-related diseases, including heart disease, diabetes, autoimmune diseases, allergies, and many cancers. Today it is not a lack of food, but rather an abundance of unhealthy food, that is the primary cause of diet-related disease.

Returning to the Garden

Change can also be positive, and globalization, transportation, and the evolution of the grocery store and farmers' markets now present us with a tremendous opportunity to return to the diet that is more in alignment with God's original dietary provision. You can now go to the grocery store in mid-January, when the ground is frozen and cold, and buy fresh fruit, broccoli, kale, and salad greens that will support the health of your body, maintain repair and regenerative processes, and provide energy and vitality, just as Adam and Eve did in January in God's original garden.

Every time you make a decision to buy, cook, or eat food, consider the source and compare it to the image of God's garden. Ask yourself if this is a creation from the hand of God. Is it made by man, processed, refined, and devoid of nutrients, or is it made by God, living, unprocessed, and full of nutrients? It is a simple question that will help you to make good decisions that lead to health and life. As you take and eat of those foods, stop and consider your Creator and His provision for life. Take a bite and intentionally focus your thoughts and thanks on Him. Enjoy His gift of food and worship Him for His complete provision for your physical and spiritual life.

Take a Minute

Take time today to thank the Lord for His provision for life and health, in food, and ask Him to help you move toward a diet based on those garden foods that will support a healthy body and draw you back into relationship with Him every time you eat. Use every meal as on opportunity to pause, focus on Him, and intentionally eat food in worship.

We need to develop an appreciation and attitude of gratitude for plant-based foods, recognizing that they are God's provision of food for our lives. I realize that breaking away from the culture of processed food and excessive animal products can be challenging, but you can be confident that ". . . my God shall supply all your need according to His riches in glory by Christ Jesus" (Philippians 4:19). Press on!

Fat Bookshelves—A Failed Strategy

*W*hen you see the word *diet,* what are the first couple of words that pop into your mind? *Weight loss, rebound weight gain, pain, sacrifice, "only thirty more days," rice cakes, frustration* and *confusion* are a few of the more common descriptors of the modern diet experience. Diets are built on the concept of sacrifice, denial, and discomfort that ultimately leaves dieters counting the days and watching the scale for that goal weight and the "end" of the diet.

But what happens after you reach your goal weight? Several studies found that the commonly recommended program of reduced caloric intake through restriction diets and increased exercise has a long-term failure rate of 95 percent.[1] Consider the implications of this information! For every one hundred people who start a diet, ninety-five will fail to maintain the weight loss. Even more concerning is that 90 percent gain back *more* weight than they lost!

This is more than just a failed system of weight loss; it is an absolute disaster. Furthermore, yo-yo dieting not only leads to feelings of failure, frustration, and hopelessness, but it can also adversely affect your metabolism and long-term health. Is there any other area of your life where you would take on a project with only a 5 percent success rate? It is safe to say that diets in general do not promote health nor lead to lasting weight loss, so save your money and time and don't follow the next big diet fad that will soon arrive at your local bookstore.

Defining Diet

The definition of *diet* that we will be using for the remainder of this book is this: *diet* is the sum total of what we eat every day. It is the food that finds its way into your shopping cart, pantry, refrigerator, and ultimately onto your fork and into your mouth. From there it is processed, assimilated, and transported directly to your cells that are awaiting the nutrients necessary for optimal function. Diet is not a weight-loss strategy but rather an opportunity to supply your body each day with the needed materials for proper body function.

The First Diet Book

When did this dietary craze begin, and what are its foundations? The first known dietary book was published in 1864 by William Banting, an English casket maker, who recommended low carbohydrates and daily alcohol in his book, *Letter on Corpulence*, after he discovered that he was unable to bend over and tie his shoes. His diet plan worked! He lost weight, tied his shoes again (for a short time), and his book planted the seeds for new $35 billion diet industry.[2]

Modern dietary and nutritional research can be traced back to the work of Wilbur O. Atwater, a founder of the United States Department of Agriculture (USDA). He was the first to show that food gives off thermal energy when it is burned, and thus the idea of calories was born.[3]

The paradigm of diet and food was forever changed in 1918 when Dr.

Lulu Hunt Peters wrote a best-selling book entitled *Diet and Health, with Key to the Calories.* Weight loss, she explained, could be attained through eating foods in 100-calorie units, a little like the modern Weight Watchers point system. She also noted in her book that the diet industry would prove to be very lucrative. She was absolutely right with recent numbers estimating a $35 billion-per-year business.[4]

Numerous dietary variations followed, including these:

- The Food Combining Diet by William H. Hay, who recommended eating proteins, starches, and sugars separately.

- The Grapefruit (or Hollywood) Diet, and the introduction of diet pills in the 1940–1950s to enhance weight loss.

- Weight Watchers was started in a home meeting in the 1960s.

- Dr. Atkins' Diet Revolution began in 1972 when Dr. Atkins released his best-selling high-protein dietary plan.

- The Pritikin Diet program hit the scene in the 1970s, recommending low-fat and high-fiber initially for those with a heart history, but was quickly endorsed for weight loss.

- The 1980s saw the rise of the Beverly Hills Diet and later the Glycemic Index that was developed to help diabetics understand how foods affect blood sugar levels and then was later adopted by a number of dietary plans to promote weight loss.

- The 1990s saw the rise of diets such as Sugar Busters Diet, The Zone, and the South Beach Diet, each promoting a new twist on carbohydrate, fat, and protein combinations for weight loss.

- More recent and outrageous diets include the Hershey Kiss Diet, the Cabbage Soup Diet, the Cookie Diet, the Lemonade Diet, and a guaranteed weight loss plan—the Tapeworm Diet![5,6]

Today, both our waistlines and bookshelves are bulging, yet every year Americans continue to search for the next easy answer to painless weight loss. Have you ever wondered what we ate before all of the hype?

Chasing the Wrong Rainbow

Despite all the expert opinions and bookshelves full of diet books, the average American has continued to gain weight. I hope that a known failure rate of 98 percent causes you to stop and ask why we haven't figured out that this system is not working. Why do so many people continue to pursue failed strategies?

I believe that four of the most powerful causes of the high failure rate are these:

1. We have abandoned the dietary foundation of God's original provision of foods that support health and life.

2. The use of weight loss as the single motivating factor, with no long-term vision for health, leaves people without an empowering "why" for change.

3. Restrictive diet plans fail to address the sinister power of food addictions.

4. A lack of nutrient-rich foods leaves the body starving for nutrients and persistently hungry.

The diet industry continues to focus on body weight as its primary objective measure for success. It is a very easily measured and visual marker of progress, but weight loss is really an uninspiring, short-term goal that lacks any long-term motivation for lasting lifestyle change. It also fails to address the more important goal of health, disease prevention, and quality of life. Does that number on the scale really ignite the fires of passion and motivation once you reach your ideal weight? Is it a goal that really gets you out of bed in the morning a year from now? Weight loss becomes motivating when there is something of greater value linked to the weight loss, such as a wedding, summer vacation, class reunion, or similar event that reaches into deeper personal motivating factors. The isolated goal of weight loss will never create lasting change, and every diet program focused primarily on weight loss will ultimately fail unless people can develop a passionate and meaningful vision for their future health.

Individuals who have successfully lost weight and changed their health have an important secret ingredient that is not necessarily found in books or programs: transformational vision. They reach a point when they have said, "That's it! I'm sick and tired of being sick and tired, and I must change!" And they begin to envision themselves as a new healthy person, leaving behind the old, unhealthy habits, and pressing on toward a new future. Their change is fueled by passion, inspiration, hope, and excitement, and they are pulled into change by the energy of their vision. Every diet program today highlights someone who caught a new vision for their life and was pulled toward that vision, rather than merely pushed by external motivators. It was not necessarily the diet program that led to the long-term change, but it was the individual's vision and resolve. It really was the transformational vision, not necessarily the diet program's plan, that created lasting change. Their new lifestyle and sacrifices took on new meaning because the joy of the vision far out-weighed the discomfort of the work along the way.

As Christians we have the greatest primary transformational vision cast before us each day. Remember, you are the living, breathing temple of the Creator of the universe. You are His ambassador and a representative here on earth. And your body is not your own but belongs to the King of kings. You also have several secondary visions that should continue to motivate you to change, including developing a body that can continue to serve and go as Christ calls, your influence in the lives of your loved ones, and the opportunity to promote a healthy body for the future. If you were to die from a preventable disease today, who would be affected and how?

Developing a transformational vision requires time in God's Word, prayer, and some honest introspection. You may find that, as you prayerfully consider your life, food has a much higher degree of importance than it should. You may also find that you use food to pacify pain or anxiety, feed food addictions, or eat for the pleasure of taste. Surrender it all to Him, and allow Him to transform you by renewing your mind.

Take a Minute

Please take some time to surrender these important realizations to the Lord and allow Him to begin to create a new vision for your life and help you realize His vision for your life: loving the Lord your God with all of your heart, mind, soul, and spirit because of His love and grace toward you. Surrender your dietary failures; feelings of guilt, failure, and fear; food struggles; and addictions to Him. Ask Him to regenerate your life and instill into you an eternal vision for your life that places your days and motives on earth in the perspective of eternity. Live for eternity, die to the flesh, and represent Him to the best of your ability every day.

What's in Your Grocery Story?

$\mathcal{H}$ere is a little exercise for you this week. The next time you take a trip to the grocery store, stop for a moment and let your eyes focus on the shelves, marketing campaigns, advertising, packaging, and presentation of food. How does the food look, how is it packaged, what colors are used, where does it come from, and what is the overarching advertising message on the package? Step back and look at all of the shelves and the incredible cornucopia of products. Then, as you stand there in the middle of the grocery store, change gears mentally and imagine that you just walked out of the garden of Eden and had never seen a grocery store. Through this lens ask yourself how the food compares with naturally occurring food that God provided, what is really necessary for life, and how many of the food choices are based on taste and pleasure. What percentage of the food in the grocery store would be considered foods that God established during creation?

The abundance and variety of choices in grocery stores is staggering. Recent estimates suggest that we have 46,852 items to choose from in the average supermarket today. Packaged foods, snack foods, and drinks comprise the majority of the aisles, and you would have to hike your way to the periphery to find naturally occurring foods that might resemble those foods in the garden. In fact, the top ten best-selling grocery items for 2009 were these:

1. Carbonated beverages

2. Milk

3. Fresh bread and rolls

4. Beer/ale

5. Salty snacks

6. Natural cheese

7. Frozen dinners/entrees

8. Cold cereal

9. Wine

10. Cigarettes[1]

None of these foods supports a healthy body. Most contribute to disease, and yet they comprise the top sellers in our nation's grocery stores.

Research has also shown that high-caloric foods, such as processed foods, candy, and snacks cost an average of $1.76 per 1,000 calories.[2] Disease-promoting foods are the least expensive, most readily available—usually within arm's reach and at eye level—and fill more than three-fourths of the space in our grocery stores today. The man-made, processed food system has made it too easy, too convenient, and too affordable to make lots of unhealthy choices.

Radical Shift

Today, studies estimate that the average person spends approximately 90 percent of his or her household food budget on processed foods and animal products.[3] Hidden within these attractively packaged and convenient foods are unnatural, man-made ingredients that contribute to the development of a host of diseases. Additives such as high-fructose corn syrup, refined flours, salt, trans fats, preservatives, color dyes, and flavor enhancers have all been shown to have detrimental effects on every system in your body. Many of these additives will powerfully stimulate your appetite, leaving you overfed yet hungry. Often these ingredients are cloaked in natural-sounding language that, on the surface, appears nonthreatening, but in reality hides their true treacherous identities.

Words like *natural coloring, cane juice,* and *natural preservatives* give the label a benign-sounding list of ingredients when, in reality, they can be very harmful when consumed consistently. Also, packed within the processed foods are hidden toxins, such as pesticides, plastic residue, and heavy metals that find their way into our modern-day food chain. Food today is not really "food" but rather a chemistry experiment to produce delicious, preserved products that fill the stomach yet starve the cells.

It's not just what is *added* to the food that promotes disease, but it's also what is *removed*. Vital minerals, vitamins, antioxidants, and phytochemicals are stripped away during the processing of food, and many of the natural enzymes and vitamins are destroyed because they are heat sensitive. Adding back processed minerals and fabricated vitamins does not make the food or product whole again or healthy. Instead, it may further contribute to lost health.[4,5] Once again man has attempted to remake food by adding back what was lost with a fabricated version made in a lab and finished on an assembly line. This is a far cry from the natural vitamins and minerals found in plants that God has prepared to support life on planet Earth.

Vitamin E is a great example of the fallacy of adding vitamins back into food. In a piece of broccoli, leafy greens, and almonds you will find eight different forms of vitamin E, each one acting slightly differently, and all eight forms work synergistically with other minerals like selenium to support the healthy function of cells. Vitamin E made in a lab is created as a single isolated form, d-alpha-tocopherol, devoid of other minerals that incompletely meets the body's needs despite satisfying the Recommended Dietary Allowance (RDA) guidelines for Vitamin E.[6] God intended us to obtain vitamins, minerals, and antioxidants from natural foods, and we are just beginning to understand the wisdom and benefits of His provision.

Plastic Food

I always tell my patients that the more times food is handled by humans, the more dangerous it becomes. Instead, the goal is to eat the majority of your food as close to its natural appearance as possible. God's plan is perfect, and the farther away we wander from God's plan, the greater the likelihood that we will reap destruction in every area of our lives, including our health.

The food we consume today is not what our relatives ate a hundred years ago. They ate food grown in gardens or organic farms, drank spring water, and ate almost no sugar or processed foods. Today, food is created in large factories, processed, preserved, and packaged for transportation all around the world. Most of the nutritional value has been stripped during the process and chemicals are added to enhance the flavor and prevent decay. Today our food comes in prefabricated packages with fancy labels, dazzling colors, and visually appealing pictures. Advertisers appeal to your emotions with words like *pure enjoyment, satisfaction, tantalizing, full-bodied, robust,* and *rich* juxtaposed against the guilt-free aspect of your choice by declaring that the food is *fat free, low calorie, sugar free, salt free,* or even *all natural.*

Recently I saw doughnuts advertised with a checkmark declaring that they were trans fat free. What a relief—I'll take a dozen! Every message is carefully designed to motivate you to purchase the product, enjoy the experience, and return to purchase the product again and again. And they defend their deceptive advertising practices by saying, "It's just business." But what happens to your health in the process of playing this dangerous game that promises guilt-free enjoyment without consideration of the future consequence to your health?

Food Tower of Babel

Mankind is also attempting to improve the food chain by altering the genes or DNA of food to make it more resistant to disease, pesticides, weeds, and pests, while improving the yield, size, and accelerate the growth time. Sounds like a good idea, doesn't it? So did the Tower of Babel to the original builders, but there was a severe consequence for their prideful and self-serving venture.

Modifying DNA, the Creator's blueprint for life, almost assuredly has a dark side. It is estimated that 75 percent of processed foods contain genetically modified foods. Research has shown that genetically modified foods can be allergenic, alter the gastrointestinal system, accelerate aging, be carcinogenic, and negatively affect nutritional values of food.[7] Animal-based research has found sterility in second- and third-generation organisms fed genetically modified (GMO) foods.[8]

Further, DNA from modified foods has been shown to cross over into bacteria in the intestines and other plants, and researchers are uncertain as to the possibility of it interacting with our own cells.[9] Studies have shown an impact on the environment with the development of super-weeds and superpests, as well as the alteration of the normal soil composition. Several foods, such soy, corn, cotton, canola, zucchini, and some papayas are common GMO crops that you should avoid. Instead, purchase organic varieties.

Food for Health and Life

We all inherently understand that food provides life, energy, and strength for the body, and we all know that without food we will die. During times of scarcity, the basic principle of Food = Life becomes readily apparent. God created food to sustain life, and He provided taste to bring enjoyment and safety to the process. But in our culture of processed and chemically contrived foods, we have moved beyond these basic principles to a new understanding of food that includes words like *enjoyment, decadent, rich, gourmet,* and how about *sinfully delicious* or Food = Fun.

As I write this, I am traveling through the Atlanta airport, walking past a modern cornucopia of food that includes pizza, hamburgers, pretzels, ice cream, french fries, candy, and a plateful of Southern fried foods. Almost all of the foods are designed to gratify taste buds and fill empty stomachs but are devoid of any real nutritional value. Modern foods leave the cells starving for nutrients and the body bulging from excess empty calories. It is truly a case of a population that is overfed and undernourished by processed foods that drive unrelenting hunger and perpetuate food addictions. We no longer eat to live, but we live to eat and ultimately eat to die from diet-related diseases, such as heart disease, diabetes, and many cancers. Eating has become another entertaining hobby that is always in search of the ever-new "Wow!" and "Pow!" Yet it consistently falls far short of its true purpose—maintaining the body.

Take a Minute

Step back and consider the food that enters your body through your mouth. Is it a part of God's original provision of naturally occurring foods for health, or is it man's modified and processed attempt to create a pleasurable, yet deficient, alternatives? What percent of your diet is comprised of food that you would have found in the original garden? How much is processed food?

Similarly, take a few minutes to consider the spiritual food that you are consuming—that which enters through the eyes and ears. How much is God's provision compared to the world's processed and fabricated attempts to feed your mind and spirit? It is strikingly similar to the change that has occurred in our food consumption. Remember to feast every day on God's best—His Word and His original food provision. May these be your primary source of spiritual, mental, and physical nutrition.

Day 10

Diseases of Diet

John is a forty-nine-year-old blue-collar worker who faced a health crisis. He was diabetic and required two medications and insulin to maintain his blood sugars within the normal range. His high blood pressure added two more medications to his daily routine, and his elevated cholesterol added yet another medication. John also struggled with his weight and during the past decade gained an extra 120 pounds. Due to his excessive weight, he developed severe back pain that required extensive treatment and injections with only limited relief.

One afternoon John sat in my office despondent and hopeless because he recognized that he was in a desperate situation. His quality of life was being eroded by a flash flood of diseases.

He sat holding his head in his hands, saying, "What am I going to do, Doc? I'm a hopeless case."

I shared with John that there was hope and that the fundamental solution to his problem was a dramatic change in his diet and lifestyle. That day, John caught the vision, and inspired by hope, he agreed to work with me to change his diet and lifestyle. He took action that afternoon by throwing out the ice cream and processed foods at home, and he spent an evening at the grocery store stocking up on the wholesome foods that God created. Gradually, over the course of nine months, John's health began to improve. Initially, the gains were small but consistent, and within three months became visible. One year later, John was 120 pounds lighter, was able to discontinue all of his medications, and had normal lab values for blood sugar, blood pressure, and cholesterol. His back pain resolved, and he returned to work and life with new energy and enthusiasm. In fact, the endocrinologist who managed his diabetes discharged him and said, "John you are free of diabetes; I don't need to see you anymore." Similarly, his primary care physician scheduled him only for a well visit the following year. John is free from the grip of disease, and his quality of life has dramatically expanded.

Millions of people around the world, just like John, are slowly killing themselves with their food choices, or as one writer said, "They are digging their graves with a fork and spoon." A large percentage of the population underestimates the critical relationship between food and disease and will eventually suffer the consequences of this tragic miscalculation. In fact, over 70 percent of premature deaths in America are related to poor diet, lack of exercise, and tobacco.[1,2]

Many of my patients acknowledge the general concept that eating poorly can lead to disease, but they are stunned to learn that the majority of heart disease, type 2 diabetes, high blood pressure, and a number of other diseases and many cancers are directly linked to a nutrient-poor diet. They are then quick to point out that they "eat healthy" but are unable to articulate what comprises a healthy diet or why their diet is considered healthy. They are even more surprised to learn that only 10 percent of Americans eat a diet consistent with the basic federal daily nutrition recommendations of three to five servings of vegetables and two to four servings of fruit.[3] How do you honestly measure up?

Diet and Disease

Over the last decade, I have learned that we really do become the food we eat, and the food we eat largely determines our health destiny and future quality of life. I have watched people burdened with the heavy yoke of disease radically transform into vibrant, healthy, and active individuals simply by changing the food they eat. A long list of chronic diseases, including heart disease, type 2 diabetes, high blood pressure, many auto-immune diseases, headaches, and numerous cancers are strongly related to diet. Let's look together at four of the most common diseases and their direct relationship to diet.

Heart Disease

Heart disease is the number one cause of death in America, accounting for one in every 2.8 deaths, just slightly less than 50 percent of all deaths.[4] That is one of two people in your home today! You have an approximately 50 percent lifetime risk of dying prematurely from heart disease, unless you make a lasting lifestyle change. Every year 1.5 million people will experience a heart attack, and 1 million will die of heart disease, or about one death every thirty seconds. Approximately 40 percent of first-time heart attacks are fatal—they don't get a second chance to change their lifestyles—and 66 percent of people who experience a heart attack never fully recover.[5]

Currently, 58 million people are diagnosed with heart disease, but the actual number of people with heart disease is much greater. In a study of young trauma victims age thirty-five or younger, 78 percent showed evidence of significant atherosclerosis (clogged arteries) at the time of death, suggesting that if you have consumed a typical Western diet and are thirty-five years or older, you likely have atherosclerosis and are at risk for a heart attack.[6]

"But my cholesterol level is within the normal range; therefore, I don't have to worry about a heart attack," my patient confidently stated. Sadly, this is not true. In fact, most heart attacks occur when cholesterol levels are 175–225 mg/dl, and shockingly 95 percent of Americans, Canadians, and Europeans have cholesterol levels above 150 mg/dl, with the average in America of 203 mg/dl. Contrast this with the fact that rural Chinese have average total cholesterol levels of 127 mg/dl. Because of the Western lifestyle, American men die at a rate seventeen times greater than Chinese men. It is not just an issue of cholesterol levels, but first of diet, and then secondarily exercise, stress, and lifestyle.[7]

The good news is that *atherosclerotic* (hardening of the arteries) heart disease is largely reversible. Both Dr. Dean Ornish and Dr. Caldwell Esselstyn have demonstrated the reversal of *atherosclerosis* (clogged arteries) through diet and lifestyle changes.[8,9] Did you notice that important word *reversal* in the last sentence? Studies utilizing cardiac catherization have shown that with aggressive dietary change the plaque begins to resolve, and the arteries open up. Heart disease in many cases can be reversed and does not need to be a death sentence for one in two Americans . . . or for you. More on the cure to come!

Diabetes

Reaching epidemic proportions, the incidence of diabetes increased 61 percent between 1991 and 2001, and in the next twenty-five years the number of people with diabetes is expected to double, increasing from 23.7 million to 44.1 million. Diabetes can be divided into two types:

1. *Type 1 diabetes* accounts for approximately 10 percent of the cases and is a problem with the production of insulin in the

pancreas due to damage of the cells. Commonly, this occurs in childhood and is thought to be unrelated to dietary excess, but it may have a relationship to dietary triggers.

2. *Type 2 diabetes* is caused by increased resistance to the action of insulin in the tissues, largely due to diet and inactive lifestyle that leads to higher blood levels of glucose or sugar. (Insulin promotes the entry of glucose into the cells.) Type 2 diabetes is genetically linked but is influenced by food and activity, and until recently, typically appeared only late in adulthood.

It is not the diabetes alone that is the concern but the multiple diseases that result from prolonged exposure to elevated blood sugars. These include

- atherosclerosis, leading to heart disease and heart attacks

- vascular disease

- amputations

- numbness of the hands and feet (peripheral neuropathy)

- nonhealing foot ulcers

- vision loss

- kidney disease and failure

- stroke[10]

The frightening aspect of this epidemic trend is the rapid rise of type 2 diabetes in our youth. In 1990, type 2 diabetes accounted for only 4 percent of the total number of cases compared to 20 percent in 2000, according to the American Academy of Pediatrics. The Center for Disease Control (CDC) estimates that 33 percent of men and 39 percent of women born after 2000 will develop diabetes, and even more concerning is that 50 percent of African-American and Hispanic children will develop diabetes. The cause for this frightening and disturbing trend can be found at the end of our forks and on the cushions of our couches. It has been estimated that 100 percent of the increase in type 2 diabetes during the second half of the twentieth century is attributed to diet and lifestyle.[11] Type 2 diabetes is directly linked to diet and exercise and is a preventable chronic disease, and importantly, it is *reversible* with appropriate dietary change.

The most tragic statistics are those of the children. Type 2 diabetes is largely preventable and should not be a diagnosis that 33–50 percent of our children face in their childhood or lifetime. Knowing that the majority of the complications of diabetes occur over time, we can assume that more children will face devastating and disabling complications at much younger ages. The good news is that they don't have to face a life of blood sugar monitoring, needles, pills, and disease, because type 2 diabetes is preventable. The better news is that multiple studies have documented the reversal of elevated blood sugars and the discontinuation of medications through simple changes in the food intake and increased activity levels.[12,13,14,15]

If you have diabetes or a family history of diabetes, this should be exciting news. Diabetes, in the majority of cases, is reversible with proper diet and some exercise. You do not have to face the future consequences and expense of this terrible disease if you are willing to make a shift toward a healthy lifestyle and diet founded on the foods that God created in that original garden.

Obesity

The front page of every major newspaper decries America's growing waistline and the increasing trend of obesity. Obesity has become the new enemy in America, and everyone is looking for opportunities both to solve and profit from this epidemic. Recent studies reveal that approximately 70 percent of US adults are overweight, and 34 percent are considered obese. The CDC estimates that 17 percent of children from six to nineteen years of age are obese, and approximately 30 percent are overweight.[16] This is an alarming trend as childhood obesity is directly linked to adulthood diseases, including:

- elevated cholesterol

- high blood pressure

- type 2 diabetes

- coronary artery disease/heart disease

- cancer

- autoimmune diseases

- osteoarthritis

Obesity has not only affected the United States, but it is now spreading, like a viral infection, to every industrialized country through the vector of the modern Western diet. A recent World Health Organization (WHO) report on obesity estimated 1 billion people worldwide are overweight and 300 million are obese, with more being added to the expanding ranks each year. The incidence of obesity increased a staggering 74 percent from 1991 through 2001, due in large part to calorie-dense, nutrient-poor foods.[17]

Fat

Despite the epidemic of obesity, fat is commonly given such benign-sounding names as "spare tire," "saddle bags," or "love handles." However, fat is never a neutral tissue on your body; it works against you and promotes disease at every level. Excess fat has been shown to generate inflammation, promote degenerative diseases, such as osteoarthritis and heart disease, stimulate estrogen release, promote angiogenesis, leading to increased risk of cancer; and accelerate degeneration of the joints. Did you know that for every added ten pounds of fat your back experiences, thirty to fifty pounds of additional stress, and your knees fifty to seventy pounds! Multiply that added stress by three thousand steps per day, and it is easy to see why joints wear down quickly and begin to fail.

The annual estimated cost of treating obesity is $117 billion, and the individual costs are devastating. This trend is driven by a number of factors, including greater disposable income, affluence, new products, convenience, expanded advertising, transportation, importation, single-parent households, and the food-away-from-home market.[18] Further evidence of the root problem is found in a recent *Roper Report* survey in 2000 that found 70 percent of Americans eighteen years old or older report that they eat "pretty much whatever they want."

Eating "pretty much whatever they want" typifies our culture that lives in the moment without thought of future consequence or cost. However, Galatians 6:7 warns, "Do not be deceived, God is not mocked; for whatever a man sows, that he will also reap." This applies to every aspect of your life from your spiritual life and decisions to your physical body. Physically sowing or "planting" seeds of health in your body through a diet built upon the foods God created, and maintaining an active and peaceful lifestyle will reap a bountiful harvest. The opposite is also true and requires careful consideration of the consequences of sowing seeds of disease that will yield a field filled with weeds.

Cancer

One of every four people will die of
cancer, making it the second leading
cause of death in the United States.
The mention of the diagnosis strikes
fear in the hearts of most people.
Every year approximately 10 million people and their families worldwide are affected by cancer. A recent
report presented at the World Cancer
Congress estimated that there will
be 15 million new cases of cancer
in 2020, and sadly 60 percent of the
people affected will be in the developing or third world where they will
not have access to any medical care.[19]

It has been estimated by the
World Cancer Research Fund
(WCRF) that three out of four cases
of cancer are directly related to lifestyle choices, including tobacco, and
40 percent of all cancers could be
prevented with changes in diet and
exercise. According to the WCRF
and American Institute of Can-
cer Research 1997, here are the most harmful and the most protective
dietary components.[20]

The Most Harmful Dietary Components (in order)

- alcohol

- meat

- animal fat and saturated fat

- salt

- grilling/BBQ

The Most Harmful Protective Dietary Components

- vegetables

- fruits

- carotenoids (antioxidants that add color to vegetables) in foods

- fiber

A quick glance at the average American dinner plate should send a
chill down the spines of many people, because it is often filled with all

of these harmful cancer-promoting foods. The most protective foods are those that God created on Day 3.

On June 21, 2010, the results and recommendations of the largest and most comprehensive study on the link between diet, exercise, and lifestyle were released to the public. The study was conducted over five years by nine independent teams from around the world, who reviewed seven thousand large studies to determine the best practices for cancer prevention. The most striking finding was that excess body fat substantially increases the risk for cancer of the colon, pancreas, esophagus, kidney, endometrium, and postmenopausal breast cancer—alarming findings for 70 percent of Americans and a world population that is adding fat to their bodies every year. Tragically, unless a global change occurs, the developing countries will face the greatest rise in new cancer cases annually because of their rising obesity rates and poor medical screening.

For cancer prevention, the report recommends the following list. (It should not be surprising because it is really a return to life as God originally intended it.)

1. Stay as lean as possible without being underweight.

2. Avoid processed meats, such as ham, bacon, lunch meats, sausage, and hot dogs.

3. Limit red meat to one serving per week.

4. Reduce or avoid salt (linked to stomach cancer).

5. Limit or avoid alcohol. Even small amounts of alcohol consumption were convincingly linked to cancers of the pharynx, larynx, esophagus, stomach, and colon.

6. Eat foods of predominantly plant origin, and plan meals around vegetables and fruits.

7. Aim to meet dietary needs through diet, and limit supplements.

8. Exercise thirty minutes per day.

9. Avoid sugar and sugary drinks and foods high in fat and calories.

10. Mothers should breastfeed.

These are very simple and intuitive solutions to a tragic problem that steals the lives of millions of loved ones every year. God's plan is always the best for every aspect of our lives.

Simple Solution

According to the CDC, more than 75 percent of chronic diseases are preventable, and often these same diseases are reversible. That is incredibly exciting if you are facing a disease right now or have a family history of disease. The food that God created on Day 3 to provide for all living things supplies the nutrients necessary for your body to heal itself and remain resistant to degenerative diseases. I want to encourage you to return to a diet comprised predominantly of foods that God made, and eat them as close to possible in their original form, avoiding processing and chemicals. The more the food is processed, the more it is likely to lead to cellular damage and systemic disease. Avoid man-made, processed foods, and watch your health improve dramatically.

Take a Minute

Think back on your diet during the past week. Consider taking a few minutes to write down everything that you ate, and don't forget those snacks! What percent would you estimate was comprised of processed or man-made foods? How about the percentage of foods that God made—vegetables, seeds, fruits, nuts, and so on? Decide how you will begin to change each meal, removing the bad and adding in the health-promoting foods as you work toward a diet comprised predominantly of foods that are naturally occurring, unprocessed, and pure. You are consciously stepping back from the world system and returning to God's system in this area of your life. Consider how you can apply this same principle to other areas of your life, including your spiritual life. Is there anything that needs to be removed or added?

$\mathcal{D}ay$ **11**

The Cost of Being Sick

$\mathcal{D}$r. Stoll, it's just too expensive to eat healthy food!" proclaimed one of my patients who, by the way, was taking ten medications, seeing five physicians, and undergoing numerous medical tests and surgeries regularly. She was adamant that she could not afford to buy fruits and vegetables, because it would "burst her food budget." It reminded me what A. J. Reb Materi said in *Our Family*: "So many people spend their health gaining wealth, and then have to spend their wealth to regain their health."

I tried to help her, but ultimately she walked out of my office, refusing to consider the benefits of a healthy diet because of her perception that it would be too expensive. Is healthy living and eating really too expensive? To answer that question, let's first look at the opposite question: how much does it cost to be sick? And in the light of the previous chapter, we can conclude that the majority of people living the industrialized lifestyle will face the significant and devastating cost of disease.

Counting the Cost

Health care costs continue to rise annually. They tripled from 1965 to 1985 and then tripled again from 1985 to 2005.[1] Currently, the costs are growing faster than our gross domestic product (GDP), and the Congressional Budget Office estimates that health-care costs will comprise 49 percent of our GDP by 2082.[2] The blistering trend of rising health-care expenditures is unsustainable, and our country, and many other countries around the world, will have to face some very difficult decisions in the very near future.

What does this mean for you? You might be thinking, *Well, I am healthy; I don't need to worry about health-care expenses.* Or, *I have good health-care coverage that will be there to pay for any unexpected illnesses.* But consider these facts:

1. The US Surgeon General's office estimates that at least 25 percent of nonelderly Americans will experience a gap in their health-care coverage, and at least 30 million Americans will be uninsured for an entire year. What if you face a crisis, such as a heart attack or cancer, during this gap in coverage? Who will be responsible for the $50,000 hospital bill?

2. Fidelity Investments estimates that retirees without employer-sponsored plans will need on average $160,000 in savings to cover medical bills, and when adjusting for inflation, this figure could rise to $500,000 for someone in their forties today. A growing percentage of the forty- to fifty-year-old population will not have employer-sponsored health care in the future, due to rising costs.

3. According to the Kaiser Family Foundation, the average family deductible has increased 30 percent in the last 2 years from $1,034 to $1,344, and PPO deductibles have increased 64 percent from $1,439 to $2,367.

4. Total out-of-pocket expenses have increased nearly 45 percent in the last decade, and the US government estimates that by 2014 out-of-pocket health-care expenses will reach an average of $3,301 per year.

5. Seniors spend on average $2,810 on prescription drugs annually with out-of-pocket expenses approaching $1,000 for medications. Annual premiums for drug coverage are expected to rise from $420 in 2006 to $816 by 2015, and at the same time, the drug deductibles will grow from $250 to $472 dollars. The infamous doughnut hole—the difference between the initial plan coverage and the catastrophic limit, or the money you will be responsible to pay—is projected to grow from $2,850 to $5,382.

6. A 2008 study by the Commonwealth Fund in New York found that 66 percent of US adults younger than age sixty-five in 2007 reported trouble paying medical bills, went without needed care because of cost, and were uninsured for a time or were underinsured.

7. The average worker lost 5.62 days of work due to illness, with smokers averaging an additional 2 days compared to nonsmokers. Average earnings and productivity losses per worker were $1,560 dollars per year. [3]

8. According to the US Department of Labor, the age sixty-five and older group spent 12.7 percent of their income on direct health-care expenses, including insurance premiums, prescription drug co-pays, and deductibles. Low-income families spent 16 percent of their income on health-care expenses, and higher income groups spent 3 to 5 percent.[4]

9. Office visit co-payments for individuals with employer-based health care doubled between 2001 and 2006.[5]

10. In 2001, 46.2 percent of the bankruptcies filed were related to medical expenses, and in 2007 that number grew to 62.1 percent.[6] The number of health-related bankruptcies has increased substantially from approximately 8 percent in 1981.[7] Each of these financial bankruptcies is marked by lives that also are facing a health crisis and potential *physical* bankruptcy.

It is very apparent: you can't afford to be sick! And if the trends continue, you will not be able to afford a significant illness in the future. Many will spend all of their wealth and time trying to regain their lost health and may end up both physically and financially bankrupt.

Counting the Hidden Cost

The financial costs alone can be overwhelming, but what about the cost of lost quality of life and opportunity? Do you remember the last time you were sick with a cold or the flu? Did your world shrink quickly? How did your illness affect your activities, service, family, and your work? Chronic degenerative diseases have similar, but more prolonged and profound effects that can be devastating and life altering. The inherent value of the lost quality of life is not measurable in economic terms, and most people facing chronic disease would spend great sums of money to regain their lost health. It is not uncommon for individuals with illness to organize their lives around their health care. The focal point of their week is their health care, or really disease care, and it soon controls the weekly calendar and scheduling. Every day is filled with doctor visits, medical tests, or procedures, and their lives become a perpetual treadmill in and out of medical offices.

If you lose your health, you will not only suffer financial loss, but a far more valuable loss of quality life and the opportunity to rise up and go forth into the day unhindered and unencumbered. As Christians, we can lose the opportunity to be of service, to go to the mission field, take care of families, help friends or neighbors in need, or serve in our churches.

The costs of treating degenerative diseases are rising rapidly, and health-care coverage is shrinking. Countless individuals are facing the tragedy of both physical and financial bankruptcy, largely because of lifestyle-related diseases. It saddens and motivates me to know that millions of people just don't know that their diet and lifestyle are both the cause and the cure for the crisis at hand.

How can you avoid many of the costs of being sick? You know the answer—it's investing in a healthy diet and lifestyle. The return on your investment will be substantial and invaluable.

One of the best ways to save money, de-stress, and improve your health is through a garden. You don't need a large space to produce an abundant crop of nutrient-rich vegetables, and your vegetable garden will never be affected by inflation. There are several great resources, such as Square Foot Gardening, that can help you turn a small area in your backyard or even basement into an abundant garden that produces food grown by God.

Take a Minute

Prayerfully consider today the link in your own life between health, disease, finances, and your lifestyle habits. Are your lifestyle habits potentially a cause for the diseases that will ultimately drain your finances and steal away your quality of life? How would the financial loss affect your life, your family, your future, and your giving? Have you ever stopped to consider the true cost of your current lifestyle? As a steward of God's resources, have you stopped to consider the potential financial and physical loss that can result from chronic disease? Ask the Lord for His wisdom as you begin to make lifestyle changes and for the strength to follow through.

Boxes, Bags, and Cans

$\mathcal{O}$ver the past one hundred years, the size and shape of both people and food have changed dramatically, and the changes are strikingly similar. Both have been supersized, are devoid of nutrients, have become chemically laden, and generally can be considered unhealthy. The supersizing trend directly parallels the trend in our growing disease burden.

In 1900 the average male high school graduate was 133 pounds, and an average female was 122 pounds. Today, the average male is 166 pounds, and a female is 144 pounds. Similarly, in 1971, only 6.5 percent of six-to-eleven-year-old kids were obese; by 2004, the figure had climbed to a shocking 19.6 percent. During that same period, the twelve-to-nineteen-year-old group rose from 5.0 percent to 18.1 percent, and in children two to five years of age, it rose from 5 percent to 10.4 percent. And it's no surprise that even the dinner plate has increased in size by 33 percent. These statistics reflect only obesity. If we include all overweight kids, the statistics show that approximately 37 percent of our children today are overweight or obese.[1,2] Even more concerning, they carry a significantly increased risk for the early development of heart disease, diabetes, cancer, and osteoarthritis. The children born after the year 2000 are predicted to be the first modern generation that does not live as long as their parents. These distressing statistics about our children should cause you to stop and ask how this tragedy occurred, and more importantly, how it can be reversed.

Historical Perspectives—the Smoking Gun

How has the American lifestyle changed over the past one hundred years? Changes in lifestyle habits have occurred almost imperceptibly during the past century. The change is much like the old analogy of the frog placed in a pot of cold water and then the heat is slowly turned up until the water boils, and it is too late for the frog to escape. Food and exercise habits have slowly changed and are now at the critical level, teetering between a life of health or disease and death.

Here are some shocking statistics: over the past one hundred years, Americans have slowly increased total sugar consumption by 175 pounds per person per year from an average of 5 pounds per person in 1890 to more than 180 pounds in 2009. We have added 60 pounds of high-fructose corn syrup; increased the consumption of processed grains, such as chips and crackers, by 62 pounds per year; added 70 pounds of oil per year to our diets; increased meat consumption by 60 pounds per year; increased cheese intake by 28 pounds per year; added 53 gallons of soft drinks per person per year; consume 30 gallons of beer per person per year (someone is drinking my share!); added 500 calories per day; reduced total home-grown fruit and vegetable intake from 131 pounds to 11 pounds per year; and become more inactive, watching on average more than four hours of TV per day.[3]

The problem is clear: America is living on a diet that promotes disease, premature death, and disability, and our basic daily decisions add up to either a life of health or disease. As the dinner plate has changed, so has the health of America. A prominent article in the prestigious medical journal *Lancet* also pointed to the lifestyle and dietary freefall as the cause of the rise in degenerative disease and obesity:

In many [Western] countries, peoples' diet changed substantially in the second half of the twentieth century, generally with increases in consumption of meat, dairy products, vegetable oils, fruit juice, and alcoholic beverages, and decreases in consumption of starchy staple foods, such as bread, potatoes, rice, and maize flour. Other aspects of lifestyle also changed, notably large reductions in physical activity and large increases in the prevalence of obesity.

It was noted in the 1970s that people in many Western countries had diets high in animal products, fat, and sugar, and high rates of cancers of the colorectum, breast, prostate, endometrium, and lung; by contrast, individuals in developing countries usually had diets that were based on one or two starchy staple foods, with low intakes of animal products, fat, and sugar, and low rates of these cancers.

These observations suggest that the diets [or lifestyles] of different populations might partly determine their rates of cancer, and the basis for this hypothesis was strengthened by results of studies showing that people who migrate from one country to another generally acquire the cancer rates of the new host country, suggesting that environmental [or lifestyle factors] rather than genetic factors are the key determinants of the international variation in cancer rates.[4]

Ever so subtly over the past fifty years, our culture has shifted dietary intakes toward processed foods (63 percent total intake) and animal products (25 percent), and away from God's original provision for life—

plants (12 percent)[5]—and that includes french fries and ketchup! The majority of the food consumed today is in a box, bag, or can and has been modified, created, and processed by industry. The consequence of straying from God's best is disease, pain, and suffering. Returning to his best, we can enjoy his rich blessings.

The Dietary Answer to Disease

The answer to the epidemic and the lost quality of life, premature death, and disability is simple—you and I must return to the foundational, natural diet of our ancestors and the first diet provided by God. It's a diet rich in fresh vegetables and fruits, beans, lentils, nuts, and seeds, with small amounts of natural animal products. We must learn to avoid all processed foods in bags, cans, and packages. The more times man handles or processes the food, the more likely it is to produce disease. The preponderance of nutritional literature and supportive passages from the Bible all point to the same conclusion: eat a diet founded on plants with foods made by God in their most natural state. So eat fewer animal products (two to three times per week), especially those rich in fats, such as cheese, and if and when you do eat animal products, make certain they are organic, and use them as a side dish. It will take some effort in the beginning as you readjust your habits, but soon the new healthy habits will become the norm, and your body will become healthier and stronger.

Take a Minute

Today I want you to look through your cupboards, pantry, and refrigerator. Make a written list of all of the processed foods you find, and make a mental note of the percentage of space that is occupied by these foods. What types of foods fills the largest part of your kitchen space? The foods that you find in your home will find their way into your body and impact your health in the future, because everything you see will end up in your stomach and will either support healthy cells or lead to progressive damage. The food that you find will give you an idea of your buying habits, and these can be shocking.

Now consider how you will change and what you will remove from your kitchen. Are there foods you won't purchase again? What will you purchase to fill up your shelves? Use this list to begin making a new healthy shopping list that focuses on living garden foods. Prayerfully commit your plans to the Lord, and He will faithfully direct your path.

Day 13

Why Do You Eat?

$\mathcal{A}t$ least three times per day we stop and pick up a fork or spoon and put food into our mouths, but have you ever stopped to consider why you eat? The knee-jerk response for most people is, "I am hungry," but I believe there are stronger forces at work, driving our decisions not only to eat but also what we put into our mouths each day.

"Breakfast, Lunch, and Dinner: I Never Miss a Meal"

For most of recorded history, people ate two meals per day with a light midday snack, and ancient authors like Galen recommended two meals per day for health. During the nineteenth century, breakfast became a sumptuous meal with eggs and meat, followed by lunch and a late-afternoon dinner. Thus, the three-meal-per-day diet is a relatively modern invention. Many people in earlier eras believed that eating before the meal or eating too much was considered gluttony.[1]

Today, we habitually eat at least three times per day and often organize our day and work around the meal times. Diet theory has also influenced our eating patterns by recommending eating small amounts of food in-between meals, and we now often stop for a snack or pick up a candy bar to "keep going." Habitual eating leads to overeating, because we are not listening to our natural physiologic signals but rather to modern culture, food addictions, and marketing that lead to excess and unhealthy choices.

Eating Is a Pleasure Experience

Food has evolved. For thousands of years the scarcity of food determined the dietary composition of local people groups, and any pleasure obtained from food was secondary to the blessing of a full stomach. The industrial revolution and advent of agribusiness led to a new abundance of food unmatched at any time in history. Instead of digging for roots and hunting days on end, while trying not be eaten, today we can shop at beautiful markets while sipping a cappuccino with an abundance of choices from around the world at our fingertips. Eating has evolved from a life-sustaining necessity to an abundant pleasure-filled experience, adding more tantalizing foods with each meal to satiate pleasure centers while unconsciously destroying health. The vast majority of the food choices today are not based on a careful assessment of nutritional needs, but rather on tantalizing tastes and pleasure-seeking desires. Today, eating has become an "experience." Many people choose foods at each meal because they are pleasing to the palate, satisfy "hunger," and fit conveniently into busy schedules. In fact, vegetables are often eschewed because they don't please the taste buds. Pleasure has become the primary principle of food in the twenty-first century, but with your help, we can make a change, first in the church and then in the culture.

"My Stomach is Growling; I Must Be Hungry"

Some people believe that hunger drives their decision to eat food at least three times per day because they "feel hungry" and note certain physical manifestations of "hunger," such as a growling stomach, light headedness, weakness, being tired, and irritability. All of these are symptoms of hunger, right? In fact, if you were to take a poll on the street and ask one hundred people where they sense hunger, the overwhelming majority would point to their stomachs.

Where *do* you sense hunger? Surprisingly, true hunger is a feeling of drawing or pulling in the back of the throat, taste sensitivity, and increased salivation. The majority of Americans today have never experienced true hunger, because they are never without food long enough to understand the critical difference between true hunger and the food-withdrawal symptoms that they believe are motivating them to seek and eat food. True hunger is your body's mechanism for directing the acquisition and consumption of a variety of foods to meet its needs. Toxic hunger is a body driven by addiction and food withdrawal cycles to consume more and more of the same destructive foods.

We Are Driven by Addiction

The number one addiction in the Western world today is not tobacco (23.1 percent of Americans regularly smoke), alcohol (only at least 8 percent meet the criteria for alcoholism), or drugs (an estimated 7–8 percent of the population is dependent on illicit drugs). The number one addiction in our culture today is food.[2] You may be thinking that is impossible. Because we have to eat to stay alive, how can we be addicted to food, a substance that we are required to eat every day? We don't have to smoke, drink, or do drugs to stay alive—these are all purely optional and typically pleasure-seeking activities and are not necessary for life.

Your logic is correct, and it is the fact that we must eat daily that makes food an even greater risk for addiction. Most people have never stopped to consider the very real possibility of food addiction, although many would readily admit that they are chocoholics or carboholics with a laugh and a smile. But food addiction is a very real force that holds millions captive to unhealthy foods through withdrawal symptoms that are easily misinterpreted as hunger signals, driving the continued consumption of unhealthy foods. An easy test for food addiction is to avoid a food for five days, watching for the telltale signs of food addiction, including weakness, irritability, mental fixation, headaches, lightheadedness, fatigue, and an extreme urge to eat that particular food. The most common food offenders are sugar, sweets, sweet drinks, dairy, meats, and breads/processed carbohydrates. Be aware of the false hunger signals triggered by these foods so that you can avoid the addiction trap.

We Like Convenience

We know that approximately 70 percent of Americans and 30 percent of children in thirty states are overweight or obese compared to 13 percent of adults and 5 percent of children between 1971 and 1974.[3] Forty years ago, the majority of Americans were thin and maintained a normal body weight, but today we are facing an epidemic of obesity. One of the notable changes during the past forty years was a shift in meal location. The average American migrated from the kitchen table to the fast-food booth and convenience store, where meals provided pleasurable new foods high in fat, calorically dense, nutritionally poor, and sugary sweet.

The fast-food industry has grown to support this trend, and today 25 percent of Americans consume fast food every day. Estimates suggest that there are 3 million fast-food restaurants worldwide and 100,000 across the United States. A USDA study found that those who consume one food or beverage item outside of the home add 33 percent more calories to their day.[4] Convenient food meets the immediate need but ultimately leads to the most inconvenient life-altering side effects of disease, disability, and untimely death.

Why Should You Eat?

With so many conflicting signals triggering the urge to eat, how can you find and focus on the green light of God's original plan for food? First, it is important to stop, look, and listen. Step back and look at the big picture of your eating patterns and consider these questions. Where do you eat? Why do you choose to eat in those locations? What motivates your decisions—taste, habits, tradition, convenience, addiction, or a genuine intent toward healthy choices? Are your lifestyle, business, and activities causing you to sacrifice your health to the tyranny of the urgent? Are you willing to change?

God gave your body signals that trigger the urge to eat and signals that tell you when to stop eating. The hunger signals can even influence the types of food you desire as your body urges you toward specific foods to fulfill specific nutritional needs. However, these signals have been silenced by the "noise" of the modern food culture, and the signals have become crossed and confused. This leads to temporary and incomplete satisfaction of the nutrient needs and an instinctual desire for more food—unsatisfied hunger. Once you are able to break free from the culture and eat the foods that God provided for nourishment, your body will regain sensitivity to these signals and wisely guide you to a diet that refuels and supports health and fully satisfies hunger signals.

God intended the daily refueling of your body to be an enjoyable yet productive experience. Ripe strawberries, raspberries, and blueberries are a very satisfying package that delivers nutrients to your cells. And green vegetables, onions, and mushrooms are a vehicle delivering antioxidants, vitamins, and minerals that support cellular repair and regeneration. The fundamental purpose of eating food is to provide the basic building blocks and nutrients to help maintain and promote optimal operation of your body systems so your body can effectively interface with life. Your body requires protein, carbohydrates, fats, water, vitamins, minerals, antioxidants, phytochemicals, and fiber to function properly.

Imagine for a moment that your body and each cell are like factories designed for a specific function and created for the purpose of producing a service or product. And just like any factory, each cell requires a steady supply of raw materials to maintain production, repair, maintenance, and service. The raw materials are supplied by food, water, and air. So food is really an elegant and creative package of these basic raw materials required by the body, and eating is the mechanism of transport of raw materials from the outside world into our cells. That beautiful strawberry, crisp apple, and piece of kale are ingenious packages used to deliver a wide variety of nutrients to your cells. God added taste and hunger for protection from poisonous or spoiled foods, to make the experience truly enjoyable, and to direct the consumption of a variety of foods to meet your body's nutritional needs. God's providential blessing to you is that you can enjoy the experience and be completely satisfied.

Take a Minute

Today, consider why you eat the foods you eat every day. What are the primary motivations that determine your choices? Be honest with yourself and with God. If you are addicted to certain foods, or you're struggling under the weight of a burdensome schedule, lay it down at the feet of God and trust that He will help you overcome. Perhaps you are eating emotionally to cover up deeper pain, fears, anger, or bitterness. Lay this down at the Father's feet, and ask Him to help you work through the issues at hand.

Take time today to really study a piece of fruit or vegetable. Notice the skin, shape, color, texture, flesh, and stem. Consider how our Creator designed that piece of food to package the raw materials that serve as building blocks for your body. Isn't it wonderful that He created such a vast variety of beautiful foods to make the process of eating enjoyable day after day? Every variety of fruit is just a little different in taste, texture, and nutrients because He wanted you to enjoy and be fully satisfied with His provision. In prayer today, give Him thanks for this great and abundant blessing, and gratefully enjoy His firstfruits.

Free From the Bondage of Food

*M*argaret is a fifty-six-year-old woman who struggled for decades with food addictions. She was unable to eat a cookie or have a piece of cake without triggering a cycle of food bingeing that led to feelings of guilt, failure, and continual struggles with her weight. If a piece of candy was in the house, her mind was consumed with that piece of candy, and she was suddenly immersed in a mighty mental and spiritual battle over the piece of candy. She felt hopeless, powerless, and defeated because of her struggle against something seemingly so small, temporal, and insignificant. But it was a giant in her life, both physically and spiritually, and she secretly prayed for freedom from her addictions.

Pleasure Fest

Eating in the twenty-first century has become a source of selfish entertainment, and the short-lived pleasure is causing millions to lose sight of the fundamental purpose of food. As we've been discussing, God's original design and plan for health has been hijacked by the fabricated, powerful, and tantalizing processed foods that fill grocery store and pantry shelves. Unnatural and powerful supertastes, created through modern processing, have taken control of appetite centers and manipulated normal hunger patterns. Our society is now driven by cravings and addictive desires for processed foods, rather than fulfilling true bodily requirements by eating naturally occurring foods. Eating has degraded to a "pleasure fest" of richly processed and nutrient-poor foods. The body is still hungry for the building blocks and nutrients necessary to maintain health, and this normal hunger signal stimulates the overconsumption of the same nutrient-poor foods, leading to excess calories and an over-fed, undernourished body. This cycle can continue for a lifetime unless the cause is identified and deliberate steps are taken to return to God's original dietary provisions.

Americans, and now much of the world, are addicted to the high-fat, high-carbohydrate, sugar-laden, processed-food-based diet that originated in the United States in the late seventies and early eighties. Bodies that are dependent on these unnatural foods must be fed every few hours, or intense and unpleasant withdrawal symptoms will compel a search for more addictive food. This unhealthy cycle of food addiction causes people to feel discouraged and powerless to create lasting change and sets them up to fall for one diet fad after another. Food addiction and withdrawal are critical concepts to understand as you begin to establish a lifelong diet that promotes health, strength, and vitality.

The minute food enters your mouth, it begins to interact with the pleasure and emotional memory centers in your brain. Taste is not just a passing pleasure, but instead a complex association of pleasure, emotion, and memories. God created this elegant system for our enjoyment, satisfaction, and fellowship with Him each time food passes through our lips. God created a powerful connection between food, memory, and emotion that promotes a spiritual sense of gratitude and worship. Satan perverted and manipulated this perfect creation and uses it to promote self-service that leads to destruction.

Sugar and Cocaine

Sugar is one of the most powerful foods, and it exerts its influence the minute it enters your mouth. A 2007 study comparing cocaine and sugar intake illuminates the intense addictive nature of sugar. Rats were allowed to choose between concentrated sugar solutions and IV cocaine. Surprisingly, 94 percent of the rats chose the sugar solution over cocaine, and rats that were addicted to cocaine chose sugar over cocaine when given the opportunity. Sugar consumption, the authors surmised, surpassed the reward experience of cocaine.[1]

In a similar study, rats that were fed a diet of 25 percent sugar demonstrated signs of withdrawal similar to drug addicts when the sugar was removed.[2] Finally, recent studies of brain activity have shown that sugar, fat, and salt all stimulate the pleasure-seeking pathways in the brain and directly interact with the dopamine receptors—the same receptors that are stimulated in nicotine, alcohol, and drug dependence. Dopamine is a chemical found in the pleasure centers of our brains that stimulates feelings of euphoria, excitement, and satisfaction. These feelings are always short lived, and following the initial dopamine "hit," another chemical, endorphin, is released to induce a feeling of pleasure and relaxation. This same powerful pathway of pleasure is stimulated by sugar, fat, salt, and sweet foods that can create patterns of addiction.

After the pleasure trip of sugary foods ends, guilt creeps in because of the failed attempts to change a diet or lack of self-control. The feelings of guilt and sense of failure can trigger the search for the next "feel-good" food experience. This dietary addiction roller coaster has devastating effects and causes people to feel exhausted, hopeless, and enslaved to food.

This is one of the reasons that 98 percent of dieters fail to maintain their weight loss after stopping a diet. Unsuspecting and unaware, they begin to return to these addictive foods a little at a time and are soon carried away by the dopamine wave. Their food choices once again become driven by withdrawal and pleasure-seeking behaviors rather than health.[3]

Overcoming Withdrawal

Food withdrawal symptoms are many of the same symptoms that drug addicts or alcoholics experience when they go "cold turkey" and include anxiety, shakiness, mental dullness, irritability, fatigue, headaches, stomachache, depression, and intense thoughts about addictive foods like chocolate. For example, "I have to find some chocolate somewhere in this house!"

With addictive foods on every corner now, we have created a population of unsuspecting food addicts who are unable to control their ever-expanding waistlines. Breaking free of these addictions takes courage and recognition of the power of these foods, but through a period of abstinence from the addictive foods; lots of vegetables, fruits, water, some light exercise; and three to five days of discomfort, you will be free. Once you are free, you will be able to walk past the vending machines, ice cream store, or coffee shop and not feel compelled to stop and partake. You won't experience that intense urge or internal conflict and mental debate about whether to purchase the unhealthy food. The addictive foods will no longer have power in your life, and you will find freedom when you shop, travel, or dine out. You will be able to say, "No, thank you" and not think about it again. It's a wonderful feeling! One word of caution, remember that these are powerful foods that can quickly set up another cycle of addiction and need to be handled with great caution. I have worked with patients who share with me that one bite can send them down a road of food addictive cycles, so it is important to know yourself, your potential for food addictions, and never underestimate the power of food.

Serotonin, the Long-Term Solution

Dopamine drives short-term pleasure, but long-term contentment is regulated in our brains through a different set of chemicals called serotonin. Serotonin levels are increased when we are pursuing worthy tasks, such as spending time with people, serving the Lord by ministering or volunteering, and pursing life passions. Fundamental lifestyle choices improve serotonin levels, including a natural plant-based diet, a full night's sleep, physical exercise, and proper stress management.

A quick glance at the modern lifestyle, and we can see that when people abuse their bodies with poor sleep patterns, unmitigated stress, the industrialized diet, alcohol, caffeine, soft drinks, and inactivity, serotonin levels drop precipitously. Depleted serotonin produces feelings of depression that may cause the individual to seek out foods like sugar, salt, carbohydrates, caffeine, and fat to obtain a dopamine hit and boost their moods. It is a self-perpetuating problem that can be stopped only by making a lasting lifelong shift to a healthy lifestyle and avoidance of addictive foods. Sometimes, in the face of strong addictions, fasting can provide an opportunity to regain perspective and learn dependence on the Lord for strength to overcome. (See "Day 37: Fasting for Health" for more information.)

Awakening

I believe in the power of prayer and that our God, who created Canis Majoris and the stars, can and does intervene directly in our lives. Frequently, believers come to my office feeling frustrated because, despite their prayers, they continue to struggle with health issues, weight gain, failed diets, and addiction to processed foods. They have earnestly followed the advice of the diet gurus for years but continue to slide back to old diet patterns. Disappointment and discouragement are waiting at the door as the weight soon reappears in those same troublesome areas.

Some people have given up, hopelessly believing that they will always be overweight and unhealthy, and that it is "just in their genes." Others have decided to live for today, eat for pleasure, and enjoy the trip here on earth, because this is not our home, and their bodies are only temporal. Both groups ultimately arrive in my office, facing a health crisis. They are abruptly awakened from their food coma to the painful reality of disease. Frustrated and fearful, they recount a similar story that has led them to this crisis moment in their lives, ending with, "I never thought this would happen to me; I was healthy."

Most of them, however, never stopped to consider that the food they eat and the addictive qualities of food have fueled their declining health and growing disease. Food is addictive, and it is these addictions to foods that hold us hostage to a disease-promoting diet that ultimately leads to a predictable, disastrous end. It is the food addictions that overcome your willpower and relentlessly draw you back to those same destructive eating patterns and comfort foods. God's original plan and provision for fueling the body did not include the foods that make up 90 percent of the American diet, and it definitely did not include the addictive foods that cause millions to struggle with weight and poor health. The most powerful one-two punch for overcoming these addictions is returning to prayer and the foods that God has provided, while avoiding man-made processed foods. By doing so, you can gain freedom.

The Power of a Name

Words are important and give intense meaning to concepts and ideas. Many of the most dangerous and addictive foods have names like snacks, treats, sweets, desserts, pick-me-ups, or "my weakness." All are endearing and cute names for foods that have been shown in numerous studies to cause disease, alter brain neurochemistry, and contribute to addictive eating cycles. It is important to recognize the foods for what they are: potentially addictive foods that affect the brain in the same way as drugs, like cocaine and methamphetamine, and when they are used regularly, always lead to chronic degenerative disease. For some people, these foods are addictive and dangerous and cause destruction both physically and mentally. For others, the dependence is less apparent, but the attraction is still strong, influencing daily food decisions, and slowly shifting food preferences, purchases, and ultimately health. Warning: handle sweet and sugary foods with great care. Remove the deceptive cloak of innocence often cast by our culture, and recognize them in their true form.

Margaret's Happy New Beginning

Margaret was stuck in a perpetual cycle of short-term, immediate pleasure that led to long-term pain and emotional and physical suffering. The only lasting and permanent solution to her desperate situation was to take immediate and dramatic steps to break the chains that held her in bondage. Prayerfully she acknowledged that she was in bondage to these foods and that, because of Christ in her life, she could do all things through Him who strengthens her. Then with renewed confidence and with the support and prayers of Christian brothers and sisters, she removed all of these addictive foods from her life for thirty days and began to exercise. After the first month, she felt much better and noticed that she had lost seven pounds. Inspired, she continued the new routine, and month by month she improved. Today Margaret has complete freedom from these addictive foods and lives a vibrant life serving the Lord. "Food," she confidently proclaims, "no longer has a hold on my life!"

Take a Minute

Right now your heart might be racing, and you may be feeling a little anxious as you consider giving up these comfort foods, but take heart because you, too, can gain freedom, just as Margaret did, from the foods that hold your health and life hostage. Your life and work are far more important than the food you eat, and I want to encourage you today to choose a life of health and freedom from addictive and destructive foods. If you believe that you struggle from food addictions, please seek the counsel of a pastor or leader who will prayerfully encourage you as you begin your journey. Spend more time in prayer and reading the Scriptures, asking God to fill and sustain you as you learn to depend more on Him. Also, a friend who has already overcome the same struggle can provide you with prayer support, wise counsel, and inspiration.

A fellow believer once shared with me that she struggled mentally during church because she knew that doughnuts were available, but she also understood that eating a doughnut would ignite a binge cycle. And so, during the service she was fighting the battle of food addiction. I believe we need to learn to be sensitive to those in our churches who struggle with food addictions and make a churchwide effort to avoid serving those sugar-based foods that contribute to addictive cycles. We are called to encourage and lift up one another to become more like Christ, and as Proverbs 27:17 says, "As iron sharpens iron, so a man sharpens the countenance of his friend." It is my opinion that, if a table full of doughnuts and sugary snacks may cause a brother or sister to slip into a binge cycle or face incredible pressure and distraction from the real reason we attend church, then in love we should find alternative snacks that will not cause them to stumble.

I want to encourage you to consider alternative foods for church picnics, Sunday services, and events that will not cause a brother or sister to struggle or face defeat. There are lots of delicious options, such as berries, bananas, apples, nuts and seeds, dried fruits, and healthy breads. Commit your body to Lord today as a holy sanctuary set apart from the world's system that leads only to death.

Emotional Eating

$\mathcal{I}$ believe that food and the process of eating have a strong spiritual component. Consider for a moment the references to eating that are closely tied to a spiritual truth. Christ said, "Take, eat; this is My body" (Matthew 26:26). In Revelation 3:20 Christ said, "Behold, I stand at the door and knock. If anyone hears My voice and opens the door, I will come in to him and dine with him, and he with Me." Here *dining* indicates a reciprocal fellowship and relationship. The Lord commanded Adam and Eve to eat freely of the fruits of the garden of Eden (Genesis 2:16). God fed the Israelites with manna from heaven, yet they craved meat and were not satisfied with His provision (Exodus 16). Jesus said, "I am the bread of Life. He who comes to Me shall never hunger, and he who believes in Me shall never thirst" (John 6:35), and believers will join Christ at a great feast in the kingdom of God (Luke 14:15). Finally, we will be given the privilege of eating of the Tree of Life in the New Jerusalem (Revelation 2:7). Food and the process of eating are God's provision for life created for relationship, enjoyment, bodily provision, and fellowship with each other. Our absolute dependence on food causes us to recognize that God is our ultimate provider and sustainer. When we hunger, it is a reminder that we are weak, that He provides for us, and that we should hunger first for a relationship with Him.

Holding a beautiful piece of fruit and noting its delicate skin and its soft, sweet, and beautifully colored flesh, we can begin to appreciate the majesty of our Creator and give thanks to Him for His incredible system of delicious food to nourish our bodies. Every opportunity to eat should remind us of our dependence on God and cause us to give thanks with a grateful heart.

Corrupted Creation

The enemy sinisterly corrupted this daily communion with God and our dependence on Him for sustenance, nourishment, and fulfillment by adding selfish gain and addiction to the equation, thus turning our eyes from God's provision to man's. Adam and Eve walked with God and enjoyed the blessing of a perfect system of food and life. God's provision of food was perfect in every way, healing to the body and pleasing to the palate. But one day, while walking in that first garden, they took their eyes off of their Creator and Sustainer when the enemy enticed them to eat food with a new motivation: And the serpent said to the woman, "you will not surely die. For God knows that in the day you eat of it your eyes will be opened, and you will be like God, knowing good and evil"(Genesis 3:4–5). And for the first time in history, God's provision of food became a vehicle of selfish gain and self-fulfillment. This is the first recorded incidence of emotional eating—eating for personal gain beyond supplying nutrients for the body.

Renewal and Freedom

Emotional eating continues to shackle millions of people with empty promises and secondary guilt. It is a never-ending cycle of mental and emotional defeat that also leads to disease as people fall into negative emotional patterns and, in the process, fall prey to food addictions. The solution is looking to God for our full and complete provision, fulfillment, nourishment, and daily sustenance.

Desiring to Be Wise

Adam and Eve ate of the prohibited fruit because they desired to be wise and to be like God, knowing good and evil. The pride of life first exhibited in this action continues to drive people to create life in their own images. Let's pick up the story in Genesis 3.

Adam and Eve were standing in the garden on another perfect day in paradise, talking with the serpent, Satan in disguise. He "set up" Eve with his first question.

"Now the serpent was more cunning than any beast of the field which the LORD God had made. And he said to the woman, 'Has God indeed said, " 'You shall not eat of every tree of the garden?' " ' " (v. 1)

Eve replied, "We may eat the fruit of the trees of the garden; but of the fruit of the tree which is in the midst of the garden, God has said, 'You shall not eat it, nor shall you touch it, lest you die'" (vv. 2–3)

And the serpent said to the woman, "You will not surely die. For God knows that in the day you eat of it your eyes will be opened, and you will be like God, knowing good and evil" (vv. 4–5).

Now here is an important verse; pay attention to Eve's response as she looked at the simple fruit hanging on the tree branch: "So when the woman saw that the tree was good for food, that it was pleasant to the eyes, and a tree desirable to make one wise, she took of its fruit and ate. She also gave to her husband with her, and he ate" (v. 6).

Why did she take the fruit and eat it? Not because she was hungry or thought it would be good for her body. No, instead, her fleshly passions were kindled by the simple fruit hanging in a tree. The lust of the flesh—the fruit appeared to be delicious. The lust of the eyes—the fruit was a delight to the eyes. And the pride of life—it would make them wise. These passions were driving Eve to reach up and take that fruit from the tree (1 John 2:16). The anticipated pleasure, power, and enjoyment of the fruit quickly eclipsed God's commandment. One bite of that fruit was all it took for sin and death to corrupt God's perfect creation. The pain and suffering of that decision continues to play out in our world today.

What Will You Choose?

Man has recreated food in his own image. It is processed, chemically contrived, and genetically enhanced to provide greater abundance and pleasure, but it is ultimately empty and leads to disease and death. Our flesh and taste buds crave it (the lust of the flesh); our eyes are delighted by the packaging, colors, and shapes (the lust of the eyes); and we consume large amounts, including the 24-ounce steak (the pride of life). Just like Adam and Eve, we are faced with opportunities to make choices about the foods we eat. We reach and take that "fruit" every day, driven by our emotions, and we eat it. In turn, it corrupts our bodies, leading to disease, decay, and death. We have similar choices every day, reaching for God's provision of food or buying the lie and taking the fruit of the world.

Eating Under the Influence

Emotional eating, or eating to pacify lusts, pain, sadness, hopelessness, insecurity, control, or fear carries with it a double whammy. Emotional eating seeks to numb our feelings, but then it perpetuates feelings of failure, guilt, and self-hatred. It is life tragically out of balance. The deep guilt, abandonment, bitterness, isolation, anger, and perhaps inferiority can only be swallowed up by the love, joy, peace, and hope of Jesus Christ and never by a bowl of ice cream or a chocolate bar. The relief is only temporary, and the pain combined with guilt and failure persist. The enemy wants you to remain in fruitless cycles that consume your life and make you powerless, weak, and sick. Freedom is found in the hope and life of Christ, and we know that God will supply all our needs according to His riches in glory by Christ Jesus (Philippians 4:19).

Adaptation

Emotional eating is really an adaptive response that uses food to provide feelings of control, safety, escape, and comfort. I have encountered people who have confided that their emotional eating is rooted in the painful memories of sexual or physical abuse. Food has become their controlled comfort and safety and biochemically provides temporary relief from the painful memories. This same food then fuels further feelings of guilt and powerlessness that grow within them. Their flesh criticizes them and emphasizes their failures. This deadly cycle created by sin completely ignores the eternal truth that the God, who created the universe, knows you and loves you and sent Christ to redeem you. The only way to truly find freedom and hope is through the power of a loving God. If you are struggling with these issues, I encourage you to seek the counsel of a biblically based counselor or pastor.

Overcoming Emotional Eating

The first step in overcoming emotional eating is to completely cast your-self upon Christ, meditating on His Word day and night and prayerfully seeking Him. His Word and the power of the Holy Spirit will guide you through the healing process, working through bitterness and anger to forgiveness and relinquishing fears and pain, knowing that God will sup-ply all your needs according to His riches in glory. You can confidently approach God, knowing that Christ, our High Priest, is our ever-present intercessor, making our requests known to God.

You Can Do All Things through Christ

Don't set yourself up for failure by saying, "I will never do it again!" It is not in your power that you will overcome but by His power. Our own willpower will eventually fail us. The diet strategy will never work because, with a 98 percent failure rate, diets only reinforce the notion that you can't be trusted and will never overcome. Ignoring the emo-tions or the events doesn't work either, because they will always demand your attention. Creating unrealistic goals or expectations will never work, because it is not something that can be overcome by sheer will, but instead by the omniscient hand of God. It is important to allow your Father to work in and through you to bring healing and strength. Here are some other suggestions to help break the bondage of emotional eating.

1. Eliminate the temptations at home that may prey on your weak moments when stresses make you susceptible. And don't fool yourself, because those moments will come. Instead of eating, try praying, singing, or memorizing Scripture.

2. Examine why you use food to feed emotions, and surrender this to God in prayer. Biblically based professional counseling may be of assistance.

3. Begin to take care of your body, and remember it belongs to the Lord.

4. Become more mindful of your eating, and listen to those child-like clues for hunger and satiety. Babies know when they are hungry and when to stop. Be aware of texture and aromas of foods, and give your body healthy options. Avoid emotional conversations at mealtimes. Study the intricacies of the beautiful foods that God created and the life cycle that brought it to your table. It is His provision.

5. Read Isaiah 40 and Romans 8 to gain a better understanding of God's love for you.

6. Create new mealtime rituals by creating a beautiful table, calm music, and Bible reading during meals.

7. Always do your best (Colossians 3:17), and don't take others' critical words personally if you did your best, because you know who you are in Christ.

8. Pursue God's passions by finding an area where God is working and join Him in that eternal work. Or as one man put it, "I look to see where God is raining down His glory, and I go and get wet!"

9. Focus your thoughts on God from the first moment you open your eyes until your last thought before drifting off to sleep. Memorize scripture to help you overcome through the power of His Word.

10. Always remember that you don't have to be a slave to sin and its lusts, because you have Christ. You are free from the bondage of sin and death, and through His strength you can overcome any temptation, including food. First Corinthians 10:13 gives us hope that we can overcome any temptation: "No temptation has overtaken you except such as is common to man: but God is faithful, who will not allow you to be tempted beyond what you are able, but with the temptation will also make the way of escape that you may be able to bear it." You can overcome because He overcame.

Take a Minute

Take an hour to really spend time in prayer and Scripture reading today. We all eat emotionally, and God intended that we feel emotions during the eating process—emotions that will inspire us to a closer relationship with others and Him. Pray today that God will restore this aspect of your life and bring you back into communion with Him with every bite you take. You may need to prayerfully, and possibly through biblical counseling, work through painful or emotional issues that have arisen while living in this fallen world. Trust it all to Him and know that He will guide your paths.

$\mathcal{D}ay$ **16**

Food Foundations

$\mathcal{W}e$ eat it several times per day, we spend our hard-earned money purchasing shopping carts full of it, we have large cabinets and pantries to store it, we have created restaurants to serve special presentations of it or make preparing and eating it more convenient and fun, and we have created multibillion-dollar companies and industries around the mass production and development of food. We all know the basic food groups, but have you ever stopped to ask yourself what is in your food that either strengthens or weakens your body? What are those all-important elements that either promote health or disease?

Food is comprised of several important components: they are macronutrients, micronutrients, and fiber.

Macronutrients are protein, carbohydrates, water, and fats—the primary source of your calories. They are important building blocks for your body and are involved in energy metabolism. Most diets today manipulate the macronutrients to alter total caloric intake, metabolism, and weight.

Micronutrients are noncaloric components of food that include vitamins, minerals, antioxidants, and phytochemicals. They are important for cellular function, enzyme activity, and preventing and repairing cell damage.

Fiber is the undigestible portion of plants that is either soluble or insoluble and helps to stabilize blood sugars, feeds gut flora, and improves nutrient absorption. Even though it is inactive, it has many health benefits.

Macronutrients

Today everyone is talking about protein, carbohydrates, and fats. This category has become the source of major diet trends and marketing campaigns, such as high-protein, low-carbohydrate, low-fat, and arduous calorie-counting diets. The next time you are at the supermarket, pay attention to all of the marketing for low-fat, no-fat, low-carbohydrate, low-calorie, high-protein, and no-sugar-added products. They're all variations on the same macronutrient theme and may help you lose weight temporarily but rarely help to maintain long-term weight loss or health.

Meanwhile, keep in mind that macronutrients keep you alive! In fact, you can live for a long time on just one group of the macronutrients, and I am sure you know people who eat predominantly protein or carbohydrates. Eventually, however, the imbalance will result in disease.

In the search of the healthiest diet, focusing only on the macronutrients leads to confusion about food and long-term weight management. Who do you believe? Stepping back to look at the bigger picture of food, we learn that there are two more important components of food that have a greater contribution to health and long-term weight management than the macronutrients.

Micronutrients

Packaged within the *macro*nutrients, like a gift, are the *micro*nutrients. If the macronutrients keep you alive, the micronutrients supply the raw materials your body needs to maintain health. Your body requires more than 90 nutrients for optimal function, including 60 different minerals, 16 vitamins, 12 amino acids, and 3 essential fatty acids. This does not include the estimated 10,000 different phytochemicals and antioxidants!

Phytochemicals are an exciting group of chemical compounds in plants that help protect the plant and the human body from disease. They offer protection at every level of cellular function, including these:

1. Antioxidants in onions, leeks, garlic, grapes, fruits, and vegetables protect against DNA damage, cellular damage, and cancer.

2. They have antibacterial effects that are found in foods like garlic, clove, and basil.

3. They regulate DNA by slowing down the cancerous cell multiplication through the saponins in beans, and capsaicin that helps to protect cells from carcinogens.

4. They stimulate enzymes to slow or prevent diseases, such as cancer, through foods like cabbage, beans, and cherries.

5. They have a hormonal effect as foods like soybeans help to balance important hormones, such as estrogen, and improve the symptoms of menopause. [1,2,3] Studies have shown that it is better to consume a variety of phytochemicals from a diversity of foods rather than a single large dose from one or two sources. They have also discovered a synergistic effect when multiple phytochemicals are consumed together, such as a large salad with a variety of vegetables.[4]

Micronutrients repair damaged cells, prevent damage to cells and DNA, as well as ensure optimal cellular and system function. They are found in large quantities in plant-based foods and in very small amounts in animal products. Today the processed food industry attempts to add micronutrients back into processed food, beverages, and supplements, but every year science uncovers more valuable micronutrients and phytochemicals in naturally occurring foods that were previously unknown. Science is demonstrating the incredibly intricate system of food that God created to protect, heal, and repair our bodies. Industry will always be miles behind God's plan.

God created the perfect package for macronutrients and micronutrients, and it is not a pill or powder. It can be grown in your backyard. The perfect package is a strawberry, blueberry, broccoli, or apple. He even added delicious taste and color to the package to make it appealing to both the eye and the palate. Everything that your body requires is delivered in a beautiful, sumptuous package that fully satisfies the body's needs and delights the palate.

Calorie Accounting

Life is in the macronutrients, and health is in the micronutrients. Consider your daily diet of approximately 2,000 calories, if you are a male, or 1,500 calories, if you are a female. You could meet your caloric needs by eating a diet of pure sugar, processed meat, cereal, french fries, or candy bars—the unfortunate diet of some in America. Your body will live on this diet as long as possible, but disease and system failure will occur at some future date when it can no longer keep up with the damage.

If, however, your goal is health, then you should strive to fill each calorie with as many micronutrients as possible—nutrient-packed calories. Dr. Joel Fuhrman developed this simple formula to describe the relationship between calories and health: Health=Nutrients/Calories or H=N/C.[5]

Consider for a moment the processed foods in the center aisle of your supermarket. That's the foods in boxes, bags, plastic, and containers. Do they contain high levels of micronutrients, such as antioxidants, phytochemicals, minerals, and naturally occurring vitamins per calorie? Compare these foods to a cup of nutrient-rich kale, broccoli, or an apple, again confirming God's perfect plan for feeding your body.

Every morning when you wake up, you have essentially 1,500 to 2,000 calories to spend on foods that keep you alive, and more importantly, keep you healthy. Imagine that each calorie is a dollar to be spent. You could waste your "dollars" on frivolous foods, or you could invest your daily dollars in the valuable items that will provide long-term returns for a lifetime. Everyone loves a great bargain and "getting the most for our money.'" Similarly, the goal of eating should be to get as many nutrients for your calories as possible. And the best place to find the nutrients is in the natural foods God created to nourish and sustain our bodies. This single principle applied each day and to each meal will lead to a healthy diet, healthy body, and healthy weight.

God's Wisdom

Your diet, the food you eat every day, is far more important than meeting your daily caloric needs, fat, protein, and carbohydrate requirements or weight management. The food you choose to put into your mouth will largely determine your future health or disease and ultimately your quality of life. Not all proteins, fats, and carbohydrates are created equal, and some will promote health while others will actually promote disease. Health is hidden in the packaging that accompanies the macronutrients. Is your package full or empty?

In general, the more processed the food or the more times it is altered from its original state, the more it will likely promote inflammation, cell injury, and future disease, because it is devoid of micronutrients and filled with processed chemicals. In contrast, the more naturally occurring the food and the less processed it is, the more it will benefit your health because it has retained its God-given qualities and micronutrient content. The more times food is manipulated and processed by humans, the more likely it is to promote disease.

God's original plan provided a wide variety of plant-based foods that are rich in macronutrients that lead to optimal health. The best dietary advice is to eat the majority of your calories from foods that God created, as close to their original state as possible, and avoid foods that humans have processed, manipulated, or created.

Take a Minute

Please take a few minutes and write down the foods that currently form the foundation of your diet, or the foods that make up the majority of your calories each day. Think about what you ate for breakfast, lunch, and dinner each day last week, and don't forget to include the snacks in between meals and at bedtime. Place them in categories, such as meats/chicken, dairy, breads/cereals, junk food/chips/sweets, soda/juices, vegetables, fruits, and condiments. Once you have completed this list, ask yourself how many of the foods and total calories you ate were health-promoting, filled with phytochemicals, antioxidants, minerals, vitamins, and fiber, compared to those that may contribute to disease through nutrient-empty calories. If you are eating a health-promoting diet, you will quickly see that the majority of your calories are coming from foods that are full of micronutrients or a plant-based diet. If, however, you find that the majority of your calories are devoid of these micronutrients, your diet is probably promoting disease, and disease is gaining a foothold in your body right now.

Use this list to assist you as you begin to make dietary changes. Start by removing the "empty" foods from your kitchen, and fill up those cupboards and refrigerators with God's food.

The Nutrient-Rich Diet

*T*hen God said, "Let the earth bring forth grass, the herb that yields seed, and the fruit tree that yields fruit according to its kind, whose seed is in itself, on the earth"; and it was so. And the earth brought forth grass, the herb that yields seed according to its kind, and the tree that yields fruit, whose seed is in itself according to its kind. And God saw that it was good. So the evening and the morning were the third day. (Genesis 1:11–13)

God's Garden

Take a moment to recall a vivid mental picture of a lush green jungle at sunrise with the mist rising through the emerald tree canopy, a bountiful garden in full summer bloom, and the deep-green, rolling hills topped with golden wheat swaying in concert to a gentle June breeze. This is God's magnificent creation, and plants are His provision of food for life on planet Earth. The entire food chain today begins and ends with plants, and in the beginning the food chain was plants. On the third day of Creation, when God created plants, He saw all that He had created and pronounced that it was good.

Our modern culture, in its attempt at deity, created food in its own image—processed, packaged, sweetened, and chemically contrived to make every eating experience more fun and pleasurable. The result? The food chain radically shifted away from God's provision to man's, and as would be expected, that move created more disease, pain, and disability for its "worshippers." God's magnificent first provision, plant-based foods, have become denigrated and even despised by some as the diet of the weak, uninformed, or radical. And many followers of Christ have unwittingly been swayed by the culture to look down on one of God's great creations and provision for life. In reality, plants are one of God's most amazing creations for both their irreplaceable food value and fundamental position in the ecosystem.

God's Original Provision for Life

If God created life and then created food to sustain life, what was His first and best plan for food? I can safely tell you it was not fast food, processed food, or junk food! Recall that Genesis 1:29–30 was God's original plan for life, and it was comprised of seed-bearing plants, fruit, and vegetation. His original provision was plant-based foods.

Later, in Genesis 9:3, God blessed Noah after the Flood and told him that he could partake of everything living, including the animals and insects. God did not make clear the reason for this instruction, but it was given for Noah and the generations that followed. Biblically it follows that God's first food provision was plants, and later He allowed the consumption of animals. This order of God's food provision serves as a good guide for your dietary patterns by building a diet on a plant-based foods foundation.

Best Source of Micronutrients

Thousands of scientific studies have documented the health benefits of a plant-based diet. They are a rich source of naturally occurring minerals, vitamins, phytochemicals, and antioxidants that are vital to the optimal function of every cell in your body. Without adequate supplies or micronutrients, your cells begin to break down, and cellular and DNA damage is not repaired, leading ultimately to cell death.[1]

On a daily basis, your cells are assaulted by *free radicals* from toxic exposures, radiation, food, and stress. Free radicals are unstable, unpaired electrons that rip through cells looking for an electron to beg, borrow, or steal to stabilize their atomic structure. They are like mini tornados, causing extensive damage in cellular towns across your body. Antioxidants are able to absorb these free radicals, stabilize them, and thus prevent further damage. If free radicals are left unchecked, extensive and rapid cellular injury and death can occur.

The greatest source of antioxidants is found in vegetables, fruits, beans, lentils, whole grains, nuts, and seeds. So eating a diet founded on these foods will provide the greatest antioxidant content per calorie and ultimately slow down or minimize cellular damage. If you are not supplying antioxidants from your diet, then your system is at risk for a host of related diseases, including heart disease and cancer.

Plants to Satisfy Hunger

Have you ever finished a large meal or fast-food dinner only to find that two hours later you're hungry? How can this occur if you have just consumed enough calories to satisfy the majority of your total daily caloric needs? Several signals beyond caloric intake, including mineral stores and food addiction, drive hunger signals. Vegetables, fruits, beans, and seeds satisfy hunger signals because of their high concentration of minerals and antioxidants. Beans, lentils, and whole grains contain resistant starches that stabilize blood sugars and silence hunger hormones. Another signal that tells your body it's satisfied is a full stomach or stretching of the stomach wall. Plants, because of their fiber content, will provide greater volume per calorie than processed foods that provide very little stretch and a large number of calories. They also help to detoxify the body and overcome food addictions, satiating hunger. A diet rich in vegetables, fruits, and plant-based foods will significantly reduce your feelings of hunger.[2]

Plant Power

There is no other food group on earth that provides such a comprehensive collection of disease-fighting vitamins, minerals, antioxidants, and phytochemicals. Cultures all over the world that consume a predominantly plant-based diet do not suffer from Western lifestyle diseases, such as heart disease and diabetes. Heart disease is virtually absent in the Tarahumara Indians of Mexico, the Papua Highlanders of New Guinea, rural-living Chinese, and Kalahari Bushmen of central Africa.[3] The scientific literature overwhelmingly supports the fact that the risk of all diseases decreases with increasing amounts of fruits and vegetables. For example, a review published by the World Cancer Research Fund in 1997 found that of the 144 published studies on the association of fruits and vegetables with cancer, all 144 studies demonstrated an inverse relationship. The greater the amount of fruits and vegetables consumed, the lower the risk of all cancers.

The number one cause of death in America today is heart disease, and it accounts for 30 percent of all deaths. Can vegetables really prevent or reverse heart disease? Research has shown that heart disease, like other diseases, decreases with as total fruit and vegetable intake increases.[4, 5, 6, 7, 8] Dr. Caldwell Esselstyn demonstrated in the longest-running study on heart disease that a plant-based diet can reverse heart disease. Angiography, (interventional evaluation of the coronary arteries), revealed that 70 percent of the study participants experienced a regression or reversal of the coronary artery narrowing caused by fatty plaques.[9] A similar five-year study by Dr. Dean Ornish also demonstrated the reversal of heart disease, reduction of cholesterol, and lowering of blood pressure with a plant-based diet.[10,11,12] Green, leafy vegetables and broccoli activate protective protein NRF2, which prevents plaque adhesions in the coronary arteries. This is incredibly exciting and freeing news for those suffering from heart disease. Diet and lifestyle change can free you from heart disease.

Similar studies of other degenerative diseases reveal the same outcome—reduced damage from disease and improved disease prevention. Multiple studies of diabetes demonstrate normalization of blood sugars with a predominantly plant-based diet that eliminates processed foods and excessive animal products.[13] The risk of developing macular degeneration, the leading cause of age-related blindness, is reduced by 86 percent if you eat greens five times per week.[14] Similarly, the risk of Alzheimer's disease significantly decreases with a dietary change toward fruits and vegetables.[15]

It is staggering to begin to review the scientific literature and see that most degenerative diseases are dramatically influenced when people simply eat more plants and less processed food—more of God's provision for life and less of man's manipulated food.

Here is a list of some of the most nutrient-rich foods, containing the highest levels of minerals, vitamins, and phytochemicals.

Kale	Asparagus	Beans
Bok Choy	Carrots	Sweet potatoes
Collards	Strawberries	Apples
Spinach	Blueberries	Cherries
Broccoli	Oranges	Cucumbers
Brussels sprouts	Lentils	Almonds
Artichokes	Melons	Grapes

Immersion

During the past two years, we have been involved in seven-day health immersions to teach people the benefits of a healthy diet founded on God's plan. I am always amazed at the end of the week when a large percentage of the diabetics have normalized their sugars and discontinued their medications. Also, high blood pressures normalize, medications are discontinued, many are liberated from pain and arthritis, and the average weight loss is twelve pounds. Incredible changes can come from just one week of a diet built upon the foundation of plants.

For the participants it is a transformational week as they begin to comprehend the new possibilities of a life free from degenerative disease. Many Christian brothers and sisters also find a renewed vigor to serve the Lord with a body that is now strong, vibrant, and healthy. One Christian brother shared with me that at the beginning of the week that he was "physically, spiritually, and emotionally done." He also shared that he experienced pain all over his body and was praying that he would be able to get up and make it through another day. By the end of the immersion, he came with tears in his eyes and said that the Lord had transformed and renewed him in every way. He had a new vision for his life, no longer had pain, and was freed from the burden that he carried into the week. Enthusiastically he exclaimed, "Dr. Stoll, I feel alive again!" The secret to this amazing success and transformation is a return to God's first provision of food—plants.

Take a Minute

Thank the Lord for His bountiful gift of life through plants. Thank Him for the plants that help to mitigate the effects of the curse on our bodies through both nutrition and medicine. You may need to repent for disregarding or minimizing His provision and pray that you will begin to really appreciate these foods as a gift directly from the creative hand of our Lord.

Spend time studying the benefits of each variety of plants, and you will begin to see that variety is also His blessing. The coloring and flavoring of each one is different so we will find true lasting enjoyment as we feast upon His creation. Prayerfully ask for God's help as you strive to depend on His plan for food and health and break free of the bondage of man-made, processed food. The food He provided will bring life to your bodies, and the Son He provided will bring peace and hope to your soul.

$\mathcal{D}ay$ **18**

Cutting-Edge Research and Timeless Wisdom

$\mathcal{E}$merging research is offering two further exciting areas that support the benefits of a plant-based diet. Both are a unique glimpse into the inner workings of cells and reveal the early stages of disease long before it is ever measured in a lab test or imaging study or its effects are felt. And this is the very place where the prevention of disease is critical—stopping the train before it even begins to gain speed and eventually become a runaway train headed for certain disaster.

The two exciting cutting-edge areas of science that add substantial support to the power of diet over genes and ultimately disease are *epigenetics* and *angiogenesis*.

Now don't be intimated by the terms, because you won't be tested on them at the end of the book! Stick with me, and I guarantee you will be excited by these revolutionary scientific concepts that reveal the truth of God's timeless wisdom.

Definitions

Angiogenesis literally means new blood vessel growth that can occur in both normal and diseased states. *Epigenetics* is the study of the interaction of the environment (including food) and genes, and is revealing an incredible picture of genes that are not static and fixed but rather fluid and flexible.[1] In other words, your genes do not fully determine your genetic future, but rather your habits and exposures influence health destiny.

Epigenetics Overview

You may have heard the old saying, "You are what you eat," but have you ever heard, "Your grandchildren are what you eat"? Science has recently discovered that your environment, such as the food you eat, toxic exposures, stress, and even exercise, modifies your genes. Once modified, the genes either support health or allow disease to progress unchecked. The environment sends a message that alters the genetic structure and output. God created a wonderfully flexible platform of DNA (genes) that allows your body to adapt to a wide variety of environments and conditions by this mechanism. And when given the proper input, it creates healthy cells and a strong body that is able to meet the immediate demands. Studies have demonstrated that diet is one of the most powerful environmental forces that will influence your genes and ultimately your health and the health of your future generations.

How Your Diet Interacts with Your Genes

Epigenetics is also defined as "control over genes." It is a broad area of emerging science that has discovered that diet, toxins, stress, thought, emotion, and exercise all affect genetic expression in real time. When you eat, the food is broken down. The molecules are transported into the cell nucleus where they attach to the DNA and alter or support the product or services provided by the cells.

Genes were once thought to be hardwired and inflexible, but recently it has been discovered that genes are flexible and influenced by the environment. This flexibility either confers protection from diseases or susceptibility to disease. A classic study of women living in the Netherlands during World War II highlights this point. This group of mothers labored during the harsh winter between 1944 and 1945 and endured starvation conditions because of the German blockade. When they gave birth, their babies were decidedly small with low birth weights and more susceptible to a host of degenerative diseases, including heart disease, diabetes, and obesity. When these infants grew into adults and had children of their own, their babies were also surprisingly small. The researchers concluded that the effects of the mothers' poor nutrition modified the genes, and this modification carried over to the third generation.[2]

This hypothesis was supported by a study in mice that demonstrated that a poor diet in mothers led to physical changes (coat color) and greater disease susceptibility in their offspring. Further studies in mice in 1998 and 2006 revealed that maternal diets rich in nutrients affected the genetic state of first- and second-generation offspring.[3,4] The mice fed a nutrient-poor diet had first- and second-generation offspring that were susceptible to disease and obesity, while the well-fed mice gave birth to healthy, strong offspring. These remarkable studies suggest that the diet of mothers may be one of the most important influences of their children and grandchildren's health future.

How Does Epigenetics Work?

One of the main mechanisms of epigenetics is a process called methylation, when a chemical called a "methyl group" is added to the DNA to alter its function. Environmental factors, such as diet, turn the genes on or off by supplying or subtracting methyl groups. This alters the gene, either turning it on or off, and then changes the gene's products and function. For example, in the Netherlands' study they examined the people born during the famine and their siblings born during times of plenty. Researchers found a distinct imprint of the famine on their genetic profiles (significantly less methylation on the IGF2 gene). This is the first time that studies demonstrated that prenatal exposures affect the genes of the baby.

This methylation process occurs billions of times every second in your body, helps repair DNA and cells, recycles detoxification for cells, supports the immune system, is involved in sleep and metabolism, controls inflammation, and maintains brain function. Diseases such as cancer, lupus, dementia, heart disease, stroke, diabetes, inflammation, osteoporosis, autism, pulmonary disease, and cataracts have all been linked to a failure of methylation. Essentially, all of the degenerative diseases that plague our country have a root in epigenetics. Not surprisingly, according to epigenetic research, the habits that deplete methlyation are alcohol, sugar, tobacco, caffeine, excessive animal protein, and saturated fats—the average American lifestyle.

Nutritional studies have revealed that, if the diet is deficient in methyl groups, then the genes are either abnormally turned on or off, making the body susceptible to disease. The nutrients and toxins serve as signals to the DNA through the methyl groups. Similar studies have also shown that healthy lifestyles and diet reduce the abnormal changes and promote healthy cell function. Several cancers, including many colon, breast, and prostate cancers, have been linked to abnormal methylation of DNA.[5] Diet is the primary source of methyl groups and disease prevention.

So the critical point is where to find these on/off methyl molecules.

Epigenetic Superfoods

Broccoli	Bok Choy	Walnuts
Brussels sprouts	Kale	Sunflower seeds
Cauliflower	Dandelions	Almonds
Spinach	Watercress	Oranges
Swiss chard	Lentils	All berries
Asparagus	Beans	Bananas
Sweet potatoes	Brazil nuts	Apples

Once again we see that a diet rich in plant-based foods offers disease protection not only for you but also for your children and grandchildren. Remember this chart and put this information on a back burner to marinate for a few minutes while we move on to angiogenesis.

Angiogenesis

Another normal process in your body is the growth of new blood vessels to damaged tissues and the inhibition of the blood vessels once the job is complete. It is a well-regulated process in a normal body. But when the body is not healthy, the process becomes unregulated and again creates disease susceptibility. Some diseases, such as cancer, psoriasis, arthritis, endometriosis, pulmonary fibrosis, obesity, and Alzheimer's disease, are the result of uncontrolled growth of new blood vessels. Others, such as neuropathies, stroke, heart attacks, peripheral arterial disease, osteoporosis, and chronic wounds result from too little growth. The goal then is to regulate angiogenesis in the body through a healthy lifestyle. And just like epigenetics, research has shown that the factors that negatively impact angiogenesis are stress, tobacco, alcohol, inactivity, and sugar.

Studies in obesity reveal that fat cells are dependent on angiogenesis to supply more oxygen and nutrients. In fact, adipose tissue or fat cells actually promote angiogenesis and contain angiogeneic stem cells that create a proangiogenic environment, which is possibly one reason that obesity is linked to high rates of cancer. Weight loss is dependent on your body's ability to shut down the new blood vessels and cut off the supply lines to the fat cells. Specific foods, which will be listed later, actually combat the abnormal blood vessels, allowing your body to shed the fat more easily. But I am sure that you can begin to guess what that list will contain.

Angiogenesis and Cancer

Every cancer cell requires a blood supply to grow and eventually spread to the rest of the body. Without this abnormal blood supply, the tumors do not grow or spread. According to William Li, MD, director of the Angiogenesis Foundation,

> Autopsy studies from people who died in car accidents have shown that about 40 percent of women between the ages of forty and fifty actually have microscopic cancers in their breasts. About 50 percent of men in their fifties and sixties have microscopic prostate cancers. And virtually 100 percent of us, by the time we reach our seventies, will have microscopic cancers growing in our thyroids. Yet, without a blood supply, most of these cancers will never become dangerous.

These all-important abnormal blood vessels are formed when cancer cells release molecules that alter the genes in normal tissue, causing them to make new blood vessels (angiogenesis). Unable to grow their own blood supplies, cancer cells recruit local cells to supply the necessary blood supply. Once the cancer cells receive the new blood supply, they have all they need to grow rapidly and to spread to other areas of the body.

The exciting news is not the potential new drug category, but rather food. Specific foods were found to block or halt the formation of the abnormal blood vessels, opening new insight into cancer prevention through diet.[6,7] *What are the foods?* you may be wondering. I think you can probably guess most of the list by now:

Artichokes	Pumpkins	Maitake mushrooms	Tomatoes
Blackberries	Cranberries	Raspberries	Blueberries
Strawberries	Cherries	Red grapes	Apples
Broccoli	Cauliflower	Brussels sprouts	Grape seeds
Bok choy	Kale	Parsley	Soy beans
Lemons	Lavender	Ginger	Turmeric
Oranges	Grapefruits	Pineapples	Licorice herb
Ginseng	Nutmeg	Olives	Green tea

Isn't that exciting? Does this list look familiar? The same foods that supply a nutrient-rich diet also detoxify the body, prevent the growth of abnormal blood vessels (angiogenesis), regulate the growth of new blood vessels, support cancer prevention, and provide for the health of the fetus in the womb (epigenetics). These are the very same foods that God gave to the earth as His first provision for food. It is also exciting that this delicious list of food can be enjoyed on a daily basis, and in the process promote healthy cells that fight and ward off disease, giving us strength and vitality to rise up and go forth.

Cancer and the Third World

A sobering statistic is that the during the next twenty years the majority (two-thirds) of new cancer diagnoses are anticipated to occur in the third world where people don't have access to any medical care. The best solution and prevention may be diet. Again Dr. William Li said, "For many people around the world, dietary cancer prevention may be the only practical solution, because not everyone can afford expensive, end-stage cancer treatments, but everyone could benefit from a healthy diet based on local, sustainable, anti-angiogenic crops." Pray that new opportunities will come to the third world to learn to grow these all-important, health-supporting foods by growing gardens around the world.

Take a Minute

That is some challenging material, and I sincerely hope that you see the bigger picture of our Creator's marvelous plan to supply health through the food that He created. Three branches of science all confirm the importance of plants in maintaining your health and warding off disease. Prayerfully thank God today for His gracious provision of plants and make a commitment to consciously choose to eat the foods from the Father's hand.

Day **19**

What about Meat?

$\mathcal{O}$ne of the primary questions I hear when discussing diet and health is, "What about the meat?" Most people agree that processed food is bad for the body and nod enthusiastically in agreement, but any recommendation to reduce meat consumption is met with great skepticism and intense criticism. People love their meat; they believe it is of prime importance and that they can't live without it. It is the source of great debate today with camps on both sides of the argument. The higher meat consumers and vegan/vegetarians all cite articles to defend their positions and justify the benefits of one diet over another. How do you know who is correct?

I believe it is important to return to the Bible as a first source of information, and then use current scientific research to clarify the concepts and test the theories. We know that God allowed Noah to eat meat after the Flood, Jesus ate fish with His disciples, and meat consumption was never directly forbidden in the New Testament, unless it was noted to cause a brother or sister to stumble.

We also need to understand that cultural ideas influence trends and beliefs and establish generally accepted norms. Our culture has become accustomed to eating meat several times per day, and a meal is considered incomplete without a piece of meat as the centerpiece. This is a modern luxury that previously was available only to royalty. Today, we even name our meals based upon the meat portion of the meal. This is a truly modern diet evolving only in the last hundred years of history with the industrialization of the food system. Similarly, a cultural myth has evolved to promote the idea that meat is necessary for protein and strength and that a diet devoid of meat will lead to frailty, disease, and premature death. This belief causes people to feel that the meal is deficient and lacking nutritious value if meat is not included.

God's Provision

God permitted Noah to eat meat, and in Genesis 9:3 He said, "Every moving thing that lives shall be food for you. I have given you all things, even as the green herbs." We know that God never intends us harm, and He was making a true provision for Noah and his descendants. Therefore, biblically, we cannot justify the exclusion of meat or animal products from the diet. But it is important to recognize the order of provision, first the plants and then the animal products. This is a good model for the construction of a healthy diet. Today this order has been reversed, and meat and animal products are consumed in excess, while vegetables are relegated to a small side dish that is buttered, fried, oiled, and overcooked.

Historically, most cultures consumed meat on rare occasion and in much smaller amounts than a typical Western diet today. The ancient Hebrews were known to consume a predominantly plant-based diet of local vegetables, grains, and fruits. They ate meat only during celebrations or on special occasions. During that period in history, animals were considered a valuable asset and were not part of the daily diet.

Similarly, throughout history, lower-class populations commonly ate meat in smaller quantities and less frequently. The royalty and leaders of society consumed meat and other processed foods in abundance and died younger from diseases linked to the excesses of affluence.

How Meat Fits into a Healthy Diet

There are several keys to understanding animal products' place in your diet. The first is nutrient density. Remember that every food is a package for nutrients. The nutrients that have been shown to promote health, reduce the risk of almost every disease, reduce cellular damage, improve healing, and regeneration are the antioxidants, phytochemicals, minerals, and vitamins, or the micronutrients. Animal products have higher levels of vitamin A, B12, and vitamin D but lack many of the other micronutrients, such as phytochemicals. Therefore, diets that contain higher levels of animal products like the American diet, are devoid of these all-important micronutrients. It is a calorie trade-off: more animal products give you fewer micronutrients and higher disease risk, or fewer animal products with more plant-based foods give you higher micronutrients and lower risk of disease.

The China Project is the most comprehensive nutritional study completed to date. The study was a joint project between Cornell University and Oxford University and looked to measure the association between diet and disease. Many of the people groups of China remain relatively isolated, rarely migrate, and maintain stable dietary patterns. This allowed researchers a unique opportunity to study the full spectrum of diets from vegetarian to more Westernized diets of refined grains and animal products. The regional differences in food led to significant differences in rates of disease. Cancer rates increased incrementally as the amount of animal-product consumption increased. In areas where animal-product consumption was very low, the rates of heart disease and cancer were also very low.[1] Similarly, the mortality data from the study revealed a very strong association between heart attacks and increasing animal protein intake.[2]

Heart disease or atherosclerotic coronary artery disease is predominantly a dietary disease, and the two greatest dietary risk factors for a heart attack are refined grains and animal protein. A large international study carefully evaluated the association between the percentage of calories from animal protein and the rate of heart disease for men ages fifty-five to fifty-nine from twenty different countries. The results demonstrated that as the percentage of animal products increased, so also did the rate of heart disease.[3] In other words, as the people's diet shifted from plant based to animal based, so did their risk for heart disease.

Similarly, another large study compared environmental factors with colon cancer rates from thirty-two countries around the world. They found that in countries where the people ate more animal protein and sugar and fewer grains and plants, they had significantly increased rates of colon cancer.[4] Can you guess the countries with the highest numbers in both categories? That's right: the United States, New Zealand, Canada, and the UK. The countries with the lowest rates of cancer were the developing countries that still subsist on plant-based diets.

Eating more chicken is not the answer either. A large dietary study followed thirty-two thousand people over twelve years. Those who avoided red meat but ate white meat instead had a 300 percent increase in colon cancer incidence over those who ate no white meat. Consuming beans, lentils, or peas twice a week was associated with a 50 percent lower risk of colon cancer.[5] Chicken also has about the same amount of cholesterol as beef, and in another study from New Zealand, chicken was found to be the largest contributor of a potent cancer-causing compound formed during grilling, heterocyclic amines (HCA).[6,7]

The preponderance of the scientific literature reveals a strong connection between excessive animal protein and a host of common degenerative diseases. Alzheimer's is a tragic disease that affects 5.3 million people in the US. It, too, is related to a diet high in refined foods and animal products and low in plant-based foods—the diet of most Americans today. Several studies have demonstrated a strong correlation between diets that are high in fat and cholesterol and the development of both Alzheimer's and heart disease.[8] This would suggest that they may share a common cause—the industrialized diet.[9]

Furthermore, as the percentage of total calories from animal products increases, so do the risks of kidney stones,[10] osteoporosis [11, 12, 13] and cancers of the colon and breast.[14] Prostate cancer has not been associated with meat consumption, but in several large studies, including one of the largest ongoing nutritional studies, the European Prospective Investigation of Cancer and Nutrition, have shown that as dairy intake increases, so does the risk of prostate cancer.[15] This association between dairy consumption and prostate cancer was supported by a 2001 Harvard review of fourteen case control studies and nine cohort studies that concluded:

> This is one of the most consistent dietary predictors for prostate cancer in the published literature. In these studies, men with the highest dairy intakes had approximately double the risk of total prostate cancer, and up to a fourfold increase in risk of metastatic or fatal prostate cancer relative to low consumers.[16]

These are striking findings that point the finger at the smoking gun—the modern, industrialized diet that is comprised of refined processed foods and excessive animal products.

It is not precisely clear why excessive animal products are so strongly linked to so many diseases. Some have speculated that it is the modern farming and ranching methods that involve large doses of medications, hormones, abnormal foods to stimulate growth, and close quarters. Others believe that it is simply too little plant-based foods and their health supporting micronutrients. Others hypothesize that the actual animal-based protein stimulates growth hormone levels, leading to cancerous growths, and the fats/protein acidify the body, leading to disease susceptibility. To date there is no conclusive answer, but the trend is apparent and well documented.

The above brief review of the scientific literature is only the tip of the iceberg in the ongoing debate of animal products and disease. Clearly, the growing preponderance of studies demonstrates that excessive intake of animal products, including organic, greater than 10 percent of total calories (average American is at 25 percent), is associated with an increased risk of most of the degenerative diseases that plague our culture today. The literature does not clearly demonstrate that a complete absence of animal products is necessary for optimal health. The ancient Hebrews fit this category of rare or limited animal product consumption, and they were known for their excellent health.

This information can be shocking, and many of my patients don't want to believe it's true. In fact, they look for excuses not to put this into practice because they believe, without a scientific basis, that more meat will make you strong, and less meat will make you weak, so they need more meat for their health. However, the exact opposite is true, and it can be verified in both the literature and lives of people whose health has been dramatically changed by a whole-foods, plant-based diet.

Tinkering with DNA

Genetically modified plants were the first foray into man's attempt to create a better and more abundant food chain. Now, scientists have modified the DNA of salmon and other animals to create superanimals that will grow larger, faster, and with less disease so they can deliver more meat to your table at a lower cost. Is there a problem here? Mankind has once again deviated from God's plan for food and is fast approaching another crisis. Tinkering with the genetic code to "improve" upon God's plan is never a good idea, and as we are already seeing in the plant-based GMO literature, it can cause devastating effects for the consumer and the environment. I believe you need to avoid all GMO foods.

Recommendations

1. *Eat fewer animal products* (two to three times per week), and make them a side dish or condiment. Serving sizes should be about 3 ounces per serving (about the size of a deck of cards). Work toward *occasional* animal product consumption, as the Hebrews did, or at the very most 9 ounces per week.

2. *Avoid all processed meats*, such as hot dogs, bacon, sausage, bratwurst, and lunch meats, as these dramatically increase your risk of disease.

3. *Replace animal products with vegetables*, beans, lentils, and chickpeas.

4. *If you are going to eat meat, eat only organic, free-range animal products* just as God intended them to grow. Even though they are a little more expensive, your health is worth the cost.

5. *You don't have to become a vegetarian* or vegan to experience the great benefits of a truly healthy diet founded on a variety of plant-based foods. However, if you are facing a disease crisis or have a significant risk of disease, you will have to abstain from animal products and all processed foods to maximize your micronutrient/phytochecmicals necessary to fight disease. Remember, if you are facing a significant disease, you are fighting a war, and you need to fight with all your might and every single bite. It may take complete abstinence from all animal products, dairy, and all processed foods to overcome diseases like diabetes and heart disease, because your body needs every nutrient it can get to fight the war.

Take a Minute

Consider what you would eat if processed food and animal products were removed from your daily diet. What would remain on your plate? What percent of your diet are animal products—milk or meat? If you don't change, how will your health be potentially affected? Do you have any significant genetic risks, such as heart disease, diabetes, or cancer, that could potentially manifest disease in your life with your current diet?

Prayerfully consider shifting your diet toward God's first provision of plant-based food and significantly decreasing animal products. The ancient Hebrew diet is a good model for a healthier diet and will, in the end, produce a healthier you.

Protein Power

$\mathcal{P}$rotein has dominated the modern industrialized diet and typically is the primary focus of meals. Ask anyone today what he or she is having for lunch or dinner, and they will describe their meal based on the protein portion. "I'm having steak, chicken, fish, pork, ribs . . . " Have you ever heard anyone reply, "I'm having broccoli and brussels sprouts," or "We are having collard greens, kale, and salad with a side of fish"?

The word *protein* is derived from the Greek word *proteios*, meaning "prime importance," perhaps explaining its preeminent position in dietary discussions. Historically, early scientists, such as Carl Voit, recommended large intakes of protein despite research showing that humans needed only 48.5 grams per day. Voit mentored W. O Atwater, who founded the first nutritional laboratory at the United States Department of Agriculture and who later recommended a protein intake of 125 grams per day. He also mentored Carl Rubner, who later stated, "A large protein allowance is the right of civilized man."

This early research focus, and the recommendation for high protein consumption by scientists created a cultural current of "more is better" and "protein equals health and life." Historically, meat became a symbol of an affluent lifestyle, while those of the lower classes consumed what was considered an "inferior" plant-based diet. This high protein cultural current persists today, evidenced in the pages of the menus of elite restaurants around the world with meat as the centerpiece of the meal.[1] Protein is an important component of a healthy diet but should not be the primary focus or centerpiece on your plate.

Why Do You Need Protein?

Protein is important for the maintenance and support of muscle mass, but protein also serves myriad other important functions. It supports frameworks for cells and the production of new cells and enzymes, provides cell movement through motility "machinery," stabilizes and controls the activity of DNA and RNA, provides transport into and out of cells, and acts as a messenger molecule. A steady supply of protein through diet is necessary to repair and replace protein structures that have been damaged or worn out. It is vital to the function of every system in the body, and without protein the body will fail.

How Much Protein Do You Need?

The FDA set standards for protein consumption based on very precise nitrogen balance studies done in the 1960s. Based upon the results, they established recommendations for protein intake with an added safety factor that actually increased the recommended daily amount above the original findings. Currently, the average male requires 0.8 mg/kg of body weight. This number also includes a safety factor of 37 percent. For the average 180-pound male, this equates to a daily consumption of 65 grams of protein. The average female weighing 130 pounds would require 47 grams per day. On average women require between 40–50 grams of protein per day, and men 50–70 grams based upon their weight. Now compare this to the average American consumption of more than 100 grams per day, and we can see that Americans are far from protein deficient.[2]

You may be wondering if this excess protein is a detrimental to your health. We can evaluate this question from several different angles to find the answer.

First, *excess protein comes with excess calories.* In fact, the extra 50 grams of protein results in an extra 200 calories per day or 73,000 calories per year.

Second, *protein is classified as an acidic food,* and an excess of acidic foods taxes your body's acid/base system and can strain the kidney and mineral balance of your body as it attempts to eliminate and neutralize the excessive acids. Research has suggested that the body will mobilize calcium from the bones in an attempt to balance the acidic wastes, and this may contribute to thinning of the bones or osteoporosis.

Third, *excessive proteins, especially those from animal sources, will alter the important and delicate ideal omega-3 and omega-6 fatty acid balance.* The ideal ratio of omega-6 to omega-3 for disease prevention is 1:1–3:1. The average American diet has a ratio of 20:1–40:1. This results in a shift toward chronic, unregulated inflammation that is associated with a number of chronic diseases, including heart disease and cancer.

Fourth, *animal protein is typically packaged with saturated fat,* which has been linked to chronic diseases, such as heart disease.

Fifth and finally, *excessive protein results in a shift away from calories that contain high health-promoting nutrient densities,* such as minerals, phytochemicals, and antioxidants that help to promote healthy cellular function and prevent chronic disease as we studied in previous days. In short, excessive protein is not beneficial to your health and, in fact, is detrimental.

Does Quality Matter?

Some people may argue that animal products are a complete protein and are, therefore, superior to all other sources of protein. This is used as a justification for the consumption of more meat and dairy. It is important to ask if your body requires a complete protein at every meal to function optimally. Let's look more closely at this question.

All proteins are formed by combining different variations of the twenty different amino acids into chains of hundreds to thousands of amino acids in length. In order for the production lines to continue their manufacturing process, a steady supply of amino acids must be available. Eight of the twenty amino acids are termed *essential amino acids*, because the only source for this group is your diet. The other twelve can be made by the body and need not necessarily come from your diet.

Through the years, various protein sources, such as meat, milk, eggs, lentils, and plants have been classified as high- or low-quality proteins based on their ability to supply all the necessary amino acids. While this can be helpful in classifying foods, it is also misleading. All eight essential amino acids don't need to be present in each protein source at every meal, but over the course of one to three days of food consumption, your body will accumulate all of the necessary amino acids to maximize protein production. God created your body with the ability to manage variability in food availability and to adapt to times of abundance and scarcity. This is the body's innate wisdom programmed by our great Creator.

Protein quality is also used to describe the efficiency with which individual food proteins promote growth. One assumption underpinning this idea is that rapid growth is a marker of good health. However, several studies would suggest that rapid growth and early maturity are risks for diseases, such as breast and prostate cancer.[3, 4] Slow and steady growth appears to promote health, especially in the golden years, just like the old oak tree in the backyard that has survived many storms through the years.

Variety Is the Secret

The primary source of your protein is not as important as obtaining protein from a variety of sources. It is also not necessary to worry about combining protein sources to provide a supply of the complete essential amino acids. For years, some vegetarians were slaves to meticulous meal planning around protein sources, but today we recognize the innate intelligence and efficiency of the body to maintain amino acid stores independently of daily variations. If you are eating a diet filled with a variety of natural foods, you will meet all of your body's daily protein requirements.

Below is a list of the protein content of several common foods. It is not surprising to see that one pound of trout, beef, steak, or chicken will independently supply your protein needs for the entire day, and please note the total calories, fat, and cholesterol associated with each source. Remember that the average daily calorie requirement for men is 2000 kcal (kcal = 1,000 calories) per day, and for females it's 1500 kcal, and that protein supplies 4 calories per gram, and fat supplies 9 calories. Protein always comes packaged with other nutrients, some of which can be detrimental, such as excess cholesterol and fat. The key to health is to consume protein that is rich in the health-promoting micronutrients—

minerals, phytochemicals, and antioxidants, or spend your necessary protein calories wisely.

Food (1lb)	Calories	Protein (g)	Total Fat (g)	Cholesterol (mg)
Salmon	984	102	60.8	272
Trout	885	97.5	51.7	249
Beef (gr)	1216	81.2	96.2	307
Steak	1316	71.0	112.0	261
Chicken	394	74.5	18	239

Source: Composition of Food, US Agriculture Handbook, Vol. 8

Protein is important for life, but equally important to your health is the package combined with the protein on your plate. Disease prevention and disease reversal depend on the micronutrients, such as antioxidants and phytochemicals that are packaged with the protein.

Consider Plant Protein

Conceptually, the protein source with the greatest level of micronutrients is plants. Believe it or not, all plants are approximately 10 percent protein. Many of my patients are surprised to find out that vegetables contain protein and often stare in disbelief when I tell them that green vegetables contain more protein per calorie than most meat, breads, and beans. For example, spinach is 51 percent protein.

"How can broccoli contain more protein per calorie than steak?" they exclaim.

It is true, 100 calories of broccoli contains twice as many grams of protein than steak. Vegetables are an excellent source of protein and come packaged with a number of other health-promoting micronutrients, including the phytochemicals, antioxidants, minerals, enzymes, and vitamins. Vegetable protein sources have been criticized because they are incomplete proteins, lacking in some of the eight essential amino acids. But when a variety of vegetables are eaten, the body is able to store and release all of the necessary amino acids and buffer any short-term variation.

Consider the mountain gorillas that eat primarily a plant-based diet and yet grow to 400 pounds and maintain amazing muscle mass. Their primary source of protein is the green plant, just like the elephant, cow, and elk. In fact, all protein originates from plants. The animals consume grasses and plants enriched by the soil, water, and sun, and they develop muscle that is then processed into steak, chicken, and pork. Even predatory fish depend on the smaller fish to eat plant sources such as algae. The food chain is built upon green plants.

Often vegetarians are viewed as unhealthy because they fail to consume enough protein. In some cases vegetarians are very unhealthy because they choose to eat a diet rich in processed carbohydrates, such as cereals and breads, and are deficient not only in protein but also all of the important micronutrients. A diet with an adequate intake of calories founded on plants, such as broccoli and green leafy vegetables, will never be deficient in protein. Table 1 on the next page provides a list of vegetables and their protein content compared with common animal protein sources based on USDA values for each food group.

Table 1[5,6]

Food	Measure	Protein grams	Protein Grams/100 calories	Percent calories from protein	Percent calories from fat
Broccoli-frozen	1 cup	5.8	11.6	44	9
Spinach-cooked	1 cup	5.4	12.9	51	10
Kale-raw	1 cup	2.2	6.6	22	11
Almonds	1/4 cup	7.4	3.5	13	74
Lentils-cooked	1 cup	16.0	10	36	3
Wheat Bread	1 slice	2.7	3.9	15	14
Navy beans	1 cup	15.8	6.1	27	4
Peas-frozen	1 cup	9.0	7.5	30	4
Rice-brown	1 cup	9.0	2.1	8	7
Ground beef	2 oz.	10.6	8.0	33	62
Salmon	2 oz.	15.5	12.6	52	48
Chicken	2 oz.	5.3	12.5	52	48
Milk-2%	1/2 c.	4.0	6.2	25	35

Protein is important to your health, and if you consumed enough calories from a 100 percent plant-based diet, you would satisfy your daily protein requirement. Simply plug in some of the numbers above into a daily caloric intake of 1500–2000 calories, and you will find that the protein requirements will always be fulfilled. A number of Olympic and professional athletes, such as Alonzo Mourning (basketball), Prince Fielder (baseball), Carl Lewis (Olympic gold medalist), Dave Scott (triathlete), and Tony Gonzales (football) have shifted their diets to a more plant-based diet because of the benefits in health, recovery, and strength. God, in His infinite wisdom, created a system of food that adequately supplies your body's protein needs through a variety of plant-based foods. You don't have to be a vegetarian, but shifting your diet to a foundation of plants will dramatically improve your health and meet all of your nutritional needs.

Take a Minute

Recognize God's perfect plan to provide food and nutrition to the world through the nutritionally packed world of plants. Prayerfully seek opportunities to reduce your consumption of processed foods and animal product intake, adding in other great protein sources, such as beans, lentils, chickpeas, nuts, seeds, and broccoli. Start by changing one meal per week to a plant-based meal, and slowly add another meal every week. When you do decide to eat meat, choose organic grass-fed or free-range sources. You can find delicious recipes on our website, Day3Health.com, as well as in our companion cookbook, *Kristen's Healthy Kitchen Recipes.*

$\mathcal{D}ay$ 21

The Toxic Garden

$\mathcal{E}$very day you face an unseen enemy that lurks around every bread corner, on every plate, and in every breath. This unseen enemy of your health insidiously damages cells and contributes to a host of diseases. Yet it is rarely considered as a potential cause of disease by modern medicine. What is it? Toxic man-made chemicals found in our food, water, houses, and air.

During an average meal, you may consume dozens of chemicals in very small amounts, and to date no studies have been done to evaluate the effects of consuming small doses of multiple chemicals over a lifetime. A recent study performed on fat samples from Americans found over seven hundred chemicals in the fatty tissue.[1]

Another concerning study performed by the Environmental Working Group in 2004 measured ten cord-blood-from-fetuses samples and found that on average each sample of blood contained two hundred toxic chemicals, ranging from pesticides to consumer products. Ten out of ten samples contained lead, mercury, polychlorinated biphenyls (PCBs), dioxin, and several other known carcinogenic chemicals.[2] We are beginning our lives in a test tube of chemicals with no known studies to evaluate the cumulative effect of two hundred chemicals on a developing body. And consider this fact that now there are over one hundred thousand chemicals in commercial use today, and 25 percent are known to be hazardous. How does this affect the epigenetics of our precious little ones?

The majority of people never stop to consider their total daily or lifetime exposure to chemicals or its potential affect on their health. In the morning they drink water and coffee filled with pesticides, chlorine, trace pharmaceuticals, and heavy metals; eat contaminated processed food; breathe contaminated air; live in a home with traces of formaldehyde and other toxins in the air; and use personal care products—shampoo, creams, lotions—that contain known chemicals and metals. By the end of the day, their bodies' detoxification systems are on high alert and working at maximum capacity to isolate and eliminate all these toxic substances. Yet the body is remarkably efficient and can maintain the pace of detoxification for decades without any noticeable side effects.

Diane is a thirty-nine-year-old marathon runner who came to see me because she was experiencing pain in her arms, rashes, and fatigue. She was unable to sleep at night due to the severe pain and itching in her arms and neck, and her symptoms were dramatically affecting the quality of her life and her family's. Her husband was exhausted because they both awoke multiple times every night, running warm baths and using lotions to quiet her pain.

An initial workup by her primary care doctor did not reveal any abnormalities, and medications were prescribed to help alleviate the symptoms. They were expensive and did not help.

When she arrived in my office, she appeared tired, drawn, and desperate. I took a careful history and discovered that she ate two to three cans of tuna fish daily—a potential source of mercury poisoning. She did not have any other exposure to mercury or heavy metals. The lab work confirmed that she was mercury toxic with levels three times the acceptable range. She underwent treatment to remove the mercury from her system and recovered completely. The takeaway lesson is that toxins from food can cause disease and should not be ignored.

Our Toxic World

What are the sources of these chemicals? They are found just about everywhere! From the carpet, paint, mattresses, and varnish in our homes. From personal care products, water, food, air, and even clothing we wear. We are exposed every day to hundreds of chemicals with unknown long-term consequences. We don't know how this affects health, but studies have been done on a number of chemicals found in your life every day that do cause disease, such as lead, methyl mercury, PCBs, polychlorinated naphthalenes (PCNs), dioxin, and organophosphates. Many have been shown to have subtle effects on hormonal balances and damage DNA.

Despite the ubiquitous daily exposures, dietary intake continues to remain a primary source of daily chemical exposure. It is also the one area where you can control and dramatically reduce your exposure and reverse damage via antioxidants. Remember, pesticides are created to kill living organisms and have been linked to a number of health problems, including cancer, hormonal system effects, pulmonary disease, skin irritation, and nervous system toxicity. They are not benign, inert substances. The deleterious effects may not be pronounced or immediate, but with time they damage your cells and strain your body's detoxification systems.

Toxic Food

Is our food really toxic? The EPA estimates that 40 percent of children tested by the CDC from 1999 to 2002 had unsafe levels of organophosphates—a now restricted pesticide that has been shown to damage the nervous system.[3] These findings were supported by a 2008 study from

Emory University, which reported that children are regularly exposed to organophosphate pesticides through their diets.[4]

Let's look at a beautiful ripe, red, juicy strawberry (a conventional one). Looks harmless and delicious on your plate, but what's lurking unseen in that bright red fruit? The USDA estimates 54 pesticide residues are found in a typical conventional strawberry. Eight are known or probable carcinogens, 24 are suspected endocrine disruptors, 11 are neurotoxins, and 12 are developmental or reproductive toxins.[5] Wow! It doesn't seem quite as appealing now, does it? Again, no one knows the potential implications of eating strawberries and other toxic-laden foods over a lifetime, but I am sure it does not improve your health, and if you are susceptible to disease, these toxins can serve as a final tipping point.

Just like fruits and vegetables, animal products also contain toxins. Animal feed contains very high levels of pesticides, which are consumed by the animals and then isolated in the fat of the animal. The USDA found 10 pesticides in beef fat[6] and known or probable carcinogens.

What about processed foods? This is where the toxin load really begins to add up. Frozen french fries, 70 pesticides; pizza, 67; milk chocolate, 93; and peanut butter, 183. The majority of food consumed today is processed, man-made food filled with unnatural chemicals. In addition, the FDA maintains a list of more than three thousand chemicals that are added today to processed foods. These substances enhance flavor, color, and texture, and the average American consumes from six to nine pounds of this chemical potpourri every year. Imagine a ten-pound bag of chemicals that you sprinkle on your food every meal. These include monosodium glutamate (MSG), which is known to cause seizures, chest pain, nausea, and numbness. Sulfur dioxide is known to cause bronchial or lung dysfunction. Benzoic acid inhibits digestive enzymes, and aspartame can cause headaches and seizures.

Every aspect of our food chain has been contaminated, and as a result, people are walking chemistry experiments. What is the solution?

The First Organic Garden

The solution is to return to the diet of that first garden, eating organically grown foods and avoiding processed man-made foods. Fresh organic fruits and vegetables will prevent exposure to the chemicals found in conventional produce and industrialized processed foods, and they will substantially reduce your current toxin load and allow your body to eliminate stored toxins in as little as five days.[5] Vegetables such as parsley, cilantro, garlic, onion, and cruciferous veggies help to isolate and remove toxins from your body through a variety of mechanisms.[6, 7, 8] They act as a clean-up crew after a large event, restoring order to the system.

This can be especially important for people who have a reduced detoxification system either genetically or through years of accumulated damage. This group experiences physical effects with much lower levels of toxins because of genetically weaker enzymes than those with more robust detoxification enzymes.[9, 10] Removing the toxic load allows their bodies to redirect energies to healing and restoring of damaged cells.

Organic foods are an important component of health for two reasons: higher micronutrient density and absence of toxins. More than thirty studies have compared more than three hundred different nutrients in conventional and organic fruits and vegetables. In 85 percent of the studies, organic produce had equal or greater nutrient content compared to conventional produce.[11] So with every bite you are giving your body more of the essential nutrients that support cellular health, limiting pesticide exposure, and assisting in detoxification.

Cost is often recognized as a limitation of organic produce. You don't have to buy 100 percent organic to significantly reduce your toxic exposures. In fact, some conventional foods have very low levels of toxins, and studies have found that it is better to consume more conventional fruits and vegetables than less because of concerns about pesticides. The Environmental Working Group published a list of the twelve most- and least-contaminated vegetables and fruits, as shown in this table:[12]

12 Most Contaminated	12 Least Contaminated
Peaches	Onions
Apples	Avocados
Sweet Bell Peppers	Sweet Corn (frozen)
Celery	Pineapples
Nectarines	Mangos
Strawberries	Asparagus
Cherries	Sweet Peas (frozen)
Pears	Kiwis
Grapes	Bananas

Similarly, any animal products you eat should be organic, free-range, and raised on natural pesticide-free food sources. You will find these products to be more expensive because of the cost to raise organic animals. However, the expense will likely determine appropriate serving sizes and frequency. The shift toward a more plant-based diet will compensate for the added expense of organic animal products.

Have No Fear

Even though the statistics can be overwhelming and you may feel as if you are swimming in a test tube, do not fear. Simply shifting your diet toward the foods found in the first garden and eating naturally occurring foods will eliminate the largest pesticide source—processed foods and drinks—and provide your body with nutrients to help detoxify. God's provision for food is always the best choice, and the further you deviate from His foods, the more likely you will encounter disease. Pesticides and toxins should not be a source of worry or fear. First we should cast our fears upon God, and second we should actively decide each day to choose healthy foods from His garden.

Take a Minute

Prayerfully recognize other areas of "toxic" exposure in your life that may be damaging your mind or spirit. Just as foreign chemical substances damage cells and cause disease, worldly toxic substances, such as some movies, books, games, and people, can damage the spirit and mind. And just like our food chain today, our culture is overflowing with toxic exposures that corrupt the mind and spirit. The solution to eliminating toxic exposure from food is to return to God's provision of naturally occurring fruits and vegetables. Similarly, the solution for detoxifying your mind and spirit is to return to His first provision, Jesus, and to feast upon His holy Word.

Day 22

Glazed America

America has an insatiable sweet tooth. Americans love desserts, sugary treats, soft drinks, and snacks, and every year the sweet tooth grows. Marketing of these products today has turned the once-a-week dessert into an expected part of two meals per day. Many believe that the day is not complete without a snack. Cookies, candy, and chocolate adorn checkout counters and shelves in every type of store. Just today I was in the office supply store, and what did I find staring back at me at the checkout stand? Dozens of candy options attractively packaged just within reach and beckoning for my impulsive purchase. *Why not? It's only a dollar.* Sugar has truly become a new staple of the American diet.

We have not always consumed this much sugar. In the 1890s, the average person consumed five pounds of sugar per year. It ballooned to 109 pounds in 1950 and now is approaching 200 pounds per person per year.[1] Think about that number for a minute—200 pounds of sugar; that is forty five-pound bags of sugar, or about the weight of an average male in America today. Imagine that in January you were given a 200-pound pile of sugar and a teaspoon and told to eat your way to the bottom by December. Most of us would be repulsed and unable to begin to spoon sugar into our mouths. But hide that sugar in every food, condiment, dessert, bagel, bread, snack, or cracker, and it suddenly becomes very easy to finish off the pile.

Incognito

Sugar is disguised in many different names: high-fructose corn syrup, evaporated cane juice, rice syrup, turbinado, maltodextrin, brown sugar, natural sweeteners, sucrose, confectioner's sugar, and molasses, to name but a few of the aliases. Maybe you have seen some of these names, and I'm sure that, if you surveyed the food in your home, you would find one of these in almost every processed food product. The names are different, but the substance and damaging effects are the same. The only way to avoid hidden sugar is to begin to read labels on any processed food items that you purchase. If you find sugar in any form, put it down and walk away. The short-term pleasure of the food or beverage is not worth the long-term harm to your body.

Collateral Damage

You have already learned about the addictive nature of sugar and its powerful effects on the brain. Just like other addictive substances that offer pleasure in exchange for disease, sugar harms the body and accelerates the disease process. In many ways it is more dangerous than tobacco or cocaine because it is found everywhere in abundance, can be purchased by anyone of any age at any time, and is consumed without any attached stigma. In fact, sugar is an acceptable addiction that is promoted across the nation by unsuspecting citizens as a harmless, pleasurable food. The reality is that sugar contributes to degeneration of the body and a number of deadly diseases.

Diabetes

When your body is consistently exposed to high blood levels of sugar, the cells become more resistant to the entry of sugar, and the body responds by increasing insulin production. Insulin is the key that opens the doors on the cells, allowing sugar to enter into the cell. The cells become more resistant over time, and eventually insulin is not able to effectively move the sugar from the blood stream into the cells. Then blood sugar levels rise, and that's when diabetes is diagnosed. Eventually the pancreas burns out, insulin levels begin to fail, and prescription insulin is then required to maintain normal blood sugar levels. The prolonged, elevated blood sugar levels harm the body by increasing fat storage, decreasing immune function, reducing the anabolic or body-rebuilding hormones, damage blood vessels, and can lead to high blood pressure and heart disease. The lifetime consequences of diabetes include heart attack, amputations, sick nerves with painful numbness, loss of vision, bladder and bowel dysfunction, stroke, and early death. It is a tragic disease that slowly eats away at the body, eventually affecting every system.[2]

Cancer

"Sugar feeds cancer" is a simple saying that has existed in health circles for decades. The quote originated from research performed by Dr. Otto Warburg, a Nobel Prize winner in 1931, who discovered that cancer cells have a very different metabolism compared to healthy cells. Cancerous cells feed on glucose (sugar) and produce lactic acid as a byproduct, creating a very acidic cellular environment.[3] The lactic acid further acidifies the body, assisting the growth of cancer cells and causing malaise and fatigue.[4] This concept was again confirmed in a more recent 2010 study that demonstrated increased cancerous cell growth with refined fructose and glucose, or refined sugars that include high-fructose corn syrup. The authors of the study suggest that reducing sugar intake, including refined fructose, may inhibit and disrupt cancer growth.[5] Also important to cancer survival is the fact that sugar suppresses the immune system. Sugar is rich fertilizer for cancerous cells, both fueling the growth of the cells and inhibiting the action of the immune system.

Heart Disease

Several studies, including a Harvard study, found that higher blood sugar levels are linked with elevated inflammation markers (CRP, IL6).[3] These inflammation markers have been strongly associated with heart disease, cancer, and diabetes and can worsen autoimmune diseases, such as rheumatoid arthritis. Elevated blood sugar levels also lead to elevated triglyceride levels and injury to the delicate cells (the endothelial cells) that line the arteries of the heart. Over time, this contributes to atherosclerosis (hardening of the arteries) and, eventually, heart disease and potentially a heart attack.

Immune System

Sugar consumption significantly reduces your immune system's function. Within ten minutes of eating approximately 8 tablespoons of sugar, the immune function is suppressed for five hours.[6] A similar study found that consuming 24 ounces of soda reduced the function of the disease-fighting white blood cells (neutrophils) by 50 percent! On a daily basis, people regularly consume 24 ounces of cola or 8 tablespoons of sugar and suffer a 40–50 percent reduction in immune system function. Imagine the implications of reduced immunity during cold and flu season. And it is also important to consider that your immune system is vital to cancer prevention.

Your gastrointestinal tract is home to trillions of bacteria that work with your body to improve the function of your immune system, stabilize blood sugar levels, prevent the growth of harmful bacteria, produce vitamins such as vitamin K and biotin, and help in the absorption of nutrients. In fact, the five hundred species of bacteria have been collectively called the "forgotten organ" because of their invaluable and symbiotic contribution to bodily function. The flora have a continuous and dynamic effect on your body's immune system and destruction of the flora—such as antibiotics, fat, and sugar—can impair the immune response.

Dr. Jeff Gordon from Washington University has shown that the gut flora of obese individuals is significantly different than the flora of lean individuals. This leads to alterations of immunity and processing of food. Obese individuals have flora that more efficiently processes indigestible foods and essentially find more calories from the same amount of food. They also found that switching from a low-fat, plant-based diet to a higher in fat and sugar diet changes the flora toward that of the obese individuals with different types and amounts of unhealthy bacteria. This has potential and far-reaching implications for impairing your immune response. Restoring normal gut flora is possible by returning to a plant-based diet with natural fermented foods and may require a probiotic supplement. Once again we see the extensive and damaging effects of sugar.

High-Fructose Corn Syrup (HFCS)

Another alarming trend is the addition of high-fructose corn syrup to just about every product you may, or may not, imagine. In 1950 the average American consumed 0 pounds of high-fructose corn syrup. Today that number has grown to 60 pounds per person per year, or about 5 pounds per month. Most of us never purchase high-fructose corn syrup for our homes, so where are the 60 pounds hidden? Look no further than most foods in boxes, bags, or cans and including fast food, ketchup, mustard, dill pickles, many lunch meats and prepackaged meals, some breads, cough syrup, cereals, crackers, some canned and packaged soups, sweetened drinks, yogurt, and even healthy bars, cereals, and salad dressings. It has become ubiquitous in our modern processed food chain.

A 2010 study from Princeton University found that rats consuming high-fructose corn syrup gained 48 percent more weight than those consuming sucrose or sugar. Also, the high-fructose corn syrup groups had higher triglycerides and more fat around the stomach.[6] Similarly, another 2010 study found a strong link between high-fructose corn syrup and nonalcoholic, fatty liver disease, leading to a higher risk of cirrhosis and liver cancer, and lower HDL (good cholesterol) levels, which is associated with an increased risk for heart disease.[7]

Let's put this into perspective. We have added to our diets 60 pounds per year of a highly processed, nonnutritious substance that likely leads to damaging effects on the liver, increases abdominal fat, increases triglycerides, and lowers beneficial HDLs, increasing your risk for heart disease. As you can imagine, controversy surrounds high-fructose corn syrup and its probable harmful effects contrasted against the large profit and ubiquitous use. But to gain clarity, we need only step back and ask, "Is this a part of God's original plan for food and nutrition?" The answer to that question is like a giant fan that quickly clears away the smoke and helps to drive us back to a diet founded on those garden foods created by God and not by man. Unprocessed, naturally occurring, naturally sweetened foods that are full of rich nutrients and fiber will nourish and strengthen the body and its systems. When natural sugars are consumed in whole foods, they contain the fibers, minerals, vitamins, and phytochemicals that modify the effect on the body. Processing removes all of these important nutrients that God wove into the food to effectively nourish the body without causing harm. All processed sugars, including agave nectar, maple syrups, rice syrup, fructose, and turbinado sugar negatively affect the body. So look to whole foods, such as dates, raisins, and bananas to naturally sweeten your recipes.

Take a Minute

Today spend time in prayer regarding sugar and its place in your life. Are you struggling with addiction to sweets and sugar? The Lord can help you gain freedom. Are you thinking right now that you can't give up sugar? Be encouraged that many have gone before you and have successfully gained freedom from its powerful grasp, and you can as well with God's strength. Don't underestimate the power of sugar, the amount you consume, or its destructive nature. It will harm your body, and if consumed long enough, may contribute to life-altering diseases, such as cancer. And just like all of the world's attempts to replace God's original plan with a better more pleasurable plan, it is an empty, sweet promise attached to a bitter end.

Rejoice and learn to enjoy the natural sweetness of God's delectable foods, such as strawberries, apples, grapes, dates, and cherries. They are His provision for enjoyment of food, and we should learn to eat and be fully content and grateful.

Healthy Fats?

$\mathcal{T}$he second love of the industrialized palate is fat. People love foods that contain fat and processed oils, yet they realize that excessive fat is unhealthy. As a result, industry has attempted to create low-fat, no-fat, non-trans-fat foods to satisfy our palates and extinguish the guilt and "gut" that follow. Over the past forty years, total fat intakes have actually decreased by approximately 13 percent, but obesity rates have risen during this same period of time with essentially unchanged activity levels.[1] The low-fat message appears to have been effective, but it has not translated into a healthier nation. Very low-fat diets have been associated with increased inflammation, reduced immune function by up to 50 percent, decreased endurance, elevated triglycerides, decreased fat-soluble vitamin absorption, fatigue, dry skin, hormonal imbalance, increased risk of depression, and cancer. Very low-fat diets are definitely not the answer to health.

Low-fat messages can lead to the assumption that fat is the enemy of health, and merely reducing fat will equate to improved health. But this is not the case. Fat is an important component of a healthy diet, but the type and sources of fat are vitally important.

- *Fat* serves several important functions in your body, including a reserve energy source, cell membrane structure, precursors for hormones, absorption of vitamins, skin maintenance, and structural covering of nerves and brain cells. Fats have been classified into several categories based on their chemical composition, and like other foods, fats come in both the processed form—oils—and the unprocessed form naturally occurring in foods.

- *Saturated fats* are found in meat, fowl, eggs, dairy, coconut oil and palm oil and are solid at room temperature. Elevated intakes of saturated fats are strongly associated with heart disease and cancer. Most dietary recommendations suggest minimizing your intake of saturated fats, but some sources, such as whole coconut, do not adversely affect the body and may be associated with positive benefits.

- *Trans fats* are a monounsaturated fat that is further processed by heating and adding a metal catalyst to create a process called hydrogenation. This process creates a superoil with a very long shelf life that can be used to fry foods over and over again without going rancid. Examples include margarine, french fries, shortening, potato chips, doughnuts, and candy bars. As you can guess, this oil is double processed and, as recent news reports have revealed, is strongly associated with diseases, such as cancer and heart disease. Trans fats are so potent that merely replacing 2 percent of the energy with unsaturated fats reduces the risk of heart disease by 53 percent.[2]

- *Monounsaturated fats* are naturally occurring and can be found in food, such as almonds, olives, avocados, and peanuts. Numerous studies have linked monounsaturated fats with lower rates of heart disease when substituted for saturated fats, but the ideal source is not oil but rather the whole olive or avocado. Monounsaturated oils, such as olive oil, are liquid at room temperature.

- *Polyunsaturated fats* are typically found in plant sources, such as whole grains, nuts, and seeds and occur in oil form such as safflower, soybean, and corn oil. This group cannot be manufactured by the body and must come from your diet and are, therefore, called "essential fatty acids." The two important components of this group include the omgea-3 fatty acids (linolenic) and omega-6 fatty acids (linoleic). Omega-3s are found in walnuts, seeds, leafy green vegetables, flaxseed, soybeans, and wild fatty fish. Omega-6 rich foods include beef, fowl, eggs, dairy, and processed vegetable oils such as soybean oil (which is now found in nearly every processed food in the industrialized diet and may account for up to 20 percent of the total calories in the American diet). From these two fats your body can manufacture the other nonessential fats. Omega-3 fat is necessary to produce two important, nonessential fats: docosahexaenoic acid (DHA) and eicosapentaenoic acid (EPA), which have powerful anti-inflammatory and health-promoting properties. Both DHA and EPA have been shown to be potent antiarrythmic agents, support blood vessel cell function, lower blood pressure, improve platelet sensitivity and clotting, and lower serum triglyceride levels.[3] In contrast, omega-6 fatty acids are converted to arachadonic acid, which is a known promoter of inflammation. High levels of omega-6 fats found in the average American diet compete with the enzymes that convert omega-3 fat to the important DHA and EPA, thus further lowering the levels of these important health promoting fats.

The ideal ratio between omega-6 and omega-3 fatty acids appears to be approximately 1:1–2:1. Not too surprisingly, the industrialized diet typically carries a staggering ratio of 20–40:1. Diets with greater omega-6 levels to omega-3 have been associated with a number of chronic diseases, including heart disease, cancer, dementia, increased risk for Parkinson's disease, increased risk for degenerative joint disease, inflammatory and autoimmune diseases, arthritis, osteoporosis, some mood disorders, and thrombotic stroke. As your ratio improves, so does your health. Studies have shown that a 4:1 ratio was associated with a 70 percent decrease in total mortality in secondary prevention of cardio-vascular disease. A ratio of 2.5:1 reduced rectal cell cancer proliferation in patients with colorectal compared to a ratio of 4:1 showing no effect. Lower ratios have been associated with a decreased risk of breast cancer, a ratio of 2–3:1 suppressed inflammation in patients with rheumatoid arthritis. And a studied ratio of 5:1 had a beneficial effect on asthma, whereas a ratio of 10:1 resulted in adverse consequences.[4] Thousands of studies like these confirm the benefits of lowering omega-6 and raising omega-3 fatty acids.

With the well-documented benefits of omega-3 fatty acids and the harmful effects of high levels of omega-6 levels, the knee-jerk solution has been to supplement omega-3s while not addressing the sources of omega-6. Again, it is important to remember that elevated omega-6 will compete with the enzymes that convert omega-3 into DHA and EPA, so that merely supplementing omega-3 is far less effective than the com-bination of reducing omega-6 and increasing omega-3. Also, high levels of saturated and trans fats will interfere with this conversion process. It becomes easy to see that the typical diet of America or any other industrialized nation compromises this delicate yet powerful balance and likely accelerates the degenerative disease process.

The Oiling of America

The one category of fat intake that has increased dramatically during the past fifty years is salad and cooking oils because of the hidden addition to processed food. It is important to remember that all oils are 120 calories per tablespoon, and just 3 additional tablespoons of oil per day can contribute 360 calories, or in 10 days it totals 1 pound of fat. The added calories from oils are rapidly transitioned to fat storage in three minutes, from the mouth to hips in three minutes! Further damaging evidence against oils is their omega-6:3 ratio that is 69:1 promoting system-wide inflammation. It is important to recognize that all oils, including olive oil, are a very processed food and all of the fiber and many of the micronutrients have been removed, making them a poor source of nutrition and empty calories.

Healthy Sources of Fat

Fat is a necessary building block for your body, and it is important to obtain fat from whole foods because it comes packaged with fiber to slow the absorption, and minerals, vitamins, lignans, phytochemicals, antioxidants, and phytosterols to reduce inflammation. Processed oils and fats are devoid of all of these health-supporting nutrients.

Let's take a look at an avocado as an example of a healthy fat. Avocado improves the absorption of other phytochemicals, such as lycopene from tomatoes and beta-carotene from salad. They contain phytosterols that reduce inflammation, provides oleic acid that reduces cholesterol, prevents breast cancer, and acts as an antioxidant—a powerful package compared to three nutritionally empty tablespoons of oil.

Nuts and seeds can also be a very healthy source of fats. Studies have shown that nuts and seeds lower cholesterol, reduce blood sugar levels, lower triglycerides, improve antioxidant activity, lower weight, prevent cardiac arrythmia, and improve the absorption of vitamins.[5,6] Nut and seed consumption was found to dramatically reduce the risk of sudden cardiac death and arrythmia, and those who consumed nuts two or more times per week had a reduced risk of sudden cardiac death by approximately 50 percent.[7,8] A similar study looked at three thousand African-American men and women and found that those who consumed nuts five times per week reduced their risk of dying of coronary heart disease by 44 percent compared to those who ate nuts one time per week.

You can begin to add 1 ounce (the amount that fits in the average palm of the hand) per day of nuts and seeds to your diet by using them as a condiment on salads or oatmeal, in soups, in homemade dressings and sauces. Always purchase raw, unroasted (roasting increases free radicals), and unsalted nuts and seeds, and try to avoid creating a large nut bowl for snacking. This always leads to one too many handfuls during the day. Nuts and seeds can also be a great source of added calories, protein, and phytochemicals for athletes.

Your body requires fat for optimal function, and the best sources are plants, such as avocado, nuts and seeds, and coconut. Try to avoid oils because they are a processed food item that contains a large number of empty calories. You can cook without oil by using a base of onions or water, or cooking on a bed of lettuce.

Take a Minute

Look through your cabinets and read the labels on the boxes, bags, and cans. What types of oils do you see? How many grams of fat and oil are contained per serving? Consider the amount of oil you use every day, and pour it into a glass. How does it look, and is that something you would want to pour into your body? Challenge yourself this week to put the oil away and cook with water. I know you will be happily surprised, and your body will thank you.

The Spice of Life

"Let it snow, let it snow, let it snow" were the words that leaped to my mind as I watched a friend salt his dinner before taking a first bite. My friend continued his conversation as the saltshaker rhythmically circled his plate for an uncomfortably long period of time. Soon a thin, pristine, white layer covered his meal, like a new-fallen snow, and then the saltshaker was replaced with a fork, and he was ready to eat. His taste buds had adapted to this new supersalty level, and food was tasteless without heaping teaspoons of salt onto it. Unfortunately, his taste buds were leading him down of a road of potential disease complications.

Salt has influenced humanity from the dawn of history because of its value in food preservation and taste enhancement. Early settlers built encampments near salt springs. Salt was traded ounce for ounce with gold in the deserts. Roman soldiers were paid part of their wage in salt—the salarium, or salary. Rome built roads throughout Europe to transport salt. And salted fish allowed sailors to cross vast oceans without starving.

Salt or sodium is a valuable mineral and critical for your body to function. Your body maintains a finely tuned level of sodium. If your sodium level rises or falls beyond a very small range, your vital organs, including brain, heart, and kidneys, will fail.

Modern table salt or sodium chloride is a processed food, and because of its availability at an inexpensive price, its use has proliferated. Every table has a saltshaker, and every processed food has added salt. This once rare commodity has become a common part of everyday life in the industrialized world.

As a result, salt consumption has risen 50 percent in the last forty years.[1] Approximately 75 percent of the daily salt intake in Western populations comes from processed foods. An additional 15 percent comes from cooking and table salt use, and the remaining 10 percent comes from naturally occurring foods.[2] Consequently, 90 percent of the total salt consumption in the US diet comes from manufactured salt, and 75 percent is hidden in processed foods. If you ate processed foods but never used a saltshaker, you would still consume too much salt.

Today the average American consumes two to four times the recommended amount of salt. The National Academy of Sciences recommends no more than 2300 mg of salt per day, and the American Heart Association recommends no more than 1500 mg per day.[3] In fact, one average restaurant meal contains 2000 mg of sodium, more than the recommended total daily intake.

Results of Consuming Too Much Salt

High levels of salt intake have been associated with cancers of the gastrointestinal (GI) tract, including the stomach.[4] Your stomach and GI tract are normally protected by a thin layer of cells that die when exposed to high levels of sodium chloride or salt, leaving the delicate layer beneath exposed. The cell damage stimulates the production of new cells that increases the likelihood of genetic errors, leading to cancer. Excessive salt intake has also been linked to kidney stones,[5] high blood pressure, and cardiovascular disease. A large review study published in *Lancet* found that a high sodium intake predicted mortality (death) and risk of cardiovascular or heart disease independent of all other factors.[6] Excessive salt intake is a primary contributor to cardiovascular disease.

Garden Spices

If you want to really enjoy your food and improve your health, you will need to begin using the natural flavor enhancers created on Day 3 of creation. These have proven health benefits and do not harm the body. Natural spices, such as cinnamon, turmeric, cloves, oregano, and garlic, not only spice up the taste but also act as potent antioxidants. Let's look at five of the most powerful spices that you can begin adding to your diet today.

Turmeric is a member of the ginger family and acts as a powerful anti-inflammatory. Studies have also found that it has anti-angiogenesis qualities, reducing the growth of cancer cells and lowering low-density lipoprotein (LDL) cholesterol. Studies have also suggested that it is beneficial in preventing the plaque formations in Alzheimer's disease and reducing the pain of arthritis. It is a bright yellow/orange spice that can be added to soups, stews, and potato dishes.

Oregano has more than forty times the antioxidant activity of an apple and is a potent antimicrobial that can help stave off infections and colds. It can be added to Italian dishes, salads, potato dishes, or salad dressings.

Cinnamon is a powerful antioxidant and anti-inflammatory spice that also helps to stabilize blood sugar levels. Sprinkle some on your oatmeal, apples, or in a smoothie.

Cloves have one of the highest antioxidant ratings of any of the spices and one-half teaspoon contains more antioxidants than one-half cup of blueberries or cranberries. This spice lowers LDL cholesterol and improves insulin function, resulting in lower blood sugar levels. It can be added to soups, stews, and East Indian cuisine.

Garlic, also known as "Russian penicillin," has very potent antibacterial qualities, as noted by Louis Pasteur in the 1800s and during World Wars I and II. The Russians relied on garlic as an antiseptic to disinfect open wounds. Albert Schweitzer also used garlic to treat cholera, typhus, and amoebic dysentery. When a garlic clove is crushed, more than one hundred sulphur-containing compounds are released that kill bacteria. Several studies have demonstrated a significant anticancer component of garlic in preventing gastric cancers.[7] Garlic can be added to any soup, stew, bean or lentil dish, and incorporated into mushrooms, wraps, or bean burgers.

The research continues to mount demonstrating the remarkable health benefits of these herbs and spices. Consider trying some of the other fresh herbs and spices that contain high levels of antioxidants, too, including parsley, peppermint, thyme, basil, and cilantro. These spices add a whole new level of taste enjoyment to food, and once they travel beyond the taste buds, they promote a healthy and strong body.

Take a Minute

Read the labels on the food in your pantry or while shopping at the store. Take a look at the sodium levels, and pay careful attention to serving size and servings per container. It is not uncommon for one serving of soup to contain nearly 1000 mg of sodium. Remind yourself that processed foods contain too much of everything unhealthy and not enough of the health-promoting nutrients. Try something new by adding some new spices to recipes in place of salt. Remember that it takes time for your taste buds to adapt and that within two to four weeks you will begin to appreciate new spices.

Also, prayerfully consider what it means to be "salt to the earth." Jesus, in Matthew 5:13, was speaking about the ability of pure salt to preserve and the worthless value of contaminated salt, such as the salt from the Dead Sea, that contained gypsum and other minerals. It is the purity of our lives for Christ that allows us to be of value to the world.

More Than Regularity

$\mathcal{F}$iber is undigestible component of plants and is classified as insoluble, fiber that is not broken down by the body; and soluble, fiber that is fermented in the large intestine. The benefits of fiber include regulating blood sugar, reducing the risk of colon cancer, reducing appetite, improving immune function, reducing cholesterol and the risk of heart disease, and alleviating constipation. Generally, fiber is found in fruits, vegetables, nuts, beans, seeds, and other plant-based foods. Foods that do not contain fiber include all animal products, refined and processed foods found in boxes, bags, cans, and packages, sweets and treats, juices, and some breads. It is yet another important building block of health that God wove into His created food.

Most of the current recommendations for increasing dietary fiber include the addition of bran, Metamucil, or psyllium husks, and for many, the primary reason to increase fiber is to prevent constipation—an important topic of conversation with many of my patients and grandparents! But is fiber merely a bulking agent to prevent constipation and reduce risk of colon cancer? Many people eat a standard industrialized diet that is deficient in fiber content and then add a half-tablespoon of fiber to compensate for poor dietary habits. It is estimated that Americans consume only 50 percent of the recommended daily fiber intake, youth alarmingly consume only 20 percent, and 95 percent of all Americans fail to consume the recommended amount.[1, 2] The current recommendation is 14 grams per 1000 calories, or about 28–35 grams of fiber per day. If you are eating a diet that requires the addition of fiber, you are putting yourself at risk for a host of diseases.

Low Fiber Intake and Disease

Low fiber intake has been associated with a number of diseases, such as colon cancer, and several studies have demonstrated dramatic reductions in cancer of up to 40 percent by doubling the intake of fiber.[3, 4] It is important to recognize that reductions in the risk of heart disease, and cancer are not associated with small or modest amounts of added fiber, such bran or psyllium, but instead are described with larger increases in daily fiber intake from natural foods.[5] The real health benefits result from the source of fiber. Fiber from fruits and vegetables is associated with significant reductions in colorectal cancer and heart disease because of the additive effect of natural soluble and insoluble fiber and the micronutrients. The wisdom of God's creation of food is once again validated by science.

The Science of Fiber

Soluble fiber, such as the pulp of fruit, is not broken down in the stomach or small intestine, but it travels to the large intestine where bacteria break down and ferment the fiber, producing a host of health-promoting products.[6] Soluble fiber is then fermented in the large intestine by the resident gut bacteria into short-chain fatty acids, such as butyric acid. These short-chain fatty acids have been shown to stabilize blood sugar, suppress cholesterol synthesis by the liver, reduce blood levels of cholesterol and triglycerides, improve the absorption of minerals, stimulate immune response, increase the proliferation of beneficial colonic bacteria, reduce inflammation, and help protect the mucosal lining of the gastrointestinal system from polyps.[7, 8]

The evidence is overwhelming that fiber is good for your health and can extend your life by lowering the risk of cancer, heart disease, respiratory diseases, and infections.[9] The individuals who consume the highest levels of fiber have a 59 percent reduction in heart disease and similar reductions for cancer. Therefore, as you begin to change your diet, the foundational foods should also be high in soluble and insoluble fiber. Foods rich in soluble fiber include peas, lentils, beans, oats, rye, chia, barley, broccoli, carrots, sweet potatoes, berries, plums, and prunes. Insoluble fiber is found in whole grains, bran, nuts and seeds, green beans, celery, cauliflower, quinoa, and psyllium.

Once again we can begin to see that plant-based foods offer everything your body needs to maintain health and prevent disease. It is evident that God's first provision of plant-based foods, those similar to the first garden, should be the foundation for your diet.

Take a Minute

Create a list of high-fiber foods that you enjoy and some that you know you need to add, and then go shopping. Restock your home with these foods. Consider adding some new whole grains, such as quinoa, millet, barley, rolled or steel-cut oats. Whole, unprocessed grains are a great source of fiber and can be made for breakfast, lunch, or dinner. Recipes are available on our website, Day3Health.com.

Day **26**

The Hidden Power of Food

*W*hat is food? Have you ever stopped to consider the many facets of food beyond the more apparent taste and calories? Why do you eat? Think about the past week and the motivators for your food choices. Do you eat primarily for taste, pleasure, and enjoyment, or do you eat because routine and habit dictate that you eat three times per day? What is your primary motivation?

Have you ever wondered why the very substance we use to refuel and replenish our bodies is the source of so many controversies, disagreements, and confusion? Food is something we need and something we absolutely love, and God created it that way. No other basic requirement for life, holds such a strong emotional attraction. Food is a powerful force is our lives, and I believe we greatly underestimate its subtle yet significant influence. God intends it for good, but the enemy has twisted this blessing into a curse of processed, artificially sweetened, chemically enhanced, genetically modified foods. As you begin to make dietary changes, it will be important to recognize and understand the forces behind the foods that motivate your decisions to eat. Let's take a look at one of the most powerful forces—taste.

Every day millions of people choose to eat for a number of reasons but rarely for the primary reason, *life,* with the intended goal of prolonging, repairing, and sustaining their bodies for another day. Excessive and deficient amounts of food will lead to disease and, ultimately, death. But few consider life and death, health and disease when making decisions about breakfast, lunch, and dinner.

Food is a powerful, hidden force in our individual lives and in our world. It carries great political power and is used as leverage against people for political ideologies, position, and military force. Food has the power to provide pleasure, even temporarily satisfying deep emotional pain. Food has power in our traditions and families to bring people together around a table from all walks of life and promote relationships. Our memories are influenced by the power of food as great meals can be recalled for years to come, and we often return to familiar meals to recreate feelings and events. Perhaps even now you are recalling a favorite family meal or holiday, and I am certain that you can almost smell and taste the food!

Thoughts of food can consume our minds, motivate our actions, and dictate our schedules. Food even has power over money, as we will willingly give up our last dollar for a loaf of bread. How does food influence your life?

Why We Eat

Today the industrialized culture eats, first, to tantalize their taste buds—often driven by food addictions—and a distant second, to fill their bellies; occasionally, to shape their bodies; and rarely, to promote health. The majority of food choices are motivated by food cravings, addictions, taste, and appearance. Did you notice the common thread? That's correct—it is self service.

Have you ever stopped to consider God's true purpose for food? Why did He create it with taste, and why are we motivated to eat by taste or cravings? Why do you and I need to eat? Simply answered—it's to nourish our bodies—providing the necessary energy and building blocks to move, repair, and maintain our bodies. God created a system of taste that helped to influence the consumption of different foods based on the body's needs at that time, and by His grace and kindness, He made the process enjoyable.

Your body is a beautifully complex machine that allows you to fully interface with the world on every level—seeing, feeling, smelling, hearing, loving, and laughing. Food provides the fuel to maintain and move the system and maximize its function. Eating is an opportunity to refuel and provide the necessary elements to maintain your body. Somewhere above the neck, we have lost sight of this very simple fact, and we choose to eat only for the now and the "Wow!" The exciting news is that you can eat for both health and taste!

Reclaiming Taste

As you begin to reshape your diet, you must first acknowledge food's great importance and power. Then you can begin to make informed and intelligent decisions about its position and influence in your life. Food is far more than satisfying your taste buds and cravings, or the extra twenty pounds around your waist. Food should be enjoyed, and the system of taste is created for this purpose.

Industry has adulterated the natural flavors that God created by refining and chemically altering natural food. The new flavors of the modern culture tantalize the taste buds just like the scantily clad men and women on magazine covers and billboards titillate the mind. Both appeal to the flesh, challenge self-control, and can lead to destructive habits. It is time to take back and reform food by returning to the original provision of God and to eat and be fully satisfied.

Tyrannical Taste Buds

Imagine for a moment that you are unable to taste food. (Perhaps you can remember a time when you had a cold and couldn't taste anything.) Every food or beverage is completely void of taste and differentiated only by texture and temperature. Ice cream is cold and smooth, meat is tough and chewy, chips are dry and crunchy, and vegetables are cool and crisp. Why would you eat? What would you eat? Would cravings, appetites, and emotions influence your choices? What would motivate you to choose certain foods: convenience, health, or texture? Now here is a challenging question: would you gain or lose weight? If you understood the health benefits and disease consequences of certain foods, would these influence your decisions? How would your life change—your thoughts about food, time spent on food, restaurants, fad diets with weight loss and weight gain? What would fill your pantry, refrigerator, and freezer? Answers to these questions may reveal the real power of taste in your food decisions. When you begin to understand the power of taste, it is easy to see that most of us are ruled by the ten thousand taste buds lining our tongues and palates. Like Mount Everest, taste can be magnificent and motivating, yet dangerous and even deadly.

Those ten thousand taste buds work in synergy with your sense of smell to create the dynamic sense of taste. This sense brings brightly colored berries and cherries to life and helps to make them more attractive.

It provides you with the opportunity to enjoy the process of refueling your body and, ultimately, should guide good choices. It is a gift of God.

Taste is also a motivator of food selection based upon bodily needs. Long before engineered and processed foods, taste guided food choices to provide the necessary building blocks and fuel for the body based upon the immediate needs. Sweet foods, such as fruits, provided immediate energy; unami taste-protein for maintenance of the musculoskeletal system and reserve energy; green plants were for minerals and health.

Taste also protects you from spoiled, harmful, or rotten foods. Bite into a piece of spoiled fruit and your first response is to spit out the fruit. Bitter or sour foods cause this aversive type reaction because most naturally occurring poisons are bitter and sour. Also, larger amounts of sour or bitter foods tend to be acidic and are not beneficial in maintaining a healthy body. In contrast, when you taste a wonderful meal or sweet piece of fruit, you let it linger on your taste buds and savor the experience.

Our industrialized culture has capitalized on the power of taste by manipulating foods, adding salt, fat, or sugar, to create new, appealing, and powerful unnatural tastes. For example, aspartame, a chemically contrived sweetener, is two thousand times sweeter than sugar. Sweet is a naturally occurring component of taste that makes foods, such as fruits, more attractive. However, white sugar is a concentrated form of naturally occurring sugars and is added in large amounts to many foods. Pick up any processed food in the store and read the ingredient list printed on the label. You will be surprised how often you find sugar in the form of sugar, corn syrup, brown rice syrup, or brown sugar added to a number of foods, including crackers, chips, pasta, bagels, and even ketchup. Our bodies have adapted to this new level of sugar exposure and, in turn, created a new standard for "sweet." The once sweet and tantalizing strawberry or raspberry quickly loses its appeal next to a bowl of your favorite ice cream or warm chocolate chip cookies. (Which one of these just evoked a memory or response in your brain?) We then begin to seek out sweeter treats to satisfy our senses, and the beautiful berries are eaten with cheesecake, pie, or whipped cream.

Frankenfoods

Dr. David Kessler, former FDA commissioner and author of the 2009 book *The End of Overeating*, describes how industry has effectively manipulated processed foods to make them more addictive. Industry scientists, he reports, manipulate the layers of sugar, fat, and salt in processed foods and restaurant meals to trigger the areas of the brain-dopamine centers to create an immediate, intense, emotional, and addictive response.[1] This results in a hedonistic emotional experience with the food driving overeating and addictive cycles. Kesler writes,

> Food manufacturers have long been using focus groups to test for cravings and then designing their product for "irresistibility" and "crave-ability." When a food scientist at Frito-Lay analyzed what determines irresistibility, five key influences were pinpointed: calories, flavor hits, ease of eating, meltdown, and early hit. Companies know this and use this.[2]

Processed foods are not just unhealthy, they are addictive and created to draw you back again and again for another "hit." The world system is at war with your spirit, mind, and body, and this is just one more example of the willful manipulation of food for profit at the expense of your health.

The Buffet Syndrome

Our passion for sweet and salt has contributed to the current state of poor health. Dr. David Katz, director of the Yale Prevention Research Center, described the concept of sensory-specific satiety in his book *The Flavor Point Diet*. This important concept sheds light on one of the causes for America's ongoing struggle against weight gain. Your body responds to the variety of tastes by either triggering or suppressing appetite. More than twenty-five years of studies have shown that when people are given a meal with a variety of tastes, their appetite increases and they typically eat more calories.[3] Can you recall being "too full" after a wedding reception or filling up on an all-you-can-eat buffet? I sure can! The multiplicity of choices and enticing tastes stimulates us to overeat.

In contrast, those who eat foods of similar taste will consistently eat less and report a decreased appetite and greater satiety. Once we reach this point of satiety, both the sight and taste of food lose their appeal, and we feel satisfied.[4] The more subtle tastes of God's created foods do not stimulate the desire for more, but rather promote contentment.

Today we are constantly battling against the pull of the culture of food because of the incredible diversity of foods and tastes available 24/7. We can stop for a pancake breakfast at midnight or a hamburger at 2 a.m. Menus read like a captivating short story, and grocery stores offer an overwhelming number of choices. When we walk through any mall or airport, our appetites are stimulated by the diverse and alluring food choices. We have grown to appreciate a wide variety of tastes and continue to seek out new and more appealing tastes once we grow tired of our typical menus.

Variety and abundance have become both friend and foe in our modern world. The secret is to eat a variety of healthy foods that will both satisfy our nutritional needs and appetites and, at the same time, avoid those foods that are powerful drivers of cravings, such as hidden flavor enhancers, sugar, salt, and chemically contrived flavors. In the days to follow I will show you how to make this transition to a diet that promotes health and satisfies your taste buds by feasting on the foods from God's hand.

Take a Minute

Recognize the delicious provision of food from the Lord. Consider carefully the wide variety of produce, plants, and spices that He has provided—think about each variety, the color, and taste. They satisfy the taste buds and gratify the needs of the body. This is God's precious gift, and it has a strong spiritual component that should direct us back to our great Provider. We have great freedom in Christ, but it is important to remember 1 Corinthians 6:12–13, which says,

> All things are lawful for me, but all things are not helpful. All things are lawful for me, but I will not be brought under the power of any. Foods for the stomach and the stomach for foods, but God will destroy both it and them. Now the body is not for sexual immorality but for the Lord, and the Lord for the body.

This is a good reminder that our liberty in Christ should be applied wisely to every area of life, including food and taste, while avoiding the temptations that enslave and encumber us.

Day 27

God's Secret to Health

*H*ave you ever stopped to consider the remarkable complexity of your body? Upon arising in the morning, your body is at your beck and call. It adjusts, adapts, compensates, repairs, produces, and coordinates to meet your most demanding and immediate requests. A healthy body can climb a 29,000-foot mountain and free dive more than 500 feet below the ocean's surface. The human body has adapted to arctic and desert life and every environment in between. Without a conscious thought, the human body begins to adapt, and within a short period of time, it has modified cells and systems to acclimate to the new environments or stresses.

Your body is a remarkable machine constructed of 100 trillion cells. As a point of comparison, there are approximately 100 billion stars in the Milky Way galaxy. Each day this dynamic symphony of cells allows you to interface with life, meet goals proposed by your mind, move, sense, feel, interact with others and the physical world, compose music, write books, paint, plant a tree, work, raise children, and reach out to help someone in need. Each task is accomplished because the individual cells work together to move your machine in the right direction. Your machine is fueled by naturally occurring sources, is self-diagnosing, is self-repairing, localizes and alerts you to problem areas, allows for instantaneous communication on multiple levels, adapts to many environments and situations, functions on all terrains, learns and recalls movement, projects and anticipates, and allows for intense interaction and connection with other people on physical, mental, emotional, and spiritual levels. You never have to think about the seventy times per minute that your heart beats, twelve breaths your lungs inhale per minute, processing of food, immune surveillance, or the functioning of the 107 billion cells of your eyes. They are constantly working and ready for any of your requests.

Train Your Taste Buds

God created your body with the amazing innate ability to adapt when it is presented new circumstances or environments. This remarkable capability is woven into the fabric of your DNA, and it allows your body to modify every system and group of cells within a very short period of time. Adaptation occurs during exercise as your body builds muscle and endurance, with mental challenges that stimulate new brain cells and increased connections, or when you move to a new climate.

Another exciting example of adaptation is your taste system. Did you know your tastes adapt? All too often, I encounter people who refuse to make the change to a healthy diet because they say that they "don't like vegetables, never have and never will." But if adaptation is true, then people can learn to enjoy the taste of vegetables. You can learn to enjoy new tastes in as little as thirty days or fifteen tries. Neuroadaptation of the taste system is well documented and occurs in thirty to ninety days when a new taste is presented consistently.[1, 2] This is very exciting because you can learn not only to *tolerate*, but actually *enjoy* foods that you may not like today.

Try It; You'll Learn to Like It!

I have a very good friend who enthusiastically changed his diet, but he said, "I don't like carrots and don't know if I will ever be able to eat them." I encouraged him to start with small amounts of carrot juice on a regular basis, and to his surprise, within three months he was actually enjoying carrots and carrot juice. You, too, can learn to love new foods and new tastes, if you are willing to simply add these foods to your diet and let your neuroadpatative response do the rest. You are only a couple of weeks away from being able to really enjoy a healthy, nutrient-rich diet.

These foods can be presented in very small, achievable sizes, such as a small leaf of lettuce cooked or juiced vegetables that can make the process very tolerable. It can even become a fun family game as every member of the family samples their new foods to the cheers of the other family members. We are working through this right now around our dinner table with mushrooms. Everyone puts a mushroom on his or her forks, and we count down to blastoff. The children laugh, and everyone eats a mushroom. Through this process, my children have learned to enjoy a number of foods that might surprise others, including salads, brussels sprouts, kale, mushrooms, cauliflower, and asparagus. In fact, they spontaneously reach for seconds on their salad greens almost every night.

The other method for altering your taste preferences is a short-term juice fast or limited raw fruit and vegetable fast for three to five days. This is further discussed in Day 37 and on our website. This period of relative rest from the world's fare will reset your taste buds and restore taste sensitivity.

What Shapes Your Body?

Your body is flexible, dynamic, and adaptable when given the opportunity to face new challenges. When challenged with an unhealthy diet, it adapts, begs, borrows, and steals as long as possible before system failures begin to overwhelm the adaptive mechanisms. Many people falsely believe that their diets are not causing any harm and that they are "healthy," when in reality their bodies are doing everything in their power to adjust to the damaging foods. Your body will also quickly adapt to a new, healthy diet with new energy, repair, detoxification, and a reversal of disease.

Origin of Change

I want to encourage you not to let rigor mortis of the mind restrain you from changing your diet. Your thoughts have great power over your future, but remember they are just intangible thoughts until they become tangible actions. Change your thoughts, and you will change your actions. Change your actions, and you will change your habits. Change your habits, and you will create a new lifestyle and future. It all begins with your thoughts and ends in your actions.

The key question then is what influences your thoughts. Is it what you read or watch, your friends or family, perhaps your history or transferable family ideas? True followers of Christ will find that their thoughts are primarily shaped and molded by spending time in God's Word and in prayer. This is the genesis of true and lasting change that will yield contentment, peace, and hope.

Take a Minute

Write down some of your closely held beliefs about your personal tastes and food preferences. What foods do you like, and why do you like them? Typically, our tastes are formed by exposure and habitual patterns. Are you willing to try some new foods? If not, why not? God created food to be enjoyed, but His foods, not the chemically manipulated and addictive, modern, processed foods. Ask God to give you the courage and strength to add more new whole foods to your diet. Give them a try—several times—and remind yourself that you will learn to enjoy these foods in time. Not only will your taste buds change, but so will your body. Give yourself, your body, and your future the opportunity for health by presenting it with a wide variety of fruits, vegetables, beans, nuts, and seeds every day.

Your Health Savings Account

*I*t is thrifty to prepare today for the wants of tomorrow," said Aesop in his story "The Ant and the Grasshopper." And Benjamin Franklin said, "If you would be wealthy, think of saving as well as getting. . . . He that goes a borrowing goes a sorrowing."They were both correct, of course, about money and about health.

Health and money will significantly impact your future; they are inextricably interwoven. Yet these two invaluable areas are neglected by millions of people. Research has shown that poor health significantly increases the probability of future financial strain, and inadequate finances can affect health by potentially limiting access to healthy foods and preventive health care.[1] Excellent health habits will not only reap physical benefits but will also create future financial margin and opportunity.

Health and Money

Your health and your money are vitally important to your current and future quality of life. Have you ever considered their similarities? Both will either improve or detract from your quality of life, require consistent investment, be influenced by inherent risk, respond to societal trends, demand your individual attention and sacrifice, and can grow rapidly or evaporate overnight. Sacrifice, wisdom, and planning are rewarded; greed and gluttony will eventually come to ruin.

You can incur debt by taking loans on your money, and you can incur a health debt through poor habits. Just like any other debt, these will always require future repayment with added interest. Ideal investment vehicles help your money to grow and provide safekeeping, just as healthy habits and lifestyles promote health and minimize future disease. I also believe there is a spiritual component of stewardship, realizing that money and health are entrusted to us, requiring responsibility and accountability, and diligence will be rewarded. How is your bottom line?

What Is a Health Bank Account?

Do you regularly save? If you do, *why* do you save? Personal savings is an investment in the future, a hedge against unforeseen events, and even disaster. Saving is a tool that is used to accomplish a future purpose or goal. It requires vision, self-discipline, and consistent effort as you plan for an uncertain future. Just as you should be saving your money for the future, so also you should be investing in your future health.

Each of us has a health bank account in which we daily make deposits and from which we make withdrawals based upon our lifestyle choices. Nutritional excellence, exercise, stress management, and adequate water are a few important daily deposits. Withdrawals from your account may include a stress-filled day, Oreos for lunch, and an evening of beer and sitcoms. Early in your life, money appears to be more important than health, but beginning about the age of forty, health quickly becomes a greater priority with each passing year.

I believe one of the most important questions about your retirement age is how much will you have saved in your *health* account? If you don't have your health, no amount of money will buy you quality of life. Sadly, many reach retirement age to find their health savings accounts are insufficiently funded for the future, and their plans and dreams are stifled by disease. They spent all their time and health to gain money, and in their retirement years, they spend their time and money to regain health! [2, 3] If you have not made regular and consistent investments during your thirties, forties, and fifties, can you honestly expect to make withdrawals in your golden years? In fact, many accounts are not only under funded, but they are filled with IOUs because they have borrowed against their health for decades.

He That Goes a Borrowing

Borrowing is always an assumption on the future. This concept is highlighted in the famous *Bogalusa Heart Study,* which demonstrated that a high intake of saturated fat early in life is strongly predictive of later heart disease.[4] A poor diet, such as the high-saturated-fat intake in the study, is a loan against future health. We are, in effect, borrowing from our future with poor diets and inactivity today. Degenerative disease is often the result of poor health savings habits, and diet is one of the primary assets or liabilities in your health portfolio. In contrast, those who choose to prepare for the future and make consistent deposits will find that their original investment is not only available but also has grown and will yield abundant health for the last quarter of life.

Begin Today

Is it too late to begin saving? No, it is never too late! However, starting later may require a larger investment. Just as money is influenced by time, so is your health. The earlier you begin a healthy lifestyle, the greater the rewards. Starting later may require first cleaning up acquired debts before you can see your health account grow. The most important advice is to start today. Taking action today and consistently applying that action daily, results in habits that will continue for a lifetime. Expert financial advice for saving money can easily also be applied to our health.

First, *learn to distinguish between wants and needs*, especially in the area of diet. It is important to begin to understand what your body needs and what your mind and emotions crave, and then choose to eat what you need not what you crave.

Second, *avoid the compulsive unhealthy "purchases,"* such as the candy bar at the checkout or the soda at the gas station.

Third, *less can be better.* You don't need to supersize the order to get the most for your money, while sacrificing your health.

Fourth, *create a food journal* to assess areas of improvement or areas that are consistently a problem. Often, journaling our food habits, or recording every bite that goes into your mouth is eye-opening. Create a long-term plan and stick to the plan with frequent reevaluation and updates quarterly. Decide today to make lifetime, lifestyle changes, and leave those detrimental habits behind.

Take a Minute

Proverbs 6:6–11 gives us the example of the ants that prepare for the future with diligent effort today. The section ends with these words: "A little extra sleep, a little more slumber, /a little folding of the hands to rest—/then poverty will pounce on you like a bandit; /scarcity will attack you like an armed robber." Today is the one day you have been given the opportunity to act. Yesterday is only history, and tomorrow is an uncertain future that will be influenced by your activity today. Faithfully use today for God's glory, and diligently sow your time and energy in activities that will yield a fruitful future. A healthy future is created today by eating (investing in) foods that God created, exercising, praying, forgiving, managing stress, drinking clean water, and taking time to rest and sleep. Ask the Lord to help you shift your lifestyle toward health, and learn to plan and prepare as the ant does.

Day 29

Physically Bankrupt or Independently Healthy

*M*argaret is a sixty-two-year-old missionary who served in overseas missions work much of her adult life. She and her husband purchased a building in Puerto Rico and converted it into an orphanage. They planned to continue serving in the orphanage well into their eighties. The busyness of life and missions work consumed their time, and they admittedly did not take care of their bodies and ate foods that were "convenient." Margaret shared that she never imagined that her health would fail or that she would develop disease.

Sitting in my office that day, Margaret was shell-shocked and couldn't believe her now desperate situation. She had always considered herself to be healthy, but in her late fifties and early sixties, disease overtook her body, her mission, and her service. She was forced to sell the orphanage, disperse the children, retire from missions work, and return to the US to fight for the rest of her life. Her physical habits and lack of concern for her health cut short her work in the missions field and affected not only her, but also her husband and all the orphans they had grown to love as their own children. The common health thieves—heart disease, diabetes, high blood pressure, arthritis, and low back pain—robbed her of her health while she was not looking. Margaret was not only financially bankrupt because of her disease, but she was facing complete physical bankruptcy. Her daily focus had shifted from service to others to service of self. Her life is now forever changed.

Lessons from Finance

We can learn from Margaret's situation. Consider how you can be the best steward of your body and avoid physical bankruptcy. Interestingly, many of the biblical principles of money management can be directly applied to your body. Both money and health are spiritual stewardship opportunities.

Financial management and investing are the allocation of limited funds in an environment of unlimited choices guided by a vision for the future. You have to save more than you spend and make decisions based on a long-term plan. God calls us to manage our finances with a kingdom view and to store up treasures in heaven, not on earth. This requires some sacrifices, biblical decision making, wise planning, and diligent execution.

Diet and health require similar management, due to the unlimited choices now available in our abundant, industrialized culture with enticing and appealing foods available twenty-four hours per day. Just like saving and investing, health also requires the formation of a long-term vision for wise management and stewardship. It also requires some sacrifices—always joyful when made for the Lord—a plan, and diligent execution that directs daily choices and encourages restraint.

Countless sermons have encouraged the wise and proper stewardship of our money, because it is God's money entrusted into our care while we are here. But very few sermons are preached on the stewardship of our physical bodies, which are also owned by God and entrusted into our care to be used for His service. In fact, we are called in Romans 12:1 to let our bodies "be a living and holy sacrifice—the kind He will find acceptable."

Do You Have a Health Budget?

A health budget is a tool to help you to distinguish between wants and needs before you sit down to a meal or go grocery shopping. Just like a financial budget, it helps to direct wise choices that support the long-term plan. Your budget can be derailed by immediate gratification and temptation, such as the break room, grocery store checkout line, and convenience stores.

Living by a health budget helps to create balance in every area and minimizes disease debt through careful planning and wise daily choices. This should include time for exercise, healthy foods, spiritual growth, and rest. It is also important to create a plan to repay the health debt. Consumer groups estimated that on average it takes three to five years to recover from credit card debt. Similarly, recovering health does not happen overnight and can take several years of consistent, dedicated effort before the damage is reversed.

One of my patients recently questioned the benefits of a healthy lifestyle because, after one and a half months of aggressive dietary change and exercise, she did not lose weight or notice any benefits.

I asked simply, "How many years did it take you to get to this point?" I wanted to make the point that she needed to change her expectations. If we are trying to pay off a large credit card debt or health debt with monthly installments, we can't expect the monthly report to read "zero" after only two months of minimum payments. Similarly, if you have a large health debt, it may take time, in some cases one to two years, to see the full effects of your lifestyle changes. Don't be discouraged. If you diligently work toward the goal, eventually the debt will be repaid, and health will be your reward.

You can begin repaying the debt today by taking an honest assessment of your incurred health debt. Have you been living to satisfy your wants with little thought of the future consequences? Take some time to review areas of your life that might be contributing to a rising health debt and those that strengthen your health savings. Are you growing debt or assets?

When tackling a health debt, it is important to choose the most pressing area, such as diet, stress, exercise, pain, or harmful habits. Then decide to make changes today, because debt will always require payment. If you don't make the effort to pay down your health debt today, larger payments in the form of a health crisis may be in the future. In contrast, have you ever paid off a credit card or loan? A great sense of accomplishment and freedom follows with the realization that your monthly budget is no longer strained.

Repaying your debts is an important step in gaining freedom from both financial and health burdens. The total debt may seem like a daunting figure, but when it is broken down into achievable steps planned over time, hope is reborn. Success can be found in both a clear vision of the goal and a stepwise plan to reach that goal. If you have a large credit card debt, paying twenty dollars per month will never repay the debt, and freedom will be only an illusion. Likewise, repaying your health debt requires more than small changes, such as cutting down on fat or exercising two times per week. If you truly want to change your health future, you must first repay the accumulated debt, and then rebuild your body. This can only come through a sincere decision to change and take aggressive action to make lifetime lifestyle changes. If this is your desire, decide today to make the changes that will reclaim your health and unlock your body's potential to heal itself.

How Do You Repay a Health Debt?

Numerous books have been written extolling biblical principles that lead to wise financial management and the repayment of debt. The Bible says that "the borrower is a slave to the lender" (Proverbs 22:7). Careless living in a culture of abundance and a multitude of affordable choices is an open door for the accumulation of both financial and health debt. The only way to repay debt and maintain healthy finances or body is to return to biblical principles and to God's original provision of food.

If you are facing a health debt, or perhaps a crisis, the most valuable currencies for repaying debt are green leafy vegetables, cruciferous vegetables, melons, juices, raw vegetables, fruits, beans, lentils, and chickpeas. These are the foods that promote healing, regeneration, and restoration of damaged cells. As the body grows healthier, it will naturally lose weight and ultimately maintain a normal, healthy body weight.

Revolving health debt that must be eliminated is sugar, white flour products, lunch meats, chips, crackers, white pasta, high-fructose corn syrup, frozen meals, fast foods, fried foods, processed meats, and some "health" products, such as cereals. Some others that should be minimized include animal-based products, processed beverages, juices, and dairy. A good rule of thumb is to eat foods as close to the natural state as possible and avoid foods that have been handled and processed multiple times.

Regular exercise, stress management, seven to eight hours of sleep, and spring water are also important components of a plan to repay debt. More information can be found on our website, Day3Health.com.

Achieve Freedom

There is great freedom and opportunity when the ledger sheet of health is cleared and the disease debt is erased. Your life will dramatically change. You can achieve freedom from the majority of diseases by following biblical principles and applying a plan that is fueled by vision and executed with diligence.

Take a Minute

Today, create a health "balance sheet" on a piece of paper with a list of assets on one side and debts on the other. Review your diet and types of food typically eaten, activity levels, sleep, stress, current diseases, medications, and family history, and place them each in the appropriate category. How does your sheet look? Where do you need to begin working on the debt, and how can you strengthen your assets? Have some fun and share your balance sheet with a loved one or spouse. Writing things down often brings a moment of honest revelation and clarity that is lost in conversation.

But My Grandfather Lived to Ninety!

$\mathcal{M}$y grandfather lived to be ninety, and he smoked and drank every day," my patient confidently exclaimed just after I finished sharing with him the importance of creating a healthy lifestyle. He, too, smoked cigarettes, was overweight, suffered from chronic low back pain, had high blood pressure and heart disease, and had no interest in changing his lifestyle at age sixty-seven. He placed great confidence in his gene pool to provide him with a long, enjoyable life and did not want to admit that his poor habits were contributing to his current health challenges that would likely compromise his future plans. This wishful thinking was not based on realistic risk management but rather a willful ignorance that perpetuated his unhealthy habits.

What confidence should you place in your genes to provide you with a healthy future free of disabling disease? If health were merely a matter of our genetic predisposition, as my patient believed, then any attempts at lifestyle changes are futile in the end. My patient gambled his future on the untested assumption that his health is predetermined by his genes and that his genes would give him the same long life that his grandfather enjoyed. However, untested assumptions can lead to perpetuated errors that can be very costly, including your life in this world and your eternal destiny. In my patient's case, he was assuming that his genes were the sole determinant of health, his genes and lifestyle were identical to his grandfather's, and his grandfather's quality of life was excellent until his death. If any of these assumptions are not true, then my patient is resting on a false sense of security, and his life is at great risk.

As you consider your own life right now, it is important to take an honest assessment of your risks and then work to protect your weaknesses. It's imperative to understand how your genes and environment (diet, exercise, toxic exposures, stress, sleep, spiritual life) influence your health. If environmental influences are important, what do you need to consider when making lifestyle choices specific to your own risks? What are your specific genetic susceptibilities based on family history? Can you influence your health future despite your risks or genetic susceptibilities?

A Chip Off the Old Block

With each of my six children, friends and family are quick to comment to my wife or me, "He/she looks just like you." While it is true that we are similar to our parents, we are also a unique expression of the two shared gene pools. There are several levels of genetic information that shape who you are today. You have genes that are expressed dominantly and will always result in the determined trait, such as brown hair. Recessive genes are expressed when matched with a similar recessive gene, such as blue eyes. Finally, you have genes called polymorphisms that are very individualized, often are involved in metabolic processes, and are influenced by environmental factors, such as diet and toxins. It is this last class of genes that is the most important in our discussion of the relationship between lifestyle habits and degenerative diseases, because you control the level of influence every day.

We are not all created equal at the genetic level, and each of us carries genetic polymorphisms that code for differing levels of disease resistance and susceptibilities—some stronger and others weaker. Perhaps you know some people who are born with a greater resistance to diseases, including the common cold, and are seemingly never sick, while others seem to catch everything going around and are constantly battling one disease after another. The answer to the disparity is in their individual health equations: Your Genes + Your Environment = Health or Disease

The Genes of the Father and Mother

Chronic degenerative diseases, such as heart disease, some cancers, and diabetes, reflect the interaction of individual genetic polymorphisms and the environment. It is a strong antioxidant polymorphism in some people that allows them to smoke five packs of cigarettes per day and not acquire lung cancer, while others are afflicted by lung cancer through secondhand smoke.[1] Unfortunately, you and I don't know which genetic weaknesses are found in our DNA and, therefore, any poor health habits are like playing Russian roulette with your future. And remember that today the environment has dramatically shifted away from God's original plan to a man-made, modern chemical milieu that cultivates disease. Every day we face more toxins and threats to our health than our ancestors of even fifty years ago, and this requires greater diligence in your health habits.

You inherit your individual disease susceptibilities and genetic variations from your parents. Then your unique lifetime environmental exposures, including diet, activity, stress, sleep, and toxin exposures, begin to exploit these weak areas. Your unique genetic variations, polymorphisms, are found in your thirty-five thousand paired genes, and they are responsible for directing everything from the metabolism of food, medications, enzymes, and toxins to the healing of skin and bone.[2] We are each a variation on the theme of our parents and extended families, and based upon your variation, you may be at more or less risk of certain diseases associated with your family history. Some diseases, such as cardiovascular disease and cancer, can show a very strong association within a family, while others, such as allergies and autoimmune diseases, appear in only some of the individuals. The intriguing question is, why are some more affected than others?

Uniquely You

We are all different, even down to our enzymes. Genetic polymorphisms increase or decrease your risk of a number of diseases, including diabetes, stroke, allergies, cancers, heart disease, dementia, some psychiatric disorders, and the immune system. For example, a very strong anti-inflammatory component of our immune system is IL-10 and is thought to assist in reducing and controlling inflammation in our bodies.

A recent study of centenarians (one hundred years old) found an association that suggests that those with higher levels of IL-10 have a greater chance of longevity and health, likely due to the reduced inflammatory levels.[3] Several other studies have reached similar conclusions on inflammation. However, inflammation does not occur without some external influence, and this is the most important point. It is your environment, including your choices of diet, habits, stress, exercise, and toxin exposure, that drive the inflammatory process and other potential disease triggers and play upon your genetic susceptibilities, like fingers on a piano. The song that is played leads to either protection or exposure to disease. Each day your health habits will "tickle the ivories" of your genetic polymorphisms. What song are they playing in your life? Hopefully, an ode to health.

Guarding Your Weaknesses

The exciting news is that your genetic weaknesses may never be manifested, if you are willing to take several simple steps to improve your health. Removing threats to your DNA in the form of pesticides, tobacco, alcohol, processed foods, and chemicals is the first step. This includes choosing some organic produce and drinking pure spring water. The most important protective factor in your health is your diet. When you remove the damaging foods and then add in the health-supporting foods, such as kale, bok choy, and broccoli, you more than double the health effect. Plant-based foods detoxify the body and repair damage through antioxidants, protect cells and DNA, and provide all of the necessary nutrition for optimal function.

God created the most elegant system of information storage, transfer, retrieval, and reproduction in the dynamic structure of DNA. He also created a system that would survive and allow for adaptation to new and challenging environments through modification of DNA. But in a fallen world touched by sin at every level, even DNA reflects the consequence of sin in the form of genetic polymorphisms for disease. You cannot control your genetic profile, but you can control your health habits and, thus, dramatically reduce your risk of disease. How can you protect yourself? By returning to God's original provision through a healthy diet founded on natural foods grown by God, exercising regularly, resting, avoiding toxins, and minimizing negative stress. If you are at risk for disease, based on a family history, don't delay in making changes. Start today. The effects of poor habits are additive over time, and disease will accumulate until it reaches the tipping point and manifests itself with devastating effects. Choose instead a lifestyle that promotes a healthy body that will be vibrant, alive, and strong for His service.

Take a Minute

Write down your potential disease risk by considering your family history of disease; habit history, including tobacco, alcohol, sleep habits, and stress; and toxin exposures, including work, food, water, pesticides, cleaners, and the like. Sometimes this is a long list, but it will help you gain some perspective and, hopefully, motivate you to make lifelong changes that promote health. Diet is one of the most powerful tools for overcoming disease and toxic habits and is the best place to begin your journey to a healthier life. Ask for the Lord's guidance and wisdom as you look through this list and know that He will give you the strength to change.

I Did It My Way

$\mathscr{I}$n an era of the "me" generation and "I did it my way," our culture often forgets that personal decisions have a ripple effect on all of the people connected to their lives. In the passionate pursuit of individualism, personal goals, and dreams, people frequently ignore the impact of their decisions on those they love. In fact, the decisions we make each day about the food we eat, exercise, and habits have consequences that extend far beyond our own bodies.

"It's my body and I can do with it whatever I want," I have often heard from patients. Another patient shared with me one afternoon in the office, "I am not hurting anyone else with my poor diet." I have encountered some who will attempt to deny this fact of connectedness, but a simple look at rising health-care costs and health care's present and coming economic impact will give credence to this concept. Our children will bear the economic burden of the daily poor health choices of most Americans. Our health-care system is straining under the weight of lifestyle-driven diseases, such as obesity, type 2 diabetes, heart disease, and smoking and related lung disease.

Six Degrees of Separation

You and I are connected to multiple people and are only separated by a surprisingly few degrees. Several studies have suggested that we are all connected in this world by only six to seven degrees of separation. Amazing, isn't it? Your family, friends, work associates, neighbors, churches, and local businesses are all more or less tied to your life and its course. It is important to recognize that your health or illness will directly impact many lives, especially those closest and dearest to you. Your decisions regarding your diet, exercise, habits, and stress will not only affect your future but the future of numerous others, especially those whom you love.

Sylvia was a sixty-five-year-old patient who initially presented to my office for chronic low back pain, knee pain, and general fatigue. She described her typical day as arising to eat breakfast, sitting on her living room chair until lunch, eating lunch, retreating to the chair for the afternoon for a nap before dinner, and then an early bedtime following dinner because she was tired. Sylvia was just surviving to see another day.

Sylvia's husband was vibrant and healthy, but he carried the burden on his furrowed brow and downtrodden face and tears marking their way down his cheeks when he spoke lovingly about his bride of forty-three years. During our initial visit, I asked Sylvia about her goals and motivations, and her husband emphatically interrupted his wife in mid-sentence, saying, "I just want my wife back." They were unable to travel to see their grandchildren on the West Coast, and the diseases that held Sylvia captive had thwarted their retirement plans. Her greatest assets were her humble teachability followed by her motivation.

When I described the hope and potential for her life and then the necessary lifestyle changes, she grabbed hold of the possibility and pursued the changes with great diligence and tenacity. Over the next three months, her pain began to resolve, and she described newfound energy, better sleep, and noticed that she was doing more around the house. After nine months, she was nearly pain free, lost thirty pounds, and was planning a trip to visit her grandchildren. Her husband was beaming when they came in for the last visit and he, too, looked renewed, hopeful, and reenergized. Her new health was a great multigenerational blessing to many, including her husband, children, and grandchildren.

Web of Influence

Imagine yourself at the center of a web of connections that graphically demonstrates your health influence. Some connections are more direct and others more distant. You are at the center of the web, and all of the threads are tied to you. Pull on one of the strings and notice that the entire web deforms. What happens when you push on the center of the web? Can you imagine the strain on each of the attached threads?

Consider for a moment in detail how each of these lives that are connected to you would be impacted if you suffered a health crisis or even premature death. The basic necessities of provision, including food, housing, and living expenses, would suffer. Your family would be forced to pick up the extra work around the house, emotional strain is felt at home, coworkers must divide up your work, friends may be asked for help, and volunteer organizations and churches must adjust due to lost help, lost mission and discipleship service, and lost charitable giving. You can begin to see that your life and health is a benefit to the lives of many, and a disease will send a ripple effect throughout your web.

Understanding and internalizing the health or disease influence of your life is critical in your decision to make lasting lifestyle changes. The foods you eat and the way you manage your health should be partially motivated by your love for your friends and family and sense of obligation to your community. It could even be argued that to continue living a disease-promoting lifestyle, once you have been enlightened to the alternative, is selfish. I believe that choosing to be healthy is another way to express your love for those closest to you. Your health influence is one more reason to invest in your health and inspire change.

Take a Minute

Create your own health web. Place yourself in the middle and draw connecting lines to everyone influenced by your life. Consider in very specific ways how their lives would be changed if you suffered a major health crisis. How would it affect your time, focus, energy, work, profession, vision, travel, patience, service, finances, and opportunities? Next, consider how their lives in each of these areas will be impacted if you are strong, healthy, and energetic. Consider how you can create a multigenerational value of health in your family by casting a greater vision for your children and the use of their bodies. A patient best summarized the core decision point in health influence when he said, "After knowing what I now know, it would be selfish of me not to change." May the Lord give you wisdom and strength for today and tomorrow.

$\mathcal{D}ay$ **32**

Accumulated Injury Tipping Point

$\mathcal{M}$ary is a forty-seven-year-old bright and busy woman who came to see me for help with her health problems and low back pain. She sat on the exam table and shared her long list of medical problems: high blood pressure, high cholesterol, borderline diabetes, low back pain, and reflux disease. Then she stopped, smiled, and exclaimed, "I just don't know what happened! It seems as if I just woke up one day and somebody had switched out my healthy body for one with a bunch of diseases!"

Have you ever felt that way? Confused and frustrated, she could not understand how her health crumbled seemingly overnight and, further-more, where all of her diseases originated. She shared with me that she thought she ate healthy food and tried to take care of herself, but fre-quently the busyness of life interfered with her best-laid plans. Now she was facing a significant health crisis and was forced to make time to reclaim her health.

Every day I see patients like Mary, who have reached this "tipping point" where degeneration and disease suddenly become apparent and steal away the quality from their lives. This tipping point is the moment when people begin to feel that they are falling apart, and it is hard for them to imagine that little things accumulated over time can lead to such dramatic pain, disease, and suffering.

Many of my patients ask, "How can my diet or lack of daily exercise have caused all these problems? I ate or drank alcohol in moderation; how could that have caused my disease? How could my old knee injury cause my severe back pain?" The answer to their questions is "accumulated injury over time." The slow but progressive wear and tear eventually overcomes the body's ability to manage the damage, and disease overtakes the system.

Degenerative disease is not the result of one event but a number of small, seemingly insignificant daily events that lead to an accumulation of cellular damage, partial healing, muscular imbalances, impaired immune function, and inadequate repair. People often ignore or downplay the significance and promise to take care of it later or make changes next year. The damage continues to accumulate under the radar until the disease presents with physical manifestations. It is similar to the damage that occurs from termites. Silently behind the walls they chew at the structural beams until one day the integrity of the house is comprised, and no one can believe the extent of the damage or the consequences.

Subclinical Disease

Modern medicine utilizes complex tests, lab work, and advanced imaging studies to measure the manifestations of disease. Then the constellation of findings and symptoms are given a name or diagnosis. Many patients falsely believe that is the first appearance of the disease. In reality, the disease process has been accumulating for years and, perhaps, decades silently beneath the surface while the body adapted and continued to perform to the best of its ability. Eventually, the body reaches a tipping point where the accumulated damage can no longer be controlled, and systems begin to fail, sometimes to the point of total failure as with an acute heart attack. This is not the beginning of a disease, but it's really a crisis point because the body has become overloaded with accumulated damage to cells and tissues. And the same process that led to one disease can also lead to others if not identified and reversed. The tipping point is a critical point in life and should become an emergency alarm signaling that your body is suffering from repeated injury and needs immediate attention.

Combating Decay

Today we live in a world that is fallen and in a state of decay. All of creation is awaiting a day of future regeneration when creation's groan (Romans 8:22) will be quieted. Until that glorious day, we are all subject to the Second Law of Thermodynamics, which imposes a state of increasing decay and randomness on everything in the universe, except our spirits that have been renewed by Christ. All we have to do is look at our aging bodies, houses, and cars to verify the truth of this law. When sin entered the world, the system began to unwind, including our bodies and DNA. Today, we all have imperfect DNA (sorry to break the bad news). Some people have weaker immune systems and greater susceptibility to certain diseases, and some suffer genetic diseases that are inherently fatal or disabling. We all live in a world that imperfectly supports life with bodies that can be affected by degeneration and disease.

Some factors in the disease process are beyond our control, but many are within the control of our daily decisions. My dad always taught me not to worry about the things beyond my control, but instead to put my full effort into those things I can control. The primary controllable factors of accumulated injury that can cause disease in your life are diet, exercise, sleep, toxic exposures—including alcohol and tobacco—and stress. These basic lifestyle choices will either promote disease or health in your life.

The potential repair, regeneration, and revitalization of your cells is determined by your daily decisions, and repeated positive choices lead to a healthier, stronger body. Poor daily decisions about the food you eat, activity, and stress will lead to cellular damage that will eventually progress to disease. The time to the tipping point is dependent on your genetic susceptibility and total daily accrued injury or repair. More bad choices in multiple areas of your lifestyle accelerate the degenerative process—add stress and you have poured fuel on the fire. The body responds very quickly to a healthy diet and lifestyle and can actually reverse accumulated damage as verified by numerous studies. When given the proper opportunity and materials, such as phytochemicals and antioxidants, the body can begin to heal itself and combat the disease and decay.

Your Body's Cry for Help

If you have reached the tipping point, listen to the message that your body is sending you: "Help! I am sick, and damage has accumulated to the point that I can't keep up. The system is overloaded."

The tipping point demands change and not just small changes in diet, stress, and exercise. Remember, you are dealing with accumulated injury that has been building up over years and even decades. Halting and reversing the process requires dedicated effort applied over time.

You may remember opening your credit card bill and being totally shocked by the large balance. I know I have been there! The debt balance accumulated over time, one purchase decision at a time. Then you look at the large balance and ask, "How did this happen?" It is a tipping point in your financial management. Spending money was easy and fun and effortless during the process, but paying back the debt takes dedicated effort over time.

Your body is just like the credit card. It is those simple daily decisions about what you eat, activity, stress, sleep, and toxic exposures that lead to accumulating debt (cellular damage) that eventually presents in the form of a bill (tipping point health crisis or new disease diagnosis). Paying back the health debt will require lifestyle changes applied over time, but the rewards are great: a strong, healthy, and vibrant body ready to be the hands and feet of Christ.

Press On

The choice is yours. The decision to fight the degeneration battle requires energy, fortitude, vision, and determination. The reward is health, vitality, quality of life, and living a life as unhindered by disease as is possible. Many have fought and won, but sadly, others have decided to succumb and surrender to the enemy and live as slaves to poor health the remainder of their years. If you decide to fight the battle, know that it will initially be challenging, but you will advance on the enemy, and the rewards awaiting you are great. Press on!

Take a Minute

Write down any areas of your life that have reached the tipping point. It doesn't have to be just physical. We can reach tipping points in our relationships and spiritual lives too. Next to each one, write down the probable sources of accumulated injury over time. Is it your diet, lack of exercise, stress, poor sleep habits, toxic exposures, lack of time in God's Word and prayer, repeated exposure to sin or temptation, harsh words to someone you love, or lack of time invested in relationships? Next, write down the solution to each of these sources of accumulated injury and decay. The solutions are all very similar and center upon returning to a Christ-centered lifestyle, putting Him first in all things, and then making daily decisions that will support health in each one of these areas of your life. It requires a separation from the culture and destructive forces that strive against us. The long-term success is found in the small choices and decisions that you make each day. May God grant you wisdom as you complete this exercise and the strength to make changes one decision at a time.

Children and Diet

$\mathcal{I}$magine for a moment that children—perhaps your own or children in your family—are like a freshly tilled garden of rich soil that has just been plowed and prepared for planting. The garden is their body, and the seeds that you will be planting are diet and lifestyle. And just like farming, the future harvest will be determined by what you plant today.

I believe that the future health of our children is largely dependent on the seeds of health and disease that are planted in the fertile soil of youth. Like seeds, they remain hidden beneath the surface for some time awaiting germination and growth. In fact, many of the seeds of disease may not sprout for years or even decades, which is well documented in many scientific studies on heart disease, diabetes, osteoporosis, and many cancers. The seeds of health are fresh vegetables, fruits, beans, lentils, whole grains, an active lifestyle, good sleep, a close relationship with God, and opportunities to give to others. The seeds of disease are high-fructose corn syrup, sugar, white flour, processed foods and meats, juices, sodas, inactivity, industrialized animal products, poor sleep, stress, and a self-focused life. It is really God's system versus the world's system. If you are a parent, you are the gardener; and over time the seeds you plant will germinate, sprout, and grow, producing a harvest of health or disease. Cultivate your little "gardens" wisely.

How Will Your Gardens Grow?

All children who have access to food will grow, and we assume that because they are growing and not showing signs of a disease they are healthy. In reality, the degenerative diseases grow slowly, subclinically, and accumulate over time until they reach a tipping point decades later. The foods that you choose to feed your children every day and the lifestyle habits you promote are foundational building blocks in their lives. I often encourage parents that your love for your children should guide you to give them the best and healthiest foods, not sweets and treats. Caving in to their cravings and satisfying the temporary pleasures of taste are really selfish pursuits, because we adults receive satisfaction when children jump for joy at junk food. But that brief, passing pleasure sets them up for unhealthy eating patterns and food addictions that will lead to disease in adulthood. We would never think of giving our children cocaine, but if you will recall what we learned on day 14, when we continually feed them sugar, we are stimulating the same cells in their brains and establishing similar addictive patterns. Remember, your children will reap what you sow into their lives.

Origin of Adult Diseases

Numerous studies have documented that many degenerative diseases have their origins in childhood. Studies of autopsies in children from five to fifteen years of age found coronary artery fatty streaks—fat in the arteries of the heart.[1] An autopsy study of young men who died in Korea with an average age of nineteen found that 77.3 percent had atherosclerosis or blockages in their coronary or heart arteries.[2]

It is important to understand that the arterial plaques, hardening of the arteries, are the body's attempt to patch or plaster areas of ongoing injury and damage to the arterial wall. The cholesterol and calcium plaques accumulate year after year, layer upon layer, inside the artery until only a small opening remains. It is very similar to a pipe or hose that becomes corroded and narrows over time. Eventually, when the child has grown into an adult, the opening becomes too small so that not enough blood is able to flow to the heart muscle, or a larger piece of the soft plaque breaks off and occludes the artery, causing an acute heart attack. The symptoms present in adulthood, but the onset of the disease process began during childhood.

Many cancers, such as colon and prostate cancer, have been linked to early and prolonged exposures that eventually manifest as disease in later adulthood.[3] Cancer begins when a cell is damaged and losses its ability to regulate its own growth. The cell begins to divide, stimulating angiogenesis, growing decade after decade until it grows large enough to begin affecting bodily function or it is measurable by modern medical tests. Until it reaches one of these two presenting points, it remains hidden, growing occultly within the body. The cancerous cells are created often in the years of youth, and the dietary habits limit the body's natural ability to identify and destroy these cells through a robust immune system. Instead, the cells are allowed to continue living and dividing, and some dietary components, such as sugar and high-fructose corn syrup, promote the cancerous cell growth.

Cultivating the Garden

"That's disgusting!" "Ick!" "It's yucky, Mommy!" If you have children, grandchildren, nephews, or nieces, you've heard these comments delivered with masterful emotion and facial contortions for added effect. How do adults typically respond? That's right, they immediately begin negotiating the amount and possible rewards for eating "just two small bites, Johnny," and ultimately cave in to the superior negotiator—a three-year-old! What are the three-year-old's powerful leverage points? More whining, crying, and a threat not to eat dinner. Adults are eventually worn down by the better negotiator and give in to their demands. The three-year-old wins again!

When you change your diet, it is challenging, but it can be much more difficult when children are involved. They tend to be more vocal and far more persistent than any other group. Often they have learned that if they can whine a little longer or a little louder, Mom or Dad will break down and give in. Have you ever been there? We have six children, and we have heard and seen it all through the years. Children are masterful in their ability to push our buttons and attempt to wear us down. A two-year-old's whining can break even the toughest marine drill sergeant.

Taste Buds Can Change

The art of winning any negotiation is to take stock of your leverage positions and clearly understand the purpose of the negotiation. In this case, the purpose is your children's health future. Children will use the time-tested negotiation tactics of whining, crying, complaining, throwing a fit, and refusing to eat. None of these are life threatening, and even if they miss a meal, children will be okay. They will eat healthy food when they are hungry.

It is important to remember that you control the purchase and preparation of food, unless your children are independent. If your children are older, you still control the majority of the food purchases for your home. You also have learned that taste buds will adapt over time, and taste preferences can change. So time is also on your side. Children can learn to enjoy healthy foods, including vegetables and fruits. This is a powerful concept to keep in mind. Through small, repeated exposures, your children can learn to enjoy foods that they may have previously rejected. Typically it takes from thirty to sixty days, or fifteen exposures to a particular food, for taste buds to begin to adapt. Slowly and consistently they will adapt, and children will not only begin to tolerate the food, but they may even surprise you when they ask for a second helping. We have used this strategy successfully with our five older children, who now truly enjoy a wide variety of vegetables, whole grains, fruits, beans, and lentils. Remember, this is a loving negotiation, not a battle or a war. Instead, you are trying to improve the quality of their lives and their future.

Strategies for Change

Make it a fun family adventure! Consider holding a fun family meeting to present the new dietary changes and the reasons you have decided to make changes as a family. Share with them that this is a family project, and the family will need to work together for success. Emphasize the biblical principles and responsibility to God to maintain the body—His temple—the consequences of disease, and the benefits of health in their future and in your own lives. Use some examples of people you have known who have suffered from disease and others who have benefited from health. Begin to teach them about their bodies, how they work, and what their bodies require for health and strength. Work together, engaging your children in the change, building meal plans, shopping, and cooking together. Learn about new vegetables and spices, and most importantly, make it fun. Laugh a lot, tell stories, and make some healthy desserts.

Creating Your Children's Eating Preferences and Habits

Your children's eating preferences and diet will be created by the food you choose to serve them. If you choose to serve pizza, noodles, and cookies, they will develop a very strong taste preference for these addictive foods and will shun healthy vegetables. Their taste preferences will determine their disease risk at forty, fifty, and sixty. Young girls or boys who only eat processed, nutrient-poor foods will suffer serious disease consequences at much earlier ages than their parents or grandparents. You should buy and serve healthy foods, and please don't give them an option by keeping unhealthy foods in the pantry or cupboards. If it is not in the house, they have no other options.

The foods you purchase and serve will become your children's body, so purchase wisely, and use the nutrient-rich foods of God's garden to build a strong healthy foundation.

Food Is Never Neutral

Often we are satisfying our desire to see our children eat, even if it's unhealthy food. Some children are praised by a proud parent for their "great appetites" as they devour their fourth hot dog. If your children decide not to eat their broccoli, don't give them more noodles, bread, or other nutrient-poor foods to just fill their bellies. Remember that food is never neutral; it either builds up or tears down the body. It is important to separate your desires and expectations from your children's plate. If they choose not to eat, it's all right. They will survive and live through the night without dinner and will come with a different attitude in the morning. Do what is right for your children, both now and for their future.

Smoothies, Using the Power of Adaptation

Smoothies are a terrific way to include vegetables, such as kale and bok choy, in your children's daily diet, and it helps to shape their taste preferences. Combining berries, pomegranate juice, and bananas with the kale hides the taste of the greens and provides a delicious, healthy breakfast. Smoothies work on the system of adaptation by frequently exposing the taste buds to fruits and vegetables. Their taste system begins to adapt to the new vegetables and fruits, and in a very short time, children actually begin to enjoy eating vegetables.

"If you eat your salad, you can have ice cream for dessert!" Frequently, adults make the mistake of promoting a conflicting view of food. Unhealthy food should never be a reward for good behavior or choices. There is no other area of life where we would give our children something damaging as a reward. We commonly describe in detail the negative effects of these foods to our children and help them to make better choices, while striking a balance to avoid making food legalistic or a healthy diet unsustainable. Instead, we encourage them to do their best, but we allow for some flexibility in situations, such as family events or holidays, striving for a 90 percent to 10 percent balance or better, eating nutrient-rich foods nine times out of ten or more. During special occasions, we allow them to choose a piece of pie or birthday cake without feelings of guilt, but we teach them to understand how that food may affect their bodies. Often my wife will bring a healthy alternative dessert for the children. A dietary plan that is too strict becomes burdensome and smothers your children's enthusiasm for a lifelong lifestyle. The goal is to assist them in learning to make wise decisions and to ultimately be self-governing individuals who will teach their families to value health and life, creating a generational legacy.

Take a Minute

Consider that you have the greatest opportunity to influence the future health of your children and set the trajectory for the rest of their lives. You also have an opportunity to establish a multigenerational value for God's food and proper maintenance of body. The food you buy and serve at home, your choice of restaurants, your habits, and your daily example will plant either the seeds of health or disease in the fertile soil of youth. Poor choices in each of these areas can enslave your beautiful children to addictive foods, weight gain, pain, heart disease, diabetes, and many cancers later in their lives. Because you love them and want the best for their lives, help them establish a healthy lifestyle early in life, and teach them why they need to avoid destructive foods and lifestyle habits. Your children's lives will be blessed by your example and leadership, and they will be grateful when they are sixty, seventy, or even eighty. Leave a legacy of health to your children and future generations to come!

Day **34**

What Happened to You?

*C*hange inevitably evokes resistance, and a change to a plant-based diet will usually be met with skepticism, long lists of questions, such as, "Where do you get your protein?" and in some cases, outright hostility. This is not uncommon and, in fact, it is similar to the challenges that you may have faced as a Christian. We have faced opposition from family and friends and I know that you may face similar challenges. I want you to be prepared for the most common questions and objections that will arise and help you put your new diet into the proper context, so that you can present a gentle and intelligent answer.

Where Do You Get Your Protein?

This will be one of the first questions people ask when you tell them you are eating a predominantly plant-based diet. The majority of the people believe that protein is found only in animal products and that a decrease or absence of these leads to protein deficiency and poor health. Cutting back on meat challenges a deeply held belief that meat equals life, health, and strength. It also challenges the modern dietary paradigm that a meal is built around meat. Remember, people are asking because they don't have all the information to make an educated decision.

Protein is found in all plants and comprises 10–15 percent of the total calories of any plant. In fact, broccoli contains more protein per calorie than steak. Multiple studies have shown that people eating a plant-based diet from a wide variety of plants, nuts, seeds, and beans consume adequate levels of protein. The average person requires 40–60 grams of protein, and in America today they average 90–100 grams per day.[1] Both the Center for Disease Control and National Institute of Health recommend protein intakes in the range of 9–10 percent of total caloric intake—the same protein content of all plants. Beans, lentils, chickpeas, fermented soy products, nuts, and seeds are excellent sources of protein. Also, as previously stated, if you choose to eat animal products, studies would suggest two to three times per week is sufficient to maintain the body and avoid disease.

I Am Healthy. Why Should I Change?

The absence of disease symptoms today can only be interpreted as a lack of disease symptoms and not necessarily the absence of disease. Please look at these startling statistics:

- Several studies have shown that at least 90 percent of Americans eating the Standard American Diet (SAD) have atherosclerosis.[2]

- The CDC released findings that 90 percent of US citizens carry a mixture of pesticides in their bodies.[3]

- About 50 percent of all Americans will die from heart disease.

- About 30 percent will die from cancer.[4]

- Approximately 30 percent have diabetes.

- One-eighth have Alzheimer's disease.

- About 70 percent are overweight or obese.

- Two-thirds of people over sixty-five have high blood pressure, putting them at risk for stroke and heart disease.

- Very few people over fifty are truly healthy.

Healthy is a term that really needs to be defined, and it is okay to ask someone how he or she would define it. You may find that healthy is defined as "disease that is controlled by medications." I have had several patients who would define health in this way. Ultimately, the choice is individual, and it is not your responsibility to convince them. If they are not interested in change or are even resistant, don't create a battle line over diet. You can offer information, statistics, and guidance, but people will never change unless they recognize their need and humbly accept the information. It is best in these cases to live as an example and love as a friend or family member so that you will have the opportunity to share with them when they are ready to receive the information.

The Bible Doesn't Promote a Diet

This is absolutely true. In fact, we are cautioned in Romans 14 to avoid disputes over diet, and in verse 13 we are encouraged with these words: "Therefore let us not judge one another anymore, but rather resolve this, not to put a stumbling block or a cause to fall in our brother's way." And later in verse 15, "Yet if your brother is grieved because of your food, you are no longer walking in love. Do not destroy with your food the one for whom Christ died." Food and diet should never be a divisive force in relationships. It is a lesser, temporal tool as both the body and food will one day pass away, but the spirit and spiritual decisions will live on eternally. However, it is important to understand that what you eat will impact your health, and this can impact the mental and spiritual aspects of life. Physical, mental, and spiritual are all intertwined in our bodies and cannot be separated—each is influenced by the health of the other.

Diet is a tool to manage the body for God's glory, just as a budget is a tool to manage finances for the Lord. So it's important to research and search for the most effective tool to manage the body for God's glory. The Bible gives some general guidance in Genesis 1:29 with God's original provision of food for life, which was plant-based, but does not give specific guidelines for a diet. We must look to science for further clarification of the foods that support health and the optimal function of the body.

We Shouldn't Be Concerned with Our Bodies, but Our Spirit

This is an unbiblical statement. Nowhere does the Bible separate the body as an unimportant aspect of who you are. This arises from Platonic Greek philosophy that imagined the body as the enemy of the soul's aspirations. As a Christian, your body has not yet been recreated and will one day be made new, but while you are here on earth, the body serves as an integral aspect of our existence. Romans 12:1 tells us to present our bodies as a "living and holy sacrifice," and in 1 Corinthians 6:19–20 we are called the "temple of the Holy Spirit" and encouraged to glorify God in our bodies. Your body is important to God, because it is the interface with life, people, spouse, loved ones, service to God, and often the manifestation of sin conceived in the heart. I encourage you to pursue the great challenge of glorifying God in your body and in every aspect of your life.

I Don't Like Those Foods

Food preferences are not fixed but rather fluid and flexible. God created within our DNA great flexibility through adaptation. Cells adapt rapidly to changes in environment to create a new norm. This includes the cells that are intricately involved in the system of taste. As previously mentioned, these cells adapt to new tastes within thirty days or with fifteen tries. And once the cells adapt, it creates the new norm. The bottom line is that taste preferences can adapt to change, and new foods can become enjoyable and eventually preferred over the previous diet. The only requirement is a willingness to continue regularly exposing taste buds to new tastes while removing some of the unhealthy foods.

You're Too Strict

This objection usually implies legalism, or the person is questioning you because they don't want to change, or they don't believe that they can change. This statement is defensive of the current status quo, and so it should be handled with a gentle answer.

First, this is not a diet based on legalism or biblical mandate. You are shifting your diet to improve your health both now and in the future and to avoid many of the diseases that plague aging Americans. The goal is to improve the quality and quantity of your life, Lord willing. As we have demonstrated, science has revealed that a predominantly plant-based diet is necessary to improve health and to prevent and reverse disease.

Second, you have decided that life and people are more important than eating addictive, damaging, processed foods. You now recognize that your health or disease will dramatically affect the lives of those you love, and you have chosen to love them by striving for good health.

Third, poor health is very expensive, and you now recognize the lifetime cost of disease and are trying to be a good steward of your finances and physical body. By simply doing your best to take care of yourself today, you can avoid the significant cost of disease later.

Fourth, you are doing your best to maintain the body that God has given to you while you are on this earth. You are joyfully stewarding the gifts of the Lord, including your body, for His glory, and why wouldn't you want to give Him your very best?

Eating Should Be Fun and Enjoyable, So Let the Kids Have Fun

God created the taste system to provide enjoyment during the refueling of our bodies and as a first line of defense against poisonous or spoiled foods. You were designed to enjoy the foods that He created, and it should be a pleasurable experience. Unfortunately, mankind hijacked the food chain and manipulated and modified foods to create supertastes that are powerfully addictive and physically destructive.

Children can have fun eating delicious foods that God created—strawberries, blueberries, frozen bananas, or fresh grapes. But when we feed children cookies, ice cream, pizza, and cheese dishes for the sole purpose of their taste pleasure, and at the expense of their future health, it is selfish and shortsighted. Also, these foods are incredibly addictive and create cycles of binging, weight gain, and guilt. Parents often say that they love their children and would do anything to improve their futures, but they don't realize that by feeding them unhealthy, addictive foods in childhood they are setting up their children for a lifetime of disease and pain.

You can create enjoyable, fun food that is healthy. It may take a little work in the beginning as you work through old habits, recipes, and traditions, but within a short period of time you can reset the course of your children's lives through healthy food that tastes great.

Eating Healthy Is Too Expensive

This is often a primary justification for not making a shift toward a healthy diet. Simply adding more vegetables and fruits to the typical industrialized diet will add substantial cost. The key is to remove processed foods and animal products during the transition. A survey in 2009 found that people were attempting to save money by buying less-healthy food and buying more hot dogs![5] Now that is shortsighted budgeting.

A study published in the *American Journal of Clinical Nutrition* compared the cost per day of unhealthy diets with those consuming very healthy foods. The authors found that on average those with the healthiest diets spent $.90 (24 percent) more per day or $27 dollars more per month. However, some of the study participants with the healthiest diets spent less ($.24/day) than the unhealthy group, illustrating that a healthy diet is not always more expensive.

The study highlighted the foods with the lowest cost and greatest health benefits, including beans, lentils, chickpeas, and whole grains, quinoa, nuts, seeds, fruits, and vegetables. Shifting money from red meat and other animal products to beans produces a great savings and even greater health advantage.[6]

Here are some suggestions to help your food budget:

- Buying in bulk can save up to 30 percent compared to packaged foods.

- Eat less red meat, fish, and chicken, and add more beans, lentils, chickpeas, and whole grains. Eden Organics brands do not have the harmful chemical bisphenol A lining the can.

- Watch for sales, buy in quantity, and create a storage place in a closet or section of the basement.

- Buy from local farmers at the farmers' market.

- Join a Community Supported Agriculture (CSA) group. Visit localharvest.org for a CSA near you.

- Avoid buying processed foods.

- Avoid pleasure purchases or foods that are purchased for the sole purpose of pleasure eating, such as ice cream, cookies, chips, crackers, and chocolate.

- Eat at home. You will save a significant amount of money by eating at home and packing your own healthy lunches.

What About Traditional Foods and Family Meals?

Again, it is important to remember that food should never be divisive, and we should love one another despite differences in diet. It is acceptable for you to share your decision to pursue a healthy dietary change and the supportive evidence. Traditional meals are often held as sacred, and the foods served become a powerful tool that provides a sense of family, togetherness, and stability. Challenging or declining the meal can often create problems, so here are several suggestions to help ease the transition, continue to enjoy family times together, improve the health of meals, and not create animosity in the process:

- Educate family and friends that this is simply a health-driven decision because of the benefits to you and your family, avoidance of disease, and spiritual commitment.

- Offer to bring a large salad and or plate of vegetables and hummus or other nutrient-rich appetizer or addition to the meal. You will find that the majority of people really enjoy these foods.

- Work to adapt the traditional recipes to make them healthier by substituting nutrient-rich ingredients removing oils, sugars, and processed ingredients.

- Recognize that it is just one meal out of the week and that dietary perfection is not the goal, but rather a healthy life. One meal will not derail your health. Eat only small amounts, and consider a raw diet or juice fast the next day.

- Avoid foods that can set up binge eating, such as sugar.

Take a Minute

Pray for those who might disagree with you, tease you, call you names, or make life difficult for you. Christ died for them and loves them just as much as He loves you. Each of us is far from perfect, and we are all in need of God's forgiveness and the forgiveness of others. You can be an example of God's great love by showing grace and kindness in the midst of challenges from those you encounter during your day, especially family members. Look to see where God is at work in their lives, and pray for them. Don't take offense at their challenges to dietary change. Press on toward your goal of glorifying God with your life. You will be surprised that over time friends and family accept and begin to embrace the dietary change as they watch you live out your convictions and see your great health. Lovingly live as an example and prayerfully trust them into the Lord's hands.

Label Reading 101

*L*iving in the twenty-first century requires skill sets that would be foreign to our ancestors. They were masters of living off the land, planting and harvesting, hunting and gathering their food. In the industrialized world, we are blessed to find all of our food twenty minutes from home all under one roof. The gathering process is much different today as we stroll through the air-conditioned supermarkets with a coffee in one hand and shopping list in the other. The only overt physical threat is another shopping cart running into your Achilles tendon!

Processed and packaged foods have replaced natural foods and now dominate the floors of every food store around the world. These foods have been manufactured with the goal of profit and ultimately erode health. So how do you know if the food you are eating supports your health or promotes disease?

Every processed food by law must have a label detailing the list of ingredients and nutritional information. In 1994 the FDA required the labeling of the majority of foods sold to the public.[1] For your health, it is imperative that you learn to read the labels of the foods you choose to eat. You will be surprised to find that some natural or organic foods may not be the healthiest choices, because they may contain sugars, excess salt, oils, or preservatives. Remember that the front of the package is not intended to give you an accurate presentation of the product, but rather it's designed to sell you the product as quickly as possible.

How to Read a Label

Rule number one is that you can't believe the front of the package—ever. Never make a decision based on the front of any package despite any of the appealing information. Rule number two is that the ingredient list is the most important information on the back of the label. If it contains any type of sugar, high-fructose corn syrup, dyes, chemicals, or names you don't know or can't pronounce, read no further. Put it back on the shelf and save your money and health.

Despite the FDA's assurance, label reading is not easy or clear-cut. So don't worry about all of the numbers or percentages; they are worthless and will not lead you to the right decision. The first important piece of information in the Nutrition Facts section is the serving size and number of food pieces per serving. One manufacturer of a small package of cookies set the serving size as two cookies with a package size of six cookies. Obviously the total calories and fat per serving appear to be significantly less, but how many people will eat only two cookies? They have been lulled into a false sense of security by the low numbers, but in reality they consume far more than they realize. The serving size and servings per container are the lenses through which to interpret the other information.

Next, look at the calories and total calories from fat. If the fat calories are greater than 20 percent of the total calories, put it down and walk away. Be very careful of the added oils, because this will show up in the ingredient list as calories from fats. Remember all oils are 120 calories/tablespoon and drive inflammation. Next, check the sodium, which should equal the calories, e.g., 130 calories containing 130 mg of sodium. If it is greater than 1:1, do not put it into your cart. Excessive sodium has been associated with hypertension[2] and gastric cancers.[3]

No Label Reading Required

The above information is helpful as you try to navigate the world of packaged foods, including some of the imposters that pose as all-natural health foods. But if you really want to be healthy and not waste your time reading a hundred labels every time you shop, choose fresh vegetables, fruits, raw nuts, seeds, beans, and small amounts of organic animal products. You will be healthier and happier that you didn't spend two hours trying to decipher the complicated and confusing information on labels that often lead you to the wrong conclusion.

Take a Minute

Look at some of the labels in your pantry and cupboards. With a discerning eye, read the marketing pitches on the fronts of the boxes. Next, flip them over and start with the ingredient lists. What do you see? Do you see any sugars or high-fructose corn syrup? What about chemicals? Do you see any notation of phytochemicals, antioxidants? Mentally compare these products to a bowl of raspberries, a green smoothie, or a plate of steamed vegetables. I hope you can see a dramatic difference. God's food is far superior! Processed foods will always leave your cells starving. Thank the Lord today for giving you the great gift of food created by His hands and that His food is designed to optimally fuel your body.

Eating for Health in the Twenty-First Century

$\mathcal{O}$ne of the most important questions my patients ask is, "How can I find the time to eat a healthy diet in the midst of my busy life?" I believe it is important to clarify the bigger picture by asking them what will happen if they don't take time to eat a healthy diet today. I ask them to consider how much time will be lost if they are sick or die prematurely. Eventually, their busy lives will come to a screeching halt, at the most inopportune time, because of disease, and sometimes they might not get a second chance. I like to tell them, "You can't afford not to make the time, because you have the time now and may not in the future." Just as I challenge them to make the time to apply a healthy lifestyle, I believe that you can't afford not to find time to make the change. Here is a helpful overview of how to make a healthy diet work in your busy schedule.

Making It Work

The first principle for making this new lifestyle and diet work is to pray daily for God's strength, wisdom, and guidance. Proverbs 3:5–6 teaches us, "Trust in the LORD with all your heart, and lean not on your own understanding; In all your ways acknowledge Him, and He shall direct your paths."

You are striving to be as healthy as possible because you are glorifying God with your body, and out of love and appreciation you're working to be the best steward of His possessions you can be. Once this foundational vision is in place, you will find a way to make it work. Through the ups and downs, successes and failures, you will succeed. Without this level of belief, you will find every excuse and opportunity to eat the convenient, more addictive foods of the industrialized diet, and one year later you'll find yourself disappointed, diseased, and distressed. The belief moves your decision from a wishy-washy "should" to a compelling and unstoppable "must." Don't quit or give up; just keep on doing your best one bite at a time. And if you have a day when you eat some unhealthy food, start fresh the next day; don't let one day derail your vision and future.

Basic Principles

Plan for success. Take some time to consider your weekly schedule and create a plan that will allow you time to shop, prepare, and consume healthy food. There is always a way to make it work, if the desire is sincere. Write your weekly schedule on a sheet of paper or in your planner. Mark those items that are essential and other items that can be modified. You will likely need to find thirty minutes to shop twice per week, or if that is difficult, you might consider ordering your produce and food through online stores that will deliver it right to your door. (See list in the Additional Resources in the back of this book.) Plan for time to prepare the food, and much of this can be completed on the weekend, if necessary.

Prepare for success. Prepare for a successful week by putting into place everything you will need to follow through with your plan. This may include preparing meals and lunches, shopping for the week, organizing or choosing recipes. If it is readily available and accessible, you will succeed.

The majority of cooking can be done on the weekend and extra portions frozen for easy, quick lunches and dinners. Stews and soups are easy, quick meals that require little preparation time and can yield multiple meals. If necessary, find time locating grocery stores and restaurants that offer healthy plant-based meals. Don't give in to the excuse that you just don't have time. Remember that you will spend your time for health either now or in the future.

Execute the plan. Execute your plan daily and consider weekly reviews of successes and challenges with trustworthy friends or family. You may find glitches and shortcomings, but don't let these derail the entire plan. If you don't eat well one day, just start fresh the next day and leave that day in the past. Don't let the failures or challenges destroy your progress, and don't let these single small failures be an excuse to stop doing what is right. If you stumble, accept the responsibility, prayerfully ask for help, learn from your mistakes, and reset your eyes on the greater vision. Or as my dad always said, "Pick yourself up, dust yourself off, and get going!" Work through these challenges, modify the plan, and keep pressing on. Every successful day added to others over the course of a year will change your life, so take five minutes each night to recast the vision and plan and prepare for the next day.

Healthy Reminders

- It is better to miss a meal than to give in to temporary hunger and cravings and eat unhealthy or fast food.

- Raw fruits and vegetables are great snacks that can travel with you wherever you go.

- Vegetables, fruits, beans, and whole grains can make a meal anywhere in the world.

- Cook large portions, and freeze the extra for future meals or lunches.

- Nuts and seeds should only be added to salads, dressings, and oatmeal, but should not be a snack. They can cause weight gain, and when used as a snack, can lead to overeating and excessive calories. Some people, such as athletes, may require more nuts and seeds to maintain a healthy weight. Recommended: 1 ounce for females and 2 ounces males.

A Day in the Life

Every morning remember the big picture. You are trying to eat as many nutrient-rich foods—foods created by God—and avoid as many foods that have been processed as possible. It is important to make the transition easy and workable. Choose recipes in the beginning that are easy and tasty; then you will have a much greater likelihood of long-term success.

For breakfast consider making a smoothie with berries, bananas, kale, and pomegranate juice, or whole slow-cooked oats or steel-cut oats with one-fourth cup of black walnuts and blueberries. Each of these takes less than five minutes to prepare and starts your day off on a nutrient-rich note.

Lunch should include a salad with beans and seeds, or use of green, leafy vegetables in a wrap or chopped into a soup or stew. Add a piece of fruit or some raw vegetables, such as cucumber or carrots. I often bring for lunch leftover soup, stew, or bean/lentils from the night before. The best advice is to pack your lunch during dinner cleanup. Avoid taking chips, crackers, granola bars, or other snacks. They may be easy, but they are not healthy.

Dinner is a wonderful opportunity to sit down, rest, and truly enjoy a wonderful meal made with delicious nutrient-rich food. Set a beautiful table, take time to pray, read God's Word, and remember that He is the provider of the food on your table. Your dinner plate should be one-half leafy greens, one-quarter cooked soup, stew, beans, lentils, or a small (the size of a deck of cards) piece of organic meat, one-quarter steamed or cooked vegetables, and a small amount of fruit. (See page xxvii for picture.)

Dessert can include a nice cup of tea, banana-based sorbet, or other tasty desserts, such as berries or fruit with a cashew-based dipping sauce. Be careful with your calories, but enjoy the dessert.

Saving Time in a Busy World

The first six months of the transition to your new diet will be the most challenging, and then it will become the new norm and will not require as much time or energy. Hang in there! It will get easier. Here are a few time savers that have helped our family.

1. Prewash and precut vegetables and greens and keep them in a bowl in the refrigerator.

2. Plan your weekly menu on the weekend, and then shop for the weekly ingredients.

3. Prewash fruit and place it in a bowl on the counter.

4. A Crock Pot is a great tool for a healthy meal on a Sunday after church.

5. Premake soups/stews or meals on the weekend, and freeze them for the week.

6. Make enough of everything so you will have extra left for lunches.

7. You can even make your smoothie the night before, put it in the freezer, and then remix it in the morning.

8. Make a standard shopping list to streamline time in the grocery store and shop during an off day.

Holiday Dinners and Family

Special events and holidays can be a challenge, because some people may not understand your diet and may feel threatened. As previously stated, food should never be divisive in these situations, and you should always present yourself with the love of Christ. Offering to bring a beautiful green salad, vegetable tray with homemade hummus, bean dish, or other cooked vegetable is a win-win situation for everyone involved.

Avoid the hors d'oeuvres, because they are very unhealthy and contain on average 70–150 calories per serving. During the meals, choose to eat more salad and vegetables, avoiding cheeses, breads, and fatty foods. Ask for a small serving of meat, or eat some of your nutrient-rich dish. For dessert, ask for tea or have a piece of fruit. If you choose to eat other desserts, enjoy one small piece and don't go back for seconds. You may find that your grace and kindness will present a better opportunity to educate your family and friends on your reasons for changing your diet. Just tell your story.

Away from Home

Traveling can pose one of the greatest challenges to maintaining a healthy diet. As a family of eight, we have traveled in and out of the country, and as a result, we have become very creative. We often stay in hotels or homes that have a small kitchen. If possible, we take a blender to make smoothies in the morning. We shop at local health food stores, Whole Foods, or grocery stores, and then we stock up for meals and snacks. This is also a great way to save money. Whole Foods has a great prepared-foods section with a wide variety of healthy options. Other restaurant choices include ethnic foods, such as Thai and Japanese. My wife is not afraid to ask for a plate of steamed vegetables, or a combination of other side dishes, and most restaurants are more than willing to adjust. Finally, in preparation for your travel day, pack some dried or dehydrated vegetables and fruits, fruit, carrots, celery, nuts, seeds, a green food bar, or one of our favorites—kale chips. That way, you will never have to face the challenge of finding food in the middle of an airport.

Take a Minute

Today spend fifteen minutes working on a plan for success in the next one month, three months, and six months. Begin making a shopping list from recipes in the cookbook or online. Make a list of kitchen items that may be helpful, such as a blender (we use the Vita Mix), food processor, choppers, and good knives, and hand them out to people as gift ideas. Organize your weekly calendar to make time for shopping and food preparation. Acquire a list of recipes that you will try in the next two weeks. And write notes to yourself and paste them around the house to recast the vision for your life change. We have written Bible verses and prayer requests—vision for the future—on our bathroom mirrors and closet doors. It is a great way to set your minds on the things above. Have fun!

$\mathcal{D}ay$ 37

Fasting for Health

$\mathcal{T}$wo men were hired to cut down trees in a small wooded valley. Both arrived early the first day with sharpened axes, steeled arms, and determination in their eyes. One face was marked by the years of experience with well-worn creases and furrows that silently told a thousand stories of a lifetime in the woods. The second face, bronzed, vibrant, and smooth, revealed the exuberance and energy of youth not yet tested by time.

The clock struck eight, and the men began chopping, the younger with great enthusiasm and strength, and the senior with skill and precision. Every three hours the senior lumberjack would take a break, and the younger man would continue to swing his ax, secretly taking pride in his strength and ability to continue working while the older woodsman had to take a break.

They worked for seven days, and the owner of the land stopped by to assess their progress. The young lumberjack stood confidently next to his pile of logs, believing that he had chopped a dozen more trees than his older coworker, who had taken a break every three hours. The elder lumberjack's pile was finally counted, and to the shock of the young woodsman, he had cut down fifteen more trees than the young man. Stunned that his strength and diligence had failed him, the young lumberjack asked the elder lumberjack how he was able to cut down so many trees while taking a break every three hours.

The wise old lumberjack, with a sparkle in his eye and smile that filled in the creases, said, "Young man, during my breaks, I sharpened my ax!"

How often are you like the young lumberjack in the management of your spiritual and physical life? Do you take time out of the busyness of life to sharpen your spiritual and physical ax? How can you effectively sharpen your life and health?

The Lost Art of Fasting

Fasting is a lost art that allows us to take a break from life and sharpen our axes. Fasting provides an opportunity to shed the weight of the world and refocus our lives on things of eternal value. It also provides a wonderful opportunity to step back from the day-to-day quest for food and satisfaction and pause to consider why we eat what we eat and how we eat it. John Piper in *A Hunger for God* wrote, "The very nature of fasting makes it an assistant to this hunger for God. The reason is that the hunger for God is spiritual, not physical. And we are less sensitive to spiritual appetites when we are in bondage to the physical ones."[1] Fasting allows our spirits to awaken from the food comas of a processed, industrialized diet and reconnect with the living God.

Let's take a look together at the lost art of fasting for both spiritual and physical health.

Fasting was a regular part of the spiritual life of the Old Testament and New Testament followers of God. Jesus fasted for forty days and nights before beginning His ministry, and He encouraged His followers to fast as well. When you fast are the words Jesus used in Matthew 6:16–17 to describe the practice of fasting. Note that he said "when," which implies that fastimg should be a normal part of every believer's spiritual life.

Fasting throughout the Bible is associated with repentance, denial of self for the purpose prayer, and seeking the Lord's will. It will always cast light on the strong yet subtle influence of our sinful nature and selfish desires that can remain hidden for a lifetime beneath the layers of life and abundance in industrialized nations. The absence of comfort foods and the lost enjoyment of eating will refocus your life away from a dependence on the bread of earth for sustenance and life to the eternal life-giving Bread of Life—Jesus. The weakness of your body and revelation of your physical desires help to clarify your true spiritual condition and need for a redeemer and sustainer. From this place of weakness, Christ becomes your strength as you depend on Him for your daily provision and direction.

The primary purpose of a fast should be to glorify God, for focused prayer, and to fellowship with God. Colossians 3:17 encourages us, saying, "And whatever you do in word or deed, do all in the name of the Lord Jesus, giving thanks to God the Father through Him." Focusing first on Christ throughout a fast makes it much easier to continue forward while depending on him for strength and sustenance rather than food. The secondary health benefits are blessings of faithful surrender and stewardship.

I know that some of you right now may be experiencing some anxiety over the word *fasting*. The very word strikes fear in some people as they consider giving up food for a period of time. One man with whom I was working exclaimed, "If I don't eat, Dr. Stoll, I'm going to die!" Maybe you feel that way, too, but I want to encourage you to read on, and remember that we can live for forty days without food, and we "can do everything through Christ, who gives [us] strength" (Philippians 4:13).

Physical Benefits of Fasting

Fasting for the purpose of health reasons has long been recognized as a method to cleanse the body and provide an opportunity for healing. There are a number of other benefits that may help to convince you to consider a short-term juice fast.

First, a short-term juice fast can dramatically enhance the transition from a conventional diet to a healthy diet. Fasting helps to more quickly overcome addictions, including food, and assists in expediting the detoxification process. The transition to a healthy diet is often much easier because the benefits are felt more immediately, and unhealthy eating habits are broken.

Second, another benefit of fasting is the body's improved ability to heal chronic disease or injuries. Metabolic energy that is normally used in digestion is diverted to the immune system to aid in repair and healing. Protein synthesis becomes more efficient, and growth hormone levels rise during a fast, promoting the repair and healing of the body. In fact, fasting is one of the best methods for supporting and increasing growth hormone levels that often fall with age.[2] Immediately after a fast, the body transitions into an anabolic or rebuilding phase that includes the formation of new muscle.

Fasting and the associated calorie restriction have been shown to increase longevity. In fact, calorie restriction is the only experimental factor to consistently increase life span and slow aging. During a fast, oxidative stress and damage to proteins, DNA, and cellular structures is significantly reduced.[3, 4] That improves the elasticity of skin and connective tissue, reduces damage to blood vessel walls, and promotes cellular detoxification.

Finally, fasting has been shown to reduce blood pressure,[5] reduce blood sugar,[6] reduce pain and improve serotonin levels and mood,[7] reduce inflammation, and improve health, vitality, and energy. Why wouldn't you want to fast?

A Quick How-To on Fasting

A simple three- to five-day juice fast can be a powerful way to break from your old ways and begin a new, healthier diet and lifestyle. Importantly, if you are a diabetic, pregnant or nursing, a child, underweight, or have severe health problems such as congestive heart failure, fasting may not be right for you at this stage in your life. If you are taking blood pressure medications or have health issues, you should meet with your physician to discuss a plan for monitoring medications during the fast. Frequently, medication dosages need to be reduced, and some medications need to be discontinued during and after the fast. If you have disease and are unable to fast, consider a five-day semi-fast free from all processed foods, animal products, oils, and sugars, focusing on predominantly raw vegetables, some fruits and beans/lentils. That is also a great way to begin to help your body heal and break food addictions.

Two days before you fast, reduce your intake of food and focus on more raw fruits and vegetables. This will make the transition into the fast more comfortable and the detoxification less severe. During the fast, avoid supplements, caffeine, nicotine, and processed beverages, including juices. Reasonable supplements include probiotics, green barley/wheat grass powders, and aloe vera juice.

Begin the morning with a glass of room-temperature lemon water to wake up your system. Then make a large green (kale, bok choy, collard greens, romaine lettuce) juice comprised of three vegetables to one fruit. Make enough to last until lunch, or if you are working, until dinner. Use a variety of fruits and vegetables, and have fun with the combinations. The excess juice can be stored easily in a thermos or mason jars in the refrigerator, and small cups can be enjoyed throughout the day. Sipping the juice more frequently can help to lessen food withdrawal symptoms, such as headaches, fatigue, light-headedness, extreme hunger, and irritability.

Hunger can be felt through the first two to three days, lessening on day three or four. Physical hunger is a reminder of the hunger that we should have for the Lord and His righteousness. Embrace the hunger and let it drive you in to prayer and the Word, thanking the Lord for His sacrifice for you.

During your fast, take time to consider your eating habits. Consider what your mind is thinking about, and what your body is craving. Be aware of eating patterns, lunches, snacks, and routines that lead to unhealthy choices. You are on the outside looking in at your life. Be conscious of what you see. Three days can be very eye opening, and you may realize that certain patterns, foods, and habits are driven by food addiction, emotional eating, or laziness and are likely contributing to disease progression.

Breaking the Fast

Breaking the fast should be done with the same intention and care. The first day, juicing is continued with the addition of melon. The second day, add in some salad (chew well), lightly steamed vegetables, soft fruits, and juice. On day three you can begin to eat cooked rice, beans, lentils, and vegetables, transitioning to a healthy long-term diet. During the transition, try to avoid adding unhealthy processed food back into your diet. You have already broken the cycle and have the momentum, so don't give up. Use this fast as an opportunity to move forward permanently.

Take a Minute

Prayerfully consider adding regular fasting to your life. It will transform your spiritual life and your physical body. Your first reaction may be to run—mine was—but I hope you will find, just as I did, that a juice fast can be one of the most powerful and instructive experiences in your life. You can start with a simple twenty-four-hour fast, and work your way up to a three-day, seven-day, or fourteen-day juice fast. Don't let fear hold you back from the blessings and benefits of fasting. Recall the words of Philippians 4:13 again: "I can do all things through Christ who strengthens me," and He will provide all that you need, including the necessary strength and sustenance during the fast. It is a marvelous opportunity to learn to depend on Christ for all of your needs. Take time to sharpen your ax. Visit our website Day3Health.com for more information.

Day **38**

The Myth of Moderation

$\mathcal{J}$n 800 BC, in his book *Works and Days*, Hesiod advised, "Everything in moderation." How often have you heard this quote as someone dives into an eight-scoop banana split? Or perhaps you have heard the saying offered as sage advice by someone who has lived a long life and is still functioning at a fairly high level. But is it really a true statement that can it be applied to health decisions? Was Hesiod thinking about chocolate cake and deep-fried candy bars when he developed this philosophy? As you begin to make healthy changes in your life, please don't let the false philosophy of moderation derail your progress.

Historically, albeit mistakenly, Aristotle is attributed as making the famous moderation statement while writing his treatise on ethics and virtue. A virtuous, purposeful life, he concluded, can be cultivated only through the moderation of a variety of virtues. He surmised that character and virtue traits in moderation and appropriate for the situation will create the right virtue in the right amount for the right time. For example, courage is the mean or moderation between fear and overconfidence. It is the right virtue for the circumstance at the right time. With this in mind, a more accurate Aristotelian dietary application of "everything in moderation" would be the right food in the right amount at the right time leads to a healthy life.

Today people take this quote out of context and often use it to justify their excesses and bad habits. Some may choose to avoid exercise or liberally dive into a big bag of chips because "everything in moderation" justifies the action. In reality, it is an excuse that is used to counter the guilt that follows or a sweet candy coating of bad habits.

Prone to Rationalization

Moderation allows people to rationalize unhealthy choices that often lead to excessive amounts and perpetuate food addictions, rather than face the challenge of overcoming these destructive foods. The definition of *rationalize* is to ascribe one's actions to causes that seem reasonable and valid but are unrelated to the true causes. Moderation does not give you the green light to continue making unhealthy choices or justify dangerous habits and addictions. Instead, be honest with yourself. If you choose to eat nutrient-poor foods, understand that you have simply chosen to eat a food that does not support your health, and if eaten repeatedly, will promote disease. Don't let the smoke and mirrors of moderation cloud clear thinking and good judgment.

How Much Is Too Much?

Moderation is an undefined term, and the limits are often subjective and very individualized. For example, is my interpretation of moderation the same as yours? What standard do you use to determine a moderate amount of ice cream, chips, steak, or cookies? At what point does moderation cross into excess, and when do you cross the line? How much is too much? What is the right amount that will either prevent or cause disease? How much will lead to disease in your life or that of a friend? How can you measure moderation?

The most important point is that moderation does not establish a goal of superior health, but rather it sets a low bar that leads only to mediocrity, malaise, and malady. Instead of living a moderately healthy life, why not choose to live an exceptionally healthy life void of disease and pain and filled with vitality and energy?

Moderation applied to daily decisions will lead to excess and disease and is often a very slippery slope. The relative standards of moderation are subject to change over time with adaptation and accommodation of new higher levels of consumption. This leads to a slow but progressive shift toward larger amounts. For example, the average daily caloric consumption has risen from 2,100 kcal/day in 1900 to 2,680 kcal in 2000, and few people have felt or recognized the upward shift because of the gradual change over decades.[1, 2]

For those with a greater genetic susceptibility, disease moderation can lead to premature disability or death. It is a principle without a standard and is established without any research, investigation, or consideration. For those with a predisposition to heart disease, eating in moderation will lead to atherosclerosis, progressive heart disease, and possibly a fatal heart attack. For those with a susceptibility to weight gain, moderation will lead to the accumulation of fat, or for those with a genetic susceptibility to cancer, it leads to a much greater likelihood of cancer.

A study done by Dr. Dean Ornish, comparing the vegetarian and more moderate American Heart Association (AHA) Diet revealed that a diet of moderation will lead to progressive heart disease, and the only way to prevent or reverse disease is to strive for nutritional excellence.[3, 4]

Overcome the Myth of Moderation

You are establishing new habits and breaking the old ones, challenging the comfortable habits that have been a part your life for years and perhaps decades. Therefore, it is important to dedicate time to pray and plan for success. Step back and honestly assess your food habits and excesses. Where are you susceptible to the slippery slope of the myth of moderation? Is it sweets and sugar, breads, meat, alcohol, or cheese? Record the actual amounts you are eating, and ask yourself if it is really necessary. Sometimes it is necessary to fast from a particular food item to break its hold on your life. You may be surprised to find that it has a stronger grip on you than you expected.

Breaking free requires a commitment to the pursuit of a worthy goal—a healthy body for God's glory. A clearly defined goal and vision, combined with a plan, squeeze out the excesses of moderation. You may need to write out a plan that includes specific amounts and acceptable times, such as, "I will allow myself to have one piece of apple pie at Thanksgiving, but not every Tuesday." You will be able to see the danger of the situation and confidently say no thank you. Be ever vigilant of the slippery slope that begins with the myth of moderation!

Moderate is not a negative term, and it is used appropriately when discussing healthy foods, such as eating a moderate amount of plums, cherries, or nuts and seeds. The amount should be clarified, but it can give some general guidance and limit excess.

Can We Live Moderately for the Lord?

Can you lead an exceptional life by following today's philosophy of moderation? Great accomplishments, including exceptional health, are the result of consistently doing the right things and minimizing those that may hinder success. Can you think of one other area in life where you would encourage moderation to achieve a goal? I don't encourage my children to study moderately or to live moderately for the Lord. During college, I did not study moderately to achieve my goal of medical school, and I certainly did not exercise moderately to make the Olympic team. Moderate effort to achieve a goal does not work in any other area of life, and we cannot believe that it will work in the area of health. If excellent health is your goal, you cannot approach your diet and exercise habits with moderation. As Christians we are called to live for the Lord, not moderately, but to love Him with all our hearts, minds, souls, and spirits, and to do everything for His glory. That does not imply living moderately, but rather giving our best, living purposely, and offering our lives—everything we are and have—as a living sacrifice.

Take a Minute

I want to encourage you to take some time to consider how you can begin to make changes, not only in your health habits, but also in other areas of your life, that will lead to a life of excellence for the Lord's glory. Most people live in reaction to their cravings (chocolate), desires (cheesecake), wants (chocolate chip cookies), moods (comfort foods), emotions (ice cream), and drives (alcohol and sugar). As Christians we are called to live with a renewed mind that transforms our lives (Romans 12:1–2) and works to bring everything under the Lord's control. We shouldn't be the repeated victim of emotions, moods, cravings, and desires, but rather victors and overcomers in Christ as He renews our minds through daily meditation on His Word. Then we can live with a godly mind that controls these desires. Prayerfully ask the Lord to give you a clear vision of a healthy body for His glory, help in creating a plan for success, and then the diligence and courage to execute your plan daily. Don't give in to the temptations carefully wrapped in appealing marketing, enticing language, and moderate philosophy. At that very moment, when you are driven by desire and before your hand reaches to partake, pray, and the Lord promises that He will provide you a way of escape and the strength to walk away.

$\mathscr{Day}$ 39

Never Give Up!

$\mathscr{O}$ne fall afternoon, our three older boys needed to burn off some energy, so we took them to the local rock-climbing wall. The two oldest boys, Dawson and Gabriel, climbed to the top of the wall and rang the bell, struggling but succeeding. Next, it was Samuel's turn. At five years of age, standing alone at the bottom, the wall seemed to double in size. He was undaunted by the size and called back to us, "Watch me ring the bell!" A true visionary!

Samuel started up the wall, hand over hand, stretching with every fiber in his body to get to the next hold. As he neared the top, he reached a point where he was unable to stretch to the next handhold because of his short arms. To our surprise, Sammy leaped across the wall, missed the hold and caught himself with one hand. Dangling at forty feet with legs flailing, he refused to let go. Fighting with all of his might, he regained his footing and steadied for a second try. Again he missed and nearly fell, catching himself by one hand. Sammy still did not quit. He regained his composure and prepared for another try. Resolved to fulfill his vision of ringing the bell, he sprang across the wall a third time, catching the next two holds. Emboldened by his success, he confidently climbed the last few feet, and then with a huge smile, he turned to look down at us, reached up, and rang the bell.

Pressing on Toward the Goal

Why do some people give up and others press on despite seemingly insurmountable odds? Perhaps you can recall an event in your life where you did not give up or give in but kept on pursuing the goal consistently day after day. What was it that caused you to press on and not give up or give in?

You may be thinking that motivation is the key element in lasting change, but what is motivation, and why do some people have more of it than others? *Motivation*, derived from *motive*, is defined as "the reason or cause for action." There can be many reasons for action, some better than others. Making healthy diet and lifestyle changes require motivation, but it must be the right cause or motive that will produce lasting change. The wrong motivation is like a match that burns brightly for a short time and then burns out. And just like the match, short-term motivation causes you to feel "burned out" and defeated. Have you ever experienced a burst of short-term motivation?

Push Pull

Motivation is either internally or externally driven—a push or a pull toward your goal. Push motivation is short-term, externally driven motivation that lasts only as long as you tolerate the motivator. The secret to lasting change is to find a pull motivation that is an intense, internally driven decision that change must occur with no excuses, no insurmountable hurdles, and no looking back. Let's take a closer look at these two types of motivation.

Return with me to a typical day in your seventh-grade gym class. You are lined up—in your gray shirt, blue shorts, extra-long tube socks, and canvas Converse tennis shoes—ready for class to begin. Your gym teacher stands in front of the class (dressed in a gray T-shirt, blue stretch shorts, white canvas Converse shoes with a whistle around his neck), and with a loud voice says, "Everyone in the push-up position, push-ups on the whistle!"

You begin doing push-ups one after another, then the shrill whistle blow seems to pick up the pace as your arms start to burn and quiver, and droplets of sweat begin to pool beneath your nose. You secretly begin to wish that he would swallow the whistle. Then, after the final whistle, you drop to the cool gym floor exhausted and unable to move, promising never again to do another push-up as long as you live!

This is an example of external or push motivation, and success is based largely on willpower. You will keep going as long as the external motivation, the coach and his whistle, are present; but as soon as it is removed you will return to a position of comfort until a new external force exerts influence. Push motivation can give you the first big push of momentum and often burns hot for a short period of time before it burns out.

Examples of push motivation include a weight-loss contest, upcoming wedding, reunion, or event, swimsuit season, or holidays. Why do people fail to integrate lasing change with push motivation? Push motivation goals are typically shortsighted and not very compelling. The vision is boring (i.e., weight), and it is not a true resolve but rather a half-hearted decision with an escape clause in the back of the mind. It is important to remember that you will always behave consistently with your vision and definition of who you are. We live out who we believe we are. Who do you believe you are, and where are you going?

Power of Pull

Pull motivation is exemplified in the lives of athletes or musicians who endure uncomfortable and exhausting workouts and significant sacrifices for a future vision. It is this detailed vision of the future that pulls them through challenges and discomfort of day-to-day life toward a perceived greater good. Paul exemplified this type of motivation when he wrote in Philippians 3:12–14,

> Not that I have already attained, or am already perfected; but I press on, that I may lay hold of that for which Christ Jesus has also laid hold of me. Brethren, I do not count myself to have apprehended; but one thing I do, forgetting those things which are behind and reaching forward to those things which are ahead, I press toward the goal for the prize of the upward call of God in Christ Jesus.

In fact, the life of Paul was marked by pull motivation, not push. He saw himself as a new creation. Forgetting the past, he suffered, endured, strove, worked, preached, and lived for the goal of knowing Christ and the future upward call of Jesus Christ. Paul was able to pursue the greater vision despite difficult circumstances and people, pain, betrayal, and suffering, because his eyes were fixed on a future day that carried far more value than the events of his today.

Paul had a substantial and compelling "why" for living out each day purposefully, and his why was Christ. There is none greater than the Creator and Redeemer of the universe saying, "Well done, good and faithful servant" (Matthew 25:21). That driving force brought purpose to his sacrifices and gave him strength to overcome the disappointments of life. Challenges look smaller and events more purposeful in the light of eternity.

Shopping for the Future

A recent study in Tel Aviv, Israel, asked two groups of people to shop for groceries. The first group was told to consider who they are now, and the second group was asked to consider who they would become. Each group's shopping carts were evaluated, and a striking difference was noted. The first group, thinking about the here-and-now, purchased chocolate, junk food, soda, and more processed food. The second group, thinking about the future, purchased more fruits, vegetables, and health-based foods. Each group had a different why, and that primary purpose directly impacted their immediate purchases and, ultimately, will affect their future health. Thinking about yourself in the here and now can cause you to lose sight of the bigger picture and, ultimately, choose immediate gratification and personal pleasure over sacrifice, but at a significant long-term price.

Paul reminds us in Colossians 3:1–2, "If then you were raised with Christ, seek those things which are above, where Christ is, sitting at the right hand of God. Set your mind on things above, not on things on the earth." Our focus should be on Christ, rather than the deceptive passing pleasures of this world. Just as in the Tel Aviv study, that vision will influence daily decisions right down to the food we choose to eat.

The Greatest "Why"

Pull motivation is "why" based, and it demands that you ask yourself why you are doing what you are doing. Changing your why will ignite long-term motivation and perseverance. If you are changing your diet, ask yourself, why am I making the change? There are different whys in your life that are either more or less motivating. Can you recall some of the whys from previous days?

For instance, weight loss is a weaker why, because it has an end point, and when that end is reached, the why is no longer pulling you to change. Changing your diet because you are facing the life-threatening diagnosis of cancer or heart disease is a much stronger why, which will likely pull you toward a lasting change. Similarly, changing your diet because you recognize that your health directly affects the lives of your loved ones is a powerful and enduring why.

The most compelling and unwavering why is found when you truly understand the purpose of your life, your 29,200 days, in the light of the supremacy of Jesus Christ, the grace offered to you by His death and resurrection, and your role as a joyful steward. Your loving response and motivation should be to hone and polish every aspect of your life, including your body, to reflect His glory. Each day and decision becomes an opportunity to offer all that you have, including your body, for His purposes, plans, and glory.

Take a Minute

Prayerfully consider your motivations, appetites, and the whys that drive your decisions to buy and eat food, exercise, and manage your body for the Lord. Perhaps you will need to repent for selfish motives around food and health. Discuss your motivations with your family and friends, and prayerfully establish a new vision for your life with motivations and whys that will lead to lasting change and a life that will shine like a bright light in this world.

Alive! and Finishing Strong

At the 1968 Olympic games in Mexico City, the marathon was the final event, culminating two weeks of grand competition. On this final day, the Olympic stadium was filled to capacity with people from around the world. The crowd cheered wildly as the first athlete sprinted to the finish line with his arms held high in victory. But miles away, on a quiet stretch of the road, hands pressed to the ground, John Stephen Akwhari of Tanzania was struggling to get back on his feet.

At 30 kilometers John's body had given up, and he had collapsed to the ground. Earlier in the race, John had suffered a knee injury that made every step painful and quickly drained the energy from his already fatigued body. John's knee was bandaged, his head pounded, and muscles screamed for rest, but his spirit remained unbroken. Slowly, he gathered himself and rose to his feet and then slowly took one step. Then another. His stride was now a skip on the good leg followed by a wincing shuffle of the bad leg.

The remaining 12 kilometers of the race John ran alone. The other runners finished, the crowds that lined the raceway dispersed, but John ran on undaunted. One hour after the winner had finished the race, John Stephen Akwhari entered the stadium that was now empty, except for a few thousand fans that remained to applaud his courage. Akwhari hobbled the final lap around the track at a painstakingly slow pace that pulled at the hearts of all who stayed to watch his heroic effort. As he rounded the final turn and limped toward the finish, the crowd rose to its feet and cheered with as much enthusiasm as they had for the winner. With one final step he collapsed across the finish line into the arms of a race official. It is one of the most heroic efforts of Olympic history. After the race, John Stephen was asked by a reporter why he had not dropped out after suffering the knee injury. He said, "My country did not send me here to start the race. They sent me to finish."[1]

We are all running the race of life. You and I are not on earth to get a good start or simply participate in the race, but instead we're here to run with endurance and finish strong for Jesus Christ. As we saw earlier, Paul raised the bar for all of us in Philippians 3:12–14 with great words of encouragement. Read them again:

> Not that I have already attained, or am already perfected; but I press on, that I may lay hold of that for which Christ Jesus has also laid hold of me. Brethren, I do not count myself to have apprehended; but one thing I do, forgetting those things which are behind and reaching forward to those things which are ahead. I press toward the goal for the prize of the upward call of God in Christ Jesus.

Paul set his vision beyond the finish line and would not stop, quit, or give up until he gave his all and then crossed that finish line and into the loving arms of Jesus. The question then is not just how will you run the race, but how will you finish?

Run the Race

Why should you strive to promote a healthy body? It is not just for the benefit of feeling good and looking healthy, or for the applause and admiration of others, nor is it to live a longer life or even to avoid disease and the pain or premature death that follows chronic disease. The primary reason that you and I, as followers of Christ, should pursue a healthy lifestyle is to bring glory and honor to our Lord. We have been blessed with liberty in Christ, but that liberty should always be directed to bring glory and honor to the Lord. There is no greater motivation, no more inspiring vision than to know the Lord and to live for Him with all of your heart, mind, soul, and body. This passionate pursuit should rise up from a profound gratitude for your salvation and your adoption as a son or daughter by the God of the universe. Then motivated by love, you will manage everything entrusted to you, including your body, for His glory.

A healthy body provides you the opportunity to run the race that is set before you with endurance, not encumbered by disease nor entangled by the sin that can so easily trip us up, such as food addictions. The key is to keep your eyes on Jesus, the champion who initiates and perfects our faith. Because of the joy awaiting Him, He endured the cross, disregarding its shame and sat down at the right hand of God. Consider Christ, who endured such hostilities at the hands of sinners lest you become weary and lose heart (Hebrews 12:1–2).

You have an opportunity during your short stay in the world to live for the Lord and bring glory to Him in everything you do. I encourage you to break the bondage of the flesh, such as food addictions, emotional eating, food cravings, and modern man-made foods, and press on in a strong, healthy body for the upward call of Jesus Christ.

Let's Go!

One aspect of your life that the world sees every day is your body. People may not always see your attitudes of the heart, charity, or prayer life, but they do see your body. It is the vehicle that carries you through life and allows you to interface with people physically, mentally, emotionally, and spiritually. Nonbelievers listen to your words, observe your actions, attitudes, and appearance, and evaluate your interactions with others. To some extent they understand the basic tenets of a Christian life, and they are always watching for fakes, frauds, and failures, often because it allows them an excuse not to sincerely consider Christ. Christians are held to a higher standard by the world, and rightly so, than non-Christians.

A recent poll suggested that one of the greatest reasons for skepticism among nonbelievers is the lack of credibility among Christians. This should cause us all to pause and consider the image of Christ that we are presenting. In other words, the world does not believe that the Christian church is demonstrating a lifestyle that is wholly consistent with Christ's message. The message to the church, growing out of that poll, could be an entire book, and the answer contains multiple layers that need to be unpacked.

In the context of this book, though, one way that you represent Christ to the world is in the care of your body. None of us is perfect or has a perfect body, but we are called to do the best we can with the bodies God gave to us. As followers of Christ, we need to set the standard for healthy, strong bodies managed with care and concern, temperance and self-discipline. And we don't do it out of self-righteousness, pride, legalism, or fear, but out of love—a deep and unsurpassable love for God, because of His great love for us. And when love is the motivation, all things are possible. When love is the motivation, change is enduring. When love is the motivation, the process is exhilarating! Love God, because He first loved us.

"Love bears all things, believes all things, hopes all things, endures all things. Love never fails" (1 Corinthians 13:7–8).

So let's go! Get to know the One true God by spending time in His Word and prayer, and then glorify Him in every aspect of your life, including your body. Live an authentic life for Christ. Love Him with all of your heart, mind, soul, and strength, and nourish His body with a diet based on foods God created on Day 3. Worship Him with each day's provision of food, and intentionally choose to eat and enjoy the foods He created for you. Then you will experience the deep spiritual and relational joy of food focusing on Him and not self and develop a body that is renewed, vibrant, and strong.

Then, let's create a movement in the church to reclaim food and health for Christ. Let's set the example of health, so that others may see our efforts and glorify God. Let's surrender all that we have to Him and begin rebuilding the temple, the bodies of believers, because we have been bought with an incalculable price, and we now wholly belong to the Lord.

Let's go, church! Come alive for the glory of God!

Notes

Day 2: Crisis in America, Crisis in the Church
1. "Tackling Obesities:The Foresight Report and Implications for Local Government Faculty of Health and Wellbeing ." *Sheffield Hallam University.* (2008).
2. *The Source: The Best of Pogo.* Edited by Mrs. Walt Kelly and Bill Crouch Jr. NY: Simon & Schuster, 1982.
3. Well, S.B. "Which way to Clergy Health? Divinity." Last modified 2002. Accessed February 15, 2007. www.pulpitandpew.duke.edu/clergy health. html.
4. Clark, Krista M., and Ken Ferraro. "Does Religion Increase the Prevalence and Incidence of Obesity and Severe Obesity in Adulthood." *Purdue University.* (2004).
5. Ferraro, Ken. Purdue University, "Purdue University News." Last modified August 24, 2006 . Accessed August 24, 2006 . http://news.uns.purdue.edu/html4ever/2006/060824.Ferraro.obesity.html.

Day 3: The Really Big Picture
1. Wikipedia, "Milky Way." http://en.wikipedia.org/wiki/Milky_Way.
2. Judson, W., Van DeVenter. "All To Jesus I Surrender." (1896).

Day 7: God's Original Diet Plan
1. Mayer. "Historical Changes in the Mineral Content of Fruits and Vegetables." *AM, Br Food.* 99. (1997): 207-211.
2. Davis, D. , and M. Epp. "Changes in USDA Food Composition Data for 43 Garden Crops." *Journal of the American College of Nutrition.* 23. no. 6 (2004): 669-682.
3. Nebeling, Yarock, J. Seymore, and J. Kimmons. "Still not Enough Can we Achieve Our Goals for American to Eat More Fruits and Vegetables in the Future?" *AM J Preven, Med..* 32. no. 4 (2007): 354-355.

Notes

Day 8: Fat Bookshelves—A Failed Strategy

1. Tsai, AG. "Systematic Review: an Evaluation of Major Commercial Weight Loss Programs in the United States." *Ann. Intern. Med.*. 142. no. 1 (2005): 55-66.
2. Girard, Keith. "Hurdles to Challenging the Mammoth Diet Industry." New York Times. January 11, 2008.
3. Banting, William. *Letter on Corpulence, Addressed to the Public.* London: Harrison 59 Pall Mall, 1864.
4. Stanford University, "Dieting." http://www.stanford.edu/group/bbeam/dieting.html.
5. Hunt Peters, Lulu. *Diet and Health with a Key to the Calories.* Chicago: Reilly and Britton, 1918.
6. Marples, Gareth. HistoryOf.net, "The History of the Atkins Diet – A Revolutionary Lifestyle!" Last modified September 10, 2008. http://www.thehistoryof.net/history-of-the-atkins-diet.html.

Day 9: What's in Your Grocery Story?

1. Information Resources Inc. (2009).
2. Drewnowski, A., and S.E. Specter. "Poverty and Obesity: The Role of Energy Density and Energy Costs." *American Journal of Clinical Nutrition.* 79. no. 1 (2004): 6-16.
3. Ingram Larson, Ivy, and Andrew Larson M.D. *Whole Foods Diet Cookbook, 200 Recipes for Optimal Health.*
4. Ziegler, R., and S. Taylor. "Nutrition and Lung Cancer." *Cancer Causes and Control.* 7. no. 1 (1996): 157-177.
5. Miller, E., R. Pastor-Barriuso, and R. Darshan Dalal. "Meta-Analysis: High-Dosage Vitamin E Supplementation May Increase All-Cause Mortality." *Ann. Intern. Med.*. 142. (205): 37-46.
6. National Institutes for Health, "Vitamin E." Last modified June 24, 2011. http://ods.od.nih.gov/factsheets/vitamine/.
7. The American Academy of Environmental Medicine, "Our Mission." Last modified 2009. www.aaemonline.org.
8. "Evaluation of Allergenicity of Genetically Modified Foods. Report of a Joint FAO/WHO Expert Consultation on Allergenicity of Foods Derived from Biotechnology." *FAO-WHO.* (2001).
9. Netherwood. "Assessing the Survival of Transgenic Plant DNA in the Human Gastrointestinal Tract." *Natural Biotechnology.* 22. (2004).

Day 10: Diseases of Diet

1. McGinnis, J.M., and W.H. Foege. "The Immediate vs. the 70%." Journal of the American Medical Association. 291. (2004): 1263-1264.
2. McGinnis, J.M., and W.H. Foege. "Actual Causes of Death in the United States." Journal of the American Medical Association. 270. (1993): 2207-2212.

3. Basiotis, P.P. "The Healthy Eating Index, 1999-2000: Charting Dietary Patterns of Americans." Family Economics and Nutrition Review. Winter. (2004).

4. Minino, A.M., M.P. Heron, and B.L. Smith. "Preliminary Data for 2004." National Vital Statistics Reports. 54. no. 19.

5. "The Burden of Chronic Diseases and Their Risk Factors." National and State Perspectives. (2004).

6. Joseph, A., D. Ackerman, and J.D. Talley. "Manifestations of Coronary Atherosclerosis in Young Trauma Victims-an Autopsy Study." J. Am. Coll. Cardiol.. 22. no. 2 (1993): 459-467.

7. Campbell, T., Colin, Parpia, Banoo, and Chen. "Diet, Lifestyle and the Etiology of Coronary Artery Disease: The Cornell China Study." Am. J. Cardiol.. 82. no. 10 (1998): 18-21.

8. Ornish, Dean, and Larry Scherwitz. "Intensive Lifestyle Changes for Reversal of Coronary Heart Disease." JAMA. 280. (1998): 2001-2007.

9. Esselstyn, Caldwell. "Resolving the Coronary Artery Disease Epidemic Through Plant-Based Nutrition." Preventive Cardiology. 4. (2001): 171-177.

10. Centers for Disease Control and Prevention, "2011 National Diabetes Fact Sheet." Last modified July 13,2011. http://www.cdc.gov/diabetes/pubs/factsheet11.htm.

11. Booth, F.W., S.E. Gordon, C.J. Carlson, and M.T. Hamilton. "Waging War on Modern Chronic Diseases: Primary Prevention Through Exercise Biology." J. Appl. Physiol.. 88. (2000): 774–787.

12. Barnard, R.J., T. Jung, and S.B. Inkeles. "Diet and Exercise in the Treatment of NIDDM." Diabetes Care. 17. (1994): 1469 –1472.

13. Barnard, R.J., L. Lattimore, R.G. Holly, S. Cherny, and N. Pritikin. "Response of Non-Insulin-Dependent Diabetic Patients to an Intensive Program of Diet and Exercise." Diabetes Care. 5. (1982): 370–374.

14. Barnard, R.J., D.A. Martin, E.J. Ugianskis, and S.B. Inkeles. "The effects of an Intensive Diet and Exercise Program on Patients with NIDDM and Hypertension." J. Cardpulm. Rehabil.. 12. (1992): 194–201.

15. Barnard, R.J., M.R. Massey, S. Cherny, L.T. O'Brien, and N. Pritikin. "Long-Term use of a High-Complex-Carbohydrate, High-Fiber, Low-Fat Diet and Exercise in the Treatment of NIDDM Patients." Diabetes Care. 6. (1983): 268 –273.

16. Centers for Disease Control and Prevention, "Overweight and Obesity." Last modified April 21,2011. http://www.cdc.gov/obesity/childhood/data.html.

17. World Health Organization Global Strategy on Physical Activity and Health, "Obesity and Overweight." Last modified 2003. http://www.who.int/hpr/NPH/docs/gs_obesity.pdf.

18. Ogden, C., S. Yanovski. "Epidemiology of Obesity." Gastroenterology. 132. no. 6 (2007): 2087-2102.

19. "Food, Nutrition, Physical Activity and Prevention of Cancer: A Global Perspective." World Cancer Research Fund. (2007).
20. Centers for Disease Control and Prevention, "Chronic Disease Prevention and Health Promotion." Last modified December 17, 2009. http://www. cdc.gov/chronicdisease/resources/publications/AAG/chronic.htm.

Day 11: The Cost of Being Sick

1. Golman, Dana, Elizabeth McGlynn. "U.S. Health Care Facts about Cost and Access and Quality." *Rand Health*. (2005).
2. Congressional Budget Office, "The Long Term Outlook for Health Care Spending." Last modified 2007. http://www.cbo.gov/ftpdocs/87xx/ doc8758/MainText.3.1.shtml.
3. *Yassin*, A.S., J.F. Martonik, and J.L. Davidson. "Office of Evaluations and Audit Analysis." *Occupational Safety and Health Administration Report*.
4. U.S. Department of Labor, "Table 47. Age of Reference Person: Shares of Average Annual Expenditures and Sources of Income." *Consumer Expenditure Survey*. (2007).
5. Claxton, G., J. Gabel, and I. Gil. "Health benefits in 2006: Premium Increases Moderate, Enrollment in Consumer-Directed Health Plans Remains Modest." *Health Aff.* Millwood. (2006).
6. Himmelstein, David U, Deborah Thorne, Elizabeth Warren, and Steffie Woolhandler. "Medical Bankruptcy in the United States, 2007: Results of a National Study." *The American Journal of Medicine*. 122. no. 8 (2009): 741-746.
7. Sullivan, T.A., E. Warren, and J.L. Westbrook. *The Fragile Middle Class: Americans in Debt.*. New Haven, Conn.: Yale University Press, 2009.

Day 12: Boxes, Bags, and Cans

1. Ogden, C.L., K.M. Flegal, M.D. Carroll, and C.L. Johnson. "Prevalence and trends in overweight among U.S. children and adolescents, 1999-2000." *JAMA*. 288. (2002):1728-32.
2. Ogden, C.L., M.D. Carroll, L.R. Curtin, M.N. Lamb, and K.M. Flegal. "Prevalence of high body mass index in U.S. children and adolescents, 2007-2008." *JAMA*. 303. no. 3 (2010): 242-249.
3. US Department of Agriculture, Food and Nutrition Service, Office of Analysis, "Nutrition and Evaluation." (2001).
4. Key, T.J., N.E. Allen, and E.A. Spencer. "The Effect of Diet on Risk of Cancer." *Lancet*. 360. no. 9336 (2002):861-868.
5. Farah Wells, Hodan, and Jean C. Buxby. USDA, "Dietary Assessment of Major Trends in U.S. Food Consumption, 1970-2005." Last modified March 2008. www.ers.usda.gov/publications/EIB33.

Notes

Day 13: Why Do You Eat?

1. Lynne Olver, "Food Timeline FAQs: meals & holiday entertaining." Last modified Februrary 13, 2011. http://www.foodtimeline.org/foodfaq7.html.
2. US Department of Health and Human Services, "Results from the 2008 National Survey on Drug use and Health."
3. Childhood Obesity, "Trends and Potential Causes; Future of Children." (2006).
4. Guthrie, J., and B. Lin. "Role of Food Prepared Away from Home in the American Diet 1977-78 versus 1994-96." *Journal of Nutrition Education and Behavior*. 34. no. 3 (2002): 140-150.

Day 14: Free From the Bondage of Food

1. Lenoir, Magalie, Fuschia Serre, Lauriane Cantin, and Serge H. Ahmed. "Intense Sweetness Surpasses Cocaine Reward." *PLoS ONE*. 2. no. 8 (2007).
2. Colantuoni, C., P. Rada, and J. McCartharthy. "Evidence That Intermittent, Excessive Sugar Intake Causes Endogenous Opioid Dependence." *Obesity Research*. 10. (2002): 478–488.
3. Farah Wells, Hodan, and Jean C. Buxby. USDA, "Dietary Assessment of Major Trends in U.S. Food Consumption, 1970-2005." Last modified March 2008. www.ers.usda.gov/publications/EIB33.

Day 16: Food Foundations

1. Top Cultures, "What are Phytochemicals?." http://www.phytochemicals.info/.
2. Nascimento, Gislene G. F., Juliana Locatelli, Paulo C. Freitas, and Giuliana L. Silva. "Antibacterial Activity of Plant Extracts and Phytochemicals on Antibiotic-Resistant Bacteria." *Braz. J. Microbiol.* 31. no. 4 (2000).
3. Young-Joon, Surh. "Cancer Chemoprevention with Dietary Phytochemicals." *Nature Reviews Cancer*. 3. October (2003): 768-780.
4. Liu, R. "Health Benefits of Fruit and Vegetables are from Additive and Synergistic Combinations of Phytochemicals." *Am. J. Clin. Nutr.*. 78. no. 3 (2003): 517-520.
5. Brown, J. *Eat to Live*. . New York: Little, Brown and Company , 2003.

Day 17: The Nutrient-Dense Diet

1. Young, I.S., J.V. Woodside. "Antioxidants in Health and Disease." *J. of Clin. Pathology*. 54. (2001): 176-186.
2. **Fuhrman, J., B. Sarter, D. Glaser**, and S. **Acocell. "**Changing Perceptions of Hunger on a High Nutrient Density Diet." *Nutrition Journal*. **9. November (2010): **51.
3. Connor, W.E., M.T. Cerqueira, and R.W. Connor. "The Plasma Lipids, Lipoproteins, and Diet of the Tarahumara Indians of Mexico." *Am. J. Clin. Nutr.*. 31. (1978): 1131-42.

Notes

4. Sinnett, P.F., and H.M. Whyte. "Epidemiological Studies in a Total Highland Population, Tukisenta, New Guinea: Cardiovascular Disease and Relevant Clinical, Electrocardiographic, Radiological and Biochemical Findings." *J. Chron. Diseases.* 26. (1973): 265.

5. Campbell, T.C., B. Parpia, and J. Chen. "Diet, Lifestyle, and the Etiology of Coronary Artery Disease: The Cornell China Study." *Am. J. Card..* 82. no. 10B (1998):18T-21T.

6. Miller, K. "Lipid Values in Kalahari Bushman." *Arch. Intern. Med..* 121. (1968): 414.

7. Oude Griep, L.M., and J. M. Geleijnse. "Raw and Processed Fruit and Vegetable Consumption and 10-year Coronary Heart Disease Incidence in a Population-Based Cohort Study in the Netherlands." *PloS One.* 25. no. 5 (2010): 10.

8. Esselsyn, Caldwell. "Resolving the Coronary Artery Disease Epidemic Through Plant Based Nutrition." *Preventive Cardiology.* 4. (2001): 171-177.

9. Ornish, D., and L. Scherwitz. "Intensive Lifestyle Changes for the Reversal of Heart Disease." *JAMA. 280. no. 23 (1998): 2001-2007.*

10. Jenkins, D.J.A., C.W.C. Kendall, A. Marchie, A.L. Jenkins, L.S.A. Augustin, D.S. Ludwig, N.D. Barnard, and J.W. Anderson. "Type 2 Diabetes and the Vegetarian Diet." *Am. J. Clin. Nutr..* 78. (2003):610-616.

11. Fraser, G.E. *Vegetarianism and Obesity, Hypertension, Diabetes, and Arthritis: In Diet, Life Expectancy, and Chronic Diseas.* Oxford, U.K.: Oxford University Press, 2003. 129 –148.

12. Nicholson, A.S., M. Sklar, N.D. Barnard, S. Gore, R. Sullivan, and S. Browning. "Toward Improved Management of NIDDM: a Randomized, Controlled, Pilot Intervention using a Low-Fat, Vegetarian Diet." *Prev. Med..* 29. (1999): 87–91.

13. Fuhrman, J. *Eat to Live.* New York: Little Brown and Company, 2011.

14. Scarmeas, N., and Y. Stern. "Mediterranean Diet and Risk for Alzheimer's Disease." *Annals of Neurology.* 59. no. 6 (2006): 921-921.

15. Hughes, T., and A. Ross. "Midlife Fruit and Vegetable Consumption and Risk of Dementia in Later Life in Swedish Twins." *American Journal of Geriatric Psychiatry.* 18. no. 5 (2010): 413-442.

Day 18: Cutting-Edge Research and Timeless Wisdom

1. Li, William, Michelle Hutnik, and Roderick Smith. The Angiogenesis Foundation, "Understanding Angiogenesis." Last modified September 7, 2011. http://www.angio.org/ua.php.

2. Heijamns, B.T., E.W. Tobi, and A.D. Stein. "Persistent Epigenetic Differences Associated with Prenatal Exposure to Famine in Humans." *Proc. Natl. Acad. Sci. U.S.A.* 105. (2008): 17046-17049.

3. Richard, E. "Inherited Epigenetic Variation." *Nature Reviews Genetics.* 7. May (2006): 395-401.

Notes

4. Wolff, G., R. Kodell, and R.Moore. "Maternal Epigenetics and Methyl Supplements Affect Agouti Gene Expression in Avy/Mice." *The FASEB Journal.* 12. (1998): 949-957.
5. Yuasa, Y., H. Nagasaki, Y. Akiyama, Y. Hashimot, T. Takizawa, K. Kojima, T. Kawano, K. Sugihara, K. Imai. and K. Nakachi. "DNA Methylation Status is Inversely Correlated with Green Tea Intake and Physical Activity in Gastric Cancer Patients." *International Journal of Cancer.* 124. (2009): 2677–2682.
6. Esteller, M, and J.G. Herman. "Cancer as an Epigenetic Disease: DNA Methylation and Chromatin Alterations in Human Tumors." *J. Pathol..* 196. no.1 (2002):1-7.
7. Dulak, J. "Nutraceuticals as Anti-Angiogenic Agents: Hopes and Reality." *J. of Physiology and Pharmacology.* 56. suppl. 1 (2005): 51-69.
8. Li, William. Angiogenesis Foundation. "Dietary Sources of Naturally-Occurring Anti-Angiogenic Substance." http://www.angio.org.

Day 19: Prime Importance

1. Chen, J., T.C. Campbell, J. Li, and R. Peto. *Diet, Lifestyle and Mortality in China: a Study of the Characteristics of 65 Chinese Counties.* Oxford, U.K.: Oxford University Press, 1990.
2. Campbell, T.C., B. Parpia, and J. Chen. "Diet, Lifestyle and the Etiology of Coronary Artery Disease: the Cornell China Study." *Am. J. Cardiol..* 82. no. 10B (1998): 18-21.
3. Jolliffe, N., and M. Archer. "Statistical Associations Between International Coronary Heart Disease Death Rates and Certain Environmental Factors." *J. Chronic. Dis..* 9. (1959): 636-652.
4. Armstrong, D., and R. Doll. "Environmental Factors and Cancer Incidence and Mortality in Different Countries with Special Reference to Dietary Practices." *Int. J. Cancer..* 15. (1975): 617-631.
5. Singh, P.N., and G.E. Fraser. "Dietary Risk Factors for Colon Cancer in a Low Risk Population." *Am. J. Epidemiol..* 148. (1998): 761-774.
6. Sinha, R., N. Rothman, and E.D. Brown. "High Concentrations of the Carcinogen 2-amino-1methyl-6-henylimidazo-(4,5-b) pyridine (PhIP) Occur in Chicken but are Dependent on the Cooking Method." *Cancer Res..* 55. no. 20 (1995): 4516-4519.
7. Thomson, B. "Heterocyclic Amine Levels in Cooked Meat and the Implications for New Zealanders." *Eur. J. Cancer Prev..* 8. no. 3 (1999): 201-206.
8. Kalmijn, S., and L.J. Launer. "Dietary Fat Intake and the Risk of Incident Dementia in the Rotterdam Study." *Ann. Neurol..* 42. (1997): 776-782.
9. Sparks, D.L., T.A. Martin, and D.R. Gross DR. "Link Between Heart Disease, Cholesterol, and Alzheimer's Disease: a Review." *Microscopy Res. Tech..* 50. (2000): 287-290.
10. Robertson, W.G. "Diet and Calcium Stones." *Miner Electrolye Metab..* 13. (1987): 228-234.

Notes

11. Wachsman, A., and D.S. Bernstein. "Diet and Osteoporosis." *Lancet.* May 4. (1968): 958-959.
12. rassetto, L.A., K.M. Todd, and C. Morris Jr. "Worldwide Incidence of Hip Fracture in Elderly Women in Relation to Consumption of Animal and Vegetable Foods." *J. Gerontology.* 55. (2000): M585-M595.
13. Abelow, B., R. Holford, and K. Insogna. "Cross-Cultural Associations Between Dietary Animal Protein and Hip Fracture: A Hypothesis." *Calcified Tissue International.* 50. (1992): 14-18.
14. Aldercreutz, H. "Western Diet and Western Diseases: Some Hormonal and Biochemical Mechanisms and Associations." *Scand. J. Clin. Lab. Invest..* 50. suppl. 201 (1990): 3-23.
15. Allen,N.E., P.N. Key, and R.C. Appleby. "Animal Foods, Protein, Calcium and Prostate Cancer Risk: the European Prospective Investigation into Cancer and Nutrition." *Br. J. Cancer.* 98. no. 9 (2008): 1574–1581.
16. Campbell, T.C., and T.M. Campbell. *The China Study.* Dallas: Benbella Books, 2004.

Day 20: Protein Power
1. Campbell, T.C., and T.M. Campbell. *The China Study.* Dallas: Benbella Books, 2004.
2. USDA, "Nutrition Search." http://search.nal.usda.gov/nutritionsearch.
3. Stoll, B.A., L.D. Walters, and S. Kivinnstand. "Does Early Physical Maturity Influence Breast Cancer Risk." *Actol. Oncol..* 32. no. 2 (1994): 171-176.
4. Choi, N.W., and G.R. Howe. "A Epidemiologic Study of Breast Cancer." *Am. J. of Epidemiology.* 107. no. 6 (1978): 510-521.
5. USDA, "Nutrition Data." Last modified December 2, 2010. http://www.ars.usda.gov/main/site_main.htm?modecode=12-35-45-00.
6. Gebhart, S. and R. Thomas. USDA, "Nutritive Value of Foods" *Home and Garden Bulletin* 72. (2002).

Day 21: The Toxic Garden
1. Stanley, J. "Characterization of HRCG/MS Unidentified Peaks from the Analysis of Human Adipose Tissue." *E.P.A. Technical Approach.* 1.
2. E.W.G. "Pollution in People: Cord Blood Contaminants in Minority New Borns." (2004).
3. Payne-Sturges, D., J. Cohen, R. Castorina, D.A. Axelrad, and T.J. Woodruff. "Evaluating Cumulative Organophosphorus Pesticide Body Burden of Children: a NationalCase Study." *Environ. Sci. Technol..* 43. no. 20 (2009): 7924-7930.
4. Lu, C., D.B. Barr, M.A. Pearson, and L.A. Waller. "Dietary Intake and its Contribution to Longitudinal Organophosphorus Pesticide Exposure in Urban/Suburban Children." *Environ. Health Perspect..* 116. no. 4 (2008): 537-42.

5. Punzi, J.S., M. Lamont, D. Haynes, and R.L. Epstein, USDA, "Pesticide Data Program: Pesticide Residues on Fresh and Processed Fruit and Vegetables, Grains, Meats, Milk, and Drinking Water." *Outlooks on Pesticide Management.* June. (2005).

6. Rahbar, A., C. Johnson, and J. Arias. "Chapter Six Designer Basic/Leucine-Zipper Proteins as Regulators of Plant Detoxification Genes." *Recent Advances in Phytochemistry.* 35. (2001): 111-130.

7. . Liska, D.J. "The Detoxification Enzyme Systems." *Altern. Med Rev..* 3. no. 40 (1998): 187-198.

8. Bland, J.S., E. Barrager, R.G. Reedy, and K. Bland. "A Medical Food-Supplemented Detoxification Program in the Management of Chronic Health Problems." *Altern. Ther. Health Med..* 1. no. 5 (1995): 62-71.

9. Lu, C., K. Toepel, R. Irish, R.A. Fenske, D.B. Barr, and R. Bravo. "Organic Diets Significantly Lower Children's Dietary Exposure to Organophosphorus Pesticides." *Environ. Health Perspect..* 114. no. 2 (2006): 260-263.

10. Furlong, C.E., N. Holland, R.J. Richter, A. Bradman, A. Ho, and B. Eskenazi. "Status of Farmworker Mothers and Children as a Predictor of Organophosphate Sensitivity." *Pharmacogenetics and Genomics.* 16. no. 3 (2006): 183.

11. Worthington, V. "Effect of Agricultural Methods on Nutritional Quality: A Comparison of Organic with Conventional Crops." *Alternative Therapies.* 4. (1998): 58-69.

12. Environmental Working Group, "2011 Shoppers Guide to Pesticides in Produce." www.EWG.org.

Day 22: Glazed America

1. Sienkiewicz, Frances. *Nutrition: Concepts and Controversies.* Thompson Wadsworth, 2006. 131.

2. Simin, Liu. "Relation Between a Diet with a High Glycemic Load and Plasma Concentrations of High-Sensitivity of C-Reactive Protein in Middle-Aged Women." *AJCN.* 75. no. 3 (2002): 492-498.

3. Warburg, O. "On the Origin of Cancer Cells." *Science.* 123. Feb. (1956): 309-14.

4. Liu, H., D. Huang, and D. McArthur. "Fructose Induces Transketolase Flux to Promote Pancreatic Cancer Growth." *Cancer Res..* 70. August (2010): 6368.

5. Sanchez, A. "Role of Sugars in Human Neutrophilic Phagocytosis." *American Journal of Clinical Nutrition.* November. (1973): 1180-1184.

6. Ringsdorf, W.M., E. Cheraskin, and R.R. Ramsey. "Sucrose, Neutrophilic Phagocytosis, and Resistance to Disease." *Am. J. Clin. Nutr..* 26. no. 2 (1973): 1180-1184.

7. Bocarsly, M.E., and E.S. Powell. "High-Fructose Corn Syrup Causes Characteristics of Obesity in Rats: Increased Body Weight, Body Fat and Triglyceride Levels." *Pharmacolology.* (2010).

8.Manal, F., Abdelmalek , Ayako,· Suzuki, and C. Guy. "Increased Fructose Consumption is Associated with Fibrosis Severity in Patients with Nonalcoholic Fatty Liver Disease." *Hepatology.* 51. no. 6 (2010): 1961-1971.

Day 23: Healthy Fats?
1. USDA Center for Nutrition Policy and Promotion. "Is Fat Consumption Really Decreasing." *Nutrition Insights.* April (1998).
2. Hu, F.B., M.J. Stampfer, J.E. Manson, and E. Rimm. "Dietary Fat Intake and the Risk of Coronary Heart Disease in Women." *N. Engl. J. Med..* 337. no. 21 (1997): 1491-1499.
3. Wijendran, V., and K.C. Hayes. "Dietary n-6 and n-3 Fatty Acid Balance and Cardiovascular Health." *Annual Review of Nutrition.* 24. July (2004): 597-615.
4. Simopoulos, A.P. "The Importance of the Ratio of Omega-6/Omega-3 Essential Fatty Acids." *Biomedicine and Pharmacotherapy.* 56. no. 8 (2002): 365-379.
5. Cortes, B., I. Nunez, and M. Cofan. "Effects of High-Fat Meals Enriched with Walnuts or Olive Oil on Post Prandial Endothelial Function." *Journal of the American College of Cardiology.* 48. no. 8 (2006): 1666-1671.
6. Hu, F.B., and M.J.Stampfer. "Nut Consumption and Risk of Coronary Heart Disease: a Review of Epidemiologic Evidence." *Curr. Atheroscler Rep..* 1. no. 3 (1999): 204-209.
7. Albert, C., M. Gaziano, and W. Willet. "Nut Consumption and Decreased Risk of Sudden Cardiac Death in the Physicians' Health Study." *Arch. Intern. Med..* 162. (2002): 1382-1387.
8. Good, D., C. Lavie, and H. Ventura. "Dietary Intake of Nuts and Cardiovascular Prognosis." *The Ochsner Journal..* 9. no. 1 (2009): 32-36.

Day 24: The Spice of Life
1. Fitzpatrick, Laura. "Brief History: Salt in U.S. Food." *Time Magazine.* April 5 (2010).
2. James, W.P., A. Ralph, and C.P. Sanchez-Castillo. "The Dominance of Salt in Manufactured Food in the Sodium Intake of Affluent Societies." *Lancet.* 1. (1987): 426-429.
3. Institute of Medicine National Academies. "Report Brief 2010: Strategies to reduce Sodium Intake in the United States." *American Heart Association.* www.heart.org.
4. Hirayama, T. "Epidemiology of Stomach Cancer in Japan: with Special Reference to the Strategy for the Primary Research." *Jpn. J. Cancer Res..* 14. (1984): 159–168.
5. He1, F.J., and G.A. MacGregor. "Effect of Modest Salt Reduction on Blood Pressure: a Meta-Analysis of Randomized Trials." *Implications for public health Journal of Human Hypertension.* 16. (2002): 761–770.

Notes

6. Eric, N., Taylor, T. Teresa, Fung, C. Gary, and Curhan. "DASH-Style Diet Associates with Reduced Risk for Kidney Stones." *JASN.* 20. October (2009): 2253-2259.
7. Bhagyalakshmi. "*Critical Reviews.*" *Food Science and Nutrition.* 45. (**2005**): 607–621.
8. Blot. "Diet and High Risk of Stomach Cancer in Shandong, China." *Cancer Research.* 48. (1998): 3518–3523.
9. Buiotti. "A Case Control Study of Gastric Cancer and Diet in Italy." *International Journal of Cancer.* **44:** 611–616.

Day 25: More Than Regularity

1. Harvard School of Public Health. "Fiber: Nutrition Source."
2. Lustig, R.H. "The 'Skinny' on Childhood Obesity: How our Western Environment Starves Kids' Brains." *Pediatr Ann.* 35. no. 12 (2006): 898–902, 905–907.
3. Bingham, S.A., N.E. Day, R. Luben, and P. Ferrari. "Dietary Fiber in Food and Protection Against Colorectal Cancer in European Protection Investigation into Cancer and Nutrition (EPIC): an Observational Study." *Lancet.* 361. no. 9368 (2003): 1496-1501.
4. Negri, E., S. Franceschi, M. Parpinel, La Veccia. "Fiber Intake and Risk of Colorectal Cancer." *Cancer Epidemiol Biomarkers Prev..* 7. no. 8 (1998): 667-671.
5. King, D.E., A.G. Mainous, B.M. Egan, R.F. Woolson, and R.E. Geesey. "Effect of Psyllium Fiber Supplementation on C-Reactive Protein. A Trial to Reduce Inflammatory Markers." *Ann. Fam. Med..* 6. no. 2 (2008):100-106.
6. Sola, R., G. Godas, and J. Ribalta. "The Effects of Soluble Fiber (Plantago Ovata Husk) on Plasma Lipids, Lipoproteins, and Apolipoproteins in Men with Ischemic Heart Disease." *J. Clin. Nutr..* 85. no. 4 (2007): 1157-63.
7. Scholz-Ahrens, K.E., P. Ade, and B. Marten. "Prebiotics, Probiotcs and Synbiotics Affect Mineral Absorption, Bone Mineral Content and Bone Structure." *J. Nutr..* 137. no. 3, suppl. 2 (2007): 838s-846s.
8. Wong, J.M., R. de Souza, C.W. Kendall, A. Emam, and D.J. Jenkins. "Colonic Health: Fermentation and Short Chain Fatty Acids." *J. Clin. Gastroenterol.* 40. no. 3 (2006): 235-43.
9. Yikyung, Park, Amy Subar, Albert Hollenbeck, and Arthur Schatzkin. "Dietary Fiber Intake and Mortality in the NIH-AARP Diet and Health Study." *Arch Intern Med.* February 14, (2011).

Day 26: The Hidden Power of Food

1. Roitman, M., and G. Stuber. "Dopamine Operates as a Subsecond Modulator of Food Seeking.". *The Journal of Neuroscience.* 24. no. 6 (2004): 126-127.
2. Raka, Jain, Mukherjee, Rajvir, and Singh. "Influence of Sweet tasting

Solutions on Opioid Withdrawal." *Brain Research Bulletin.* 64. no. 4 (2004): 319-322.

3. Katz, David. *The Flavor Point Diet: the Delicious, Breakthrough Plan to Turn Off Your Hunger and Lose the Weight for Good.* New York: Rodale, 2005.

4. Rolls, E.T., B.J. Rolls, and E.A. Rowe. "Sensory-Specific and Motivation-Specific Satiety for the Sight and Taste of Food and Water in Man." *Physiol. Behav..* 30. no. 2 (1983): 185-192.

Day 27: I Don't Like Vegetables!

1. Mattes, R.D. "The taste for Salt in Humans." *Am. J. Clin. Nutr..* 65. no. 2 (1997): 692S-697S.

2. Shell, E.R. "The Hungry Gene." *New Your: Atlantic Monthly Press.* (2002).

3. Douglas, Lisle, and Alan Goldhammer. "The Pleasure Trap. Mastering the Hidden Force that Undermines Health and Happiness." *Healthy Living Publications.* (2003).

Day 28: Your Health Savings Account

1. Himmlestein, D.E. Warren, D. Thorne, and S. Woolhander. "Illness and Injury as Contributors to Bankruptcy." *Health Affairs.* (Web Exclusive) February. (2005).

2. US Department of Health and Human Services, "2004 Survey." http://www.ahrq.gov/.

3. Fidelity Investments. "Press Release." March. (2006).

4. Freedman, D.S., W.H. Dietz, S.R. Srinivasan, and G.S. Berenson. "The Relation of Overweight to Cardiovascular Risk Factors Among Children and Adolescents: the Bogalusa Heart Study." *Pediatrics.* 103. no. 6 pt. 1 (1999):1175-1182.

Day 30: But My Grandfather Lived to 90!

1. Taioli, E., S. Benhamou,and L. Cascorbi. "Myeloperoxidase G-463A Polymorphism and Lung Cancer: a Huge Genetic Susceptibility to Environmental Carcinogens Pooled Analysis." *Genet. Med..* 9. no. 2 (2007): 67-73.

2. Shu, Ye. "Polymorphism of Matrix Metalloproteinase Gene Promoters: Implication in Regulation of Gene Expression and Susceptibility of Various Diseases." *Matrix Biology.* 19. no. 7 (2000): 623 -629.

3. Lio, D., L. Scola, A. Crivello, and G. Colonna-Romano. "Gender-Specific Association Between -1082 IL-10." *Promoter Polymorphism and Longevity.* 3. no. 1 (2002): 30-33.

Day 33: Children and Diet

1. Kortelainen, M. "Adiposity, Cardiac Size and Precursors of Coronary Atherosclerosis in 5 to 15-year-old Children: a Retrospective Study of 210

Violent Deaths." *Int. J. Obes. Relat. Metab. Disord.*. 21. no. 8 (1997): 691-697.

2. Virmani, R., M. Robinowitz, J.C. Geer, P.P. Breslin, J.C. Beyer, and H.A. McAllister. "Coronary Artery Atherosclerosis Revisited in Korean War Combat Casualties." *Arch. Pathol. Lab. Med.*. 111. no. 10 (1987): 972-976.

3. Feinberg, A., and B. Tyck. "Timeline: The History of Cancer Epigenetics." *Nature Reviews Cancer.* 4. February (2004): 143-153.

4. Venat Narayan, K.M., J. Boyle, and T. Thompson. "Lifetime Risk for Diabetes Mellitus in the United States." *JAMA.* 290. no. 14 (2003): 1884-1890.

Day 34: What Happened to You?

1. Fulgoni, V. III. "Current Protein Intake in America: Analysis of the National Health and Nutrition Examination Survey, 2003–2004." *American Journal of Clinical Nutrition.* 87. no. 5 (2008).

2. Jollifee, N., and M. Archer. "Statistical Associations Between International Coronary Heart Disease Death Rates and Certain Environmental Factors." *J. Chronic Disease.* 9. (1959): 636-652.

3. Armstrong, D., and R. Doll. "Environmental Factors and Cancer Incidence and Mortality in Different Countries, with Special Reference to Dietary Practices."

4. Chen, J., T.C. Campbell, and J. Li. *Diet, Lifestyle and Mortality in China. A Study of the Characteristics of 65 Rural Chinese Counties.* Oxford, U.K.: Oxford University Press, 1990.

5. "Economic Impact Market Segmentation Study." (2009).

6. Bernstein, A., D. Bloom, B. Rosner, M. Franz, and W. Willet. "Relation of Food Cost to Healthfulness of Diet Among US Women." *Am. J. Clin. Nutr.*. 92. no. 5 (2010): 1197-1203.

Day 35: Label Reading 101

1. FDA, "Dietary Supplement and Health Education Act of 1994." www. FDA.gov.

2. Sacks, F.M., L.P. Svetkey, W.M. Vollmer, L.J. Appel, G.A. Bray, D. Harsha, E. Obarzanek, P.R. Conlin, E.R. Miller 3rd, and D.G. Simons-Morton. "Effects on Blood Pressure of Reduced Dietary Sodium and the Dietary Approaches to Stop Hypertension (DASH) diet." *N. Engl. J. Med.*. 344. no.1 (2001): 3-10.

3. Tsugane, S. "Salt, Salted Food Intake, and Risk of Gastric Cancer: Epidemiologic Evidence." *Cancer Sci.*. 96. no. 1 (2005): 1-6.

Day 37: Fasting for Health

1. Piper, John. *A Hunger for God: Desiring God through fasting and prayer.* Weaton, Ill.: Crossway, 1997.

Notes

2. Ho, K.Y., J.D. Veldhuis, and M.L. Johnson. "Fasting Enhances Growth Hormone Secretion and Amplifies the Complex Rhythms of Growth Hormone Secretion in Man." *J. Clin. Invest.*. 81. no. 4 (1988): 968–975.
3. Gredilla, Ricardo, and Gustavo Barja. "Minireview: The Role of Oxidative Stress in Relation to Caloric Restriction and Longevity." *Endocrinology.* 146. no. 9: 3713-3717.
4. Kagawa, Y. "Impact of Westernization on the Nutrition of Japanese: Changes in Physique, Cancer, Longevity, and Centenarians." *Prev. Med.*. 7. (1978): 205-217.
5. Goldhamer, Alan C., Douglas J. Lisle, Peter Sultana, Scott V. Anderson, Banoo Parpia, Barry Hughes, and T. Colin Campbell. "Medically Supervised Water-Only Fasting in the Treatment of Borderline Hypertension." *The Journal of Alternative and Complementary Medicine.* 8. no. 5 (2002): 643-650.
6. Skrha, J., M. Kunesova, and J. Hilgertova. "Short-Term Very Low Calorie Diet Reduces Oxidative Stress in Obese Type 2 Diabetic Patients." *Physiol. Res.*. 54. no. 1 (2005): 33-39.
7. Michalsen, Andreas. "Prolonged Fasting as a Method of Mood Enhancement in Chronic Pain Syndromes: A Review of Clinical Evidence and Mechanisms." *Current Pain and Headache Reports.* 14. no. 2: 80-87.

Day 38: The Myth of Moderation

1. USDA, "FoodReview: Major Food Trends a Century in Review." (2000).
2. Barnard, N. "Trends in Food Availability 1909-2007." *Am. J. Clin. Nutr.*. 91. no. 5 (2010): 1530S-1536S.
3. Ornish, D., S.E. Brown, L.W. Scherwitz, J.H. Billings, W.T. Armstrong, T.A. Ports, S.M. McLanahan, R.L. Kirkeeide, R.J. Brand, and K.L. Gould. "Can Lifestyle Changes Reverse Coronary Heart Disease? The Lifestyle Heart Trial." *Lancet.*. 336. (1990): 129-133.
4. Pischke, Elliott-Eller. "Clinical Events in Coronary Heart Disease Patients With an Ejection Fraction of 40 percent or Less: 3-Year Follow- Up." *Journal of Cardiovascular Nursing.* 25. no. 5 (2010): E8-E15.

Day 39: Never Give Up!

1. "A recent study in Tel Aviv," p. 259.

Day 40: Alive! and Finishing Strong

1. Olympics, "Sydney 2000." (2000).

Appendices

- Additional Resources
- Index
- Personal Health Notes

Additional Resources

Books

A Hunger for God: Desiring God through Fasting and Prayer. John Piper (Crossway Books: Wheaton, IL 1997)

Breaking the Food Seduction: The Hidden Reasons Behind Food Cravings—And 7 Steps to End Them Naturally. Neal Barnard, M.D. (St. Martin's Griffin: New York, NY 2004)

The China Study: The Most Comprehensive Study of Nutrition Ever Conducted and the Startling Implications for Diet, Weight Loss, and Long-Term Health. T. Colin Campbell, Thomas M. Campbell II, Howard Lyman, and John Robbins (BenBella Books: Dallas, TX 2006)

Diet for a New America. John Robbins, 2nd edition (HJ Kramer: Belvedere Tiburon, CA 1998)

Don't Drink Your Milk! Frank Lski, M.D. (TEACH Services, Inc.: Ringgold, GA 2010)

Dr. Neal Barnard's Program for Reversing Diabetes: The Scientifically Proven System for Reversing Diabetes without Drugs. Neal Barnard, M.D. (Rodale Books: Emmaus, PA 2008)

Eat to Live: The Amazing Nutrient-Rich Program for Fast and Sustained Weight Loss, revised edition. Joel Fuhrman, M.D. (Little, Brown and Company: New York, NY 2011)

Never be Sick Again: Health Is a Choice, Learn How to Choose It. Raymond Franics and Kester Cotton (HCI: Deerfield Beach, FL 2002)

The Omnivore's Dilemma: A Natural History of Four Meals. Michael Pollan (Penguin Press: New York, NY 2007)

Pain Free: A Revolutionary Method for Stopping Chronic Pain. Pete Egoscue and Roger Gittines (Bantam Books: New York, NY 2000).

Prevent and Reverse Heart Disease: The Revolutionary, Scientifically Proven, Nutrition-Based Cure. Caldwell Esselstyn, M.D. (Avery Trade: New York, NY 2008)

Food Delivery
www.doortodoororganics.com
www.localharvest.org
www.suburbanorganics.com (East Coast)
www.Farmfreshtoyou.com (West Coast)

Gardening
www.squarefootgardening.com
www.organicgardening.com
Green Superfoods Powders and Bars
www.amazinggrass.com

Inspiration
www.Facebook.com/Jesus Daily

Kitchen Accessories
www.Day3Health.com for recommendations and reviews
www.vitamix.com - Blenders
www.Omegajuicers.com-Juicers and blenders
www.cuisinart.com - Food Processors

Recipes and Meal Planning

www.Day3Health.com
www.EatRightAmerica.com
www.wholefoodsmarket.com

Supplements

www.Day3Health.com-Information and guidance

Index

Personal Health Notes

Personal Health Notes

Personal Health Notes

Personal Health Notes

Personal Health Notes